# The Foundations of Structuralism

# The Foundations of Structuralism

## A CRITIQUE OF LÉVI-STRAUSS AND THE STRUCTURALIST MOVEMENT

**SIMON CLARKE**
*Lecturer in Sociology, University of Warwick*

THE HARVESTER PRESS · SUSSEX
BARNES & NOBLE BOOKS · NEW JERSEY

First published in Great Britain in 1981 by
THE HARVESTER PRESS LIMITED
*Publisher: John Spiers*
16 Ship Street, Brighton, Sussex
and in the USA by
BARNES & NOBLE BOOKS
81 Adams Drive, Totowa, New Jersey 07512

*British Library Cataloguing in Publication Data*

Clarke, Simon
    The foundations of structuralism.
    1. Structuralism
    I. Title
    149′.96        B841.4

ISBN 0-85527-978-8

BARNES & NOBLE
ISBN 0-389-20115-4

Photoset and printed by Photobooks (Bristol) Ltd

# Contents

Preface     vii

I Lévi-Strauss and the Foundations of Structuralism     1

II The Crisis in French Philosophy in the 1930s     6

  1 The complementarity of structuralism and phenomenology     6
  2 The intellectual orthodoxy of the Third Republic     9
  3 The inter-war intellectual crisis     16
  4 Reaction to the Crisis—the existentialist philosophy of Sartre     24
  5 Lévi-Strauss' rejection of phenomenology     30

III The Origins of Structuralism     34

  1 Lévi-Strauss and Durkheimian philosophy     36
  2 Lévi-Strauss and Durkheimian sociology     38
  3 Towards a solution: Lévi-Strauss, Mauss and the theory of reciprocity     42
  4 From the theory of reciprocity to *The Elementary Structures*     48

IV The Elementary Structures of Kinship     53

  1 The General Theory of Reciprocity     56
    a) The general theory of reciprocity and the prohibition of incest     56
    b) The social function of reciprocity     58
    c) Towards a psychological theory of reciprocity     59
    d) Reciprocity in systems of kinship and marriage     68

  2 The Elementary Structures of Kinship     72
    a) Social classification and the regulation of marriage     72
    b) The elementary structures     78
    c) Systems of kinship and marriage     80

V The Impact of *The Elementary Structures of Kinship*     86

  1 The theory of kinship     86
  2 Feminism and the exchange of women     91
  3 From structures to structuralism     96
  4 Anthropological structuralism     109

## VI  Structuralism in Linguistics                                    117

1  Saussure and the objectivity of language                          119
2  Positivism and phenomenology in the study of language             125
3  Positivism and formalism: from Bloomfield to Chomsky              129
4  Form and function: the Prague Linguistic Circle                   145

## VII  Lévi-Strauss and the Linguistic Analogy                        157

1  The encounter with linguistics                                    157
2  Language and mind: the 'structural unconscious'                   164
3  The structural analysis of meaning                                173

## VIII  The Structural Analysis of Myth                               184

1  Early approaches to myth                                          185
2  The logic of untamed thought                                     189
3  *Mythologiques*                                                   194
4  Positivism and formalism                                         206

## IX  The Structuralist Human Philosophy                              210

1  Lévi-Strauss' human philosophy                                    212
2  Sartre's incorporation of structures in the dialectic            220
3  Lévi-Strauss' subordination of the dialectic to structure        223
4  The complementarity and irreconcilability of structural and
   dialectical intelligibility                                      226
5  Conclusion                                                        230

*Abbreviations*                                                      237
*The Published Works of Claude Lévi-Strauss*                         239
*Bibliography*                                                       255

# Preface

This book is the result of ten years of intermittent work on Lévi-Strauss and the structuralist movement. The original research was for a PhD thesis on Lévi-Strauss ('The Structuralism of Claude Lévi-Strauss', University of Essex. 1975), parts of which have subsequently been published in a modified form. Lest the reader immediately return this book to the shelves with horror, I should add that the book has been almost completely rewritten so as to expunge all traces of the boredom and pedantry that seems to be an inevitable part of writing a thesis. Direct quotation and footnote references have been kept to a minimum, and endless reservations and qualifications eliminated, while the central argument has been brought out and developed and a considerable amount of new material added.

Although the scholarly apparatus of a thesis has been abandoned the reader might be reassured by the knowledge that the book is the result of extensive and intensive research over a long period so that claims and assertions are not made lightly. Those who feel lost without footnotes are invited to pore over the original thesis and published articles. This particularly applies to the technical discussion of the theory of kinship, only the conclusions of which are reported here.

One cannot write a book like this without incurring enormous debts to many people. The greatest debt is owed to Claude Lévi-Strauss, without whom it would never have been possible. Although the book is sharply critical of Lévi-Strauss' work as a contribution to the social sciences, to read his books is a tremendously rewarding experience. As literary works they make a vitally important contribution to our culture, inspiring great humility through the unfolding of the cultures that he has come to love and to whose preservation he has dedicated himself. It is perhaps not his fault that the impact of his work has been quite different from that which he intended.

Thanks are also due to Alasdair MacIntyre, who was the original supervisor of my thesis, and to Herminio Martins, who saw it come to fruition; to Margaret Boden, who has been a very sympathetic editor; and to Celia Britton, Bob Fine and Simon Frith who have been very helpful commentators on various drafts of the work. Last, but by no means least, thanks to Lin, Sam and Becky who have had to bear the strain and to whom the book is dedicated.

Parts of Chapters II and III originally formed part of an article in *Sociology* ('The Origins of Lévi-Strauss' Structuralism', *Sociology*, 12, 3, 1978, pp. 405 – 39) while Chapter VIII is a modified version of an article that appeared originally in *The Sociological Review* (Lévi-Strauss' Structural Analysis of Myth', *Sociological Review*, 25, 4, 1977, pp. 743 – 774).

I am grateful to the editors of both for permission to publish the material here.

Abbreviated footnote references refer to the bibliography of Lévi-Strauss' works.

# I. Introduction. Lévi-Strauss and the Foundations of Structuralism

THIS book presents a fundamental critique of what is known as 'structuralism' through an examination, primarily, of the work of an anthropologist, Claude Lévi-Strauss. This approach to the subject requires some explanation.

'Structuralism' is associated more with a set of names: Lévi-Strauss, Althusser, Foucault, Lacan (and, perhaps, Barthes, Derrida, *Tel Quel*) and a number of provocative slogans: 'the death of the subject', 'the assault on realism', than with a clearly defined programme or doctrine. It is indeed the case that there are many differences between these thinkers, and that each has developed the basic ideas of structuralism in his own way. However there is a basic theme at the heart of structuralism and it is largely from the work of Lévi-Strauss that this theme comes. In developing a critique of Lévi-Strauss' work it is with this theme that I am primarily concerned.

For structuralists Lévi-Strauss has shown the way to resolve once and for all the dilemma that has plagued the human and social sciences since their inception of providing a scientific account of the human world which can fully recognize that world as a world of meanings.

For structuralists Lévi-Strauss' work makes the fundamental break with the pre-structuralist era, which was divided between primitive positivist attempts to reduce the human sciences to a branch of the natural sciences and romantic (and usually irrationalist) attempts to hold the sciences at bay by insisting on the irreducibly subjective character of human experience. For structuralism any attempt to understand the human world must be based on an implacable opposition to the evils of 'positivism' ('naturalism' or 'realism') and 'humanism', marked by the naive belief in the existence of a reality independent of human apprehension or in the existence of a humanity that could create its own world. It is Lévi-Strauss who shows the human and social sciences the way to get beyond these infantile delusions.

Lévi-Strauss makes it possible to set the study of human institutions on a genuinely scientific foundation by redefining the object of the human sciences. Lévi-Strauss' achievement is to isolate an autonomous order of reality, the symbolic order, which exists independently of the things that are symbolized and the people who symbolize. Cultural meanings are inherent in the symbolic orders and these meanings are independent of, and prior to, the external world, on the one hand, and human subjects, on the other. Thus the world only has an objective existence in the symbolic orders that represent it.

It is the symbolic orders that create the illusion of an external reality for human subjects, and the illusion of human subjects for whom the world has reality. Since we can only live within these symbolic orders, we can have no knowledge of anything beyond them. Naturalism and humanism express the twin fallacies that we can know a world independently of its symbolic representation and that we can know ourselves independently of the symbolism that constitutes a particular conception of ourselves.

The claim of structuralism to have isolated symbolic orders as a privileged reality of which we can have direct knowledge depends on its ability to identify the meanings constituted by such orders independently of any particular subjective interpretation of these meanings. Structuralism seeks to discover the objective residue of meaning that remains when abstraction has been made from all such subjective interpretations. This objective meaning cannot be identified with any conscious meaning the symbolic order might have either for a particular participant in the order or for a particular analyst of it. This objective meaning can only be an unconscious meaning. Structuralism therefore directs our attention away from the illusions of consciousness to the unconscious substratum of meaning. It is the unconscious that mediates between us and the world, creating the twin illusions of reality and subjectivity.

It is this theme that pervades structuralism and that provides the basis for the structuralist claim to offer a scientific approach to humanity. It is a theme that is developed rather differently in the work of different structuralists. Althusser has developed the structuralist arguments largely in epistemological terms, recapitulating the neo-positivist critique of naturalism and of humanism. Foucault has developed it in a sustained relativist critique of the ideological pretensions of contemporary society. Lacan has developed it in a linguistic idealist reinterpretation of Freud. A comprehensive critical examination of structuralism would therefore require several volumes. However these different variations are developments of a common theme, and it is a theme that was introduced, at least in the structuralist form, in the work of Lévi-Strauss.

Examination of Lévi-Strauss' work not only has the advantage of directing our attention to the foundations of structuralism in this sense. It has two other advantages as well. Firstly, the work of Althusser, Lacan and Foucault is often extremely ambiguous, if not obscure, and is full of the most sweeping generalizations that make their claims very difficult to pin down. Lévi-Strauss, by contrast, developed the structuralist approach in the examination of particular symbolic systems, above all those of kinship and of myth, that makes his claims concrete and specific, and so amenable to rational evaluation. We can therefore examine in some detail Lévi-Strauss' attempt to characterize the objective unconscious meaning of particular symbolic systems to discover whether the structuralist method does give us access to a privileged order of reality. This makes it possible to develop a critique of structuralism that does not only rest on philosophical argument, but that also has some purchase on the supposed accomplishments of structuralism.

Secondly, through an examination of the work of the founder of structuralism it is possible to evaluate the structuralist claim to originality by examining the sources of the structuralist approach in Lévi-Strauss' work. This examination will reveal that structuralism is not as original as it presents itself to be. Its philosophical roots are planted firmly in the positivist tradition, to which Lévi-Strauss is related through the French positivist sociologist Emile Durkheim and through positivist linguistics. The central argument of structuralism is in essence a restatement of the discredited argument of linguistic positivism that language is the only reality since knowledge can only be expressed and communicated in linguistic form. Again the work of Lévi-Strauss presents us with an opportunity to examine these arguments not only in philosophical terms, which would simply involve us in a recapitulation of the history of neo-positivism, but in terms of the substantive implications of the attempt to discover the reality expressed in language. Lévi-Strauss has leant very heavily on the authority of the achievements of positivist linguistics, and so in examining his work it is appropriate to direct our attention to these supposed achievements.

Although most structuralists would agree in regarding Lévi-Strauss as the founder of the tradition, few relate uncritically to his work. The attempt to develop a critique of structuralism through a close study of the work of one structuralist might therefore appear to be compromised. Only a further detailed examination of the work of, for example, Althusser, Foucault, and Lacan could hope to persuade the sceptic that the basic critique does indeed apply to the work of the latter. For the more sympathetic reader, however, it might be in order to indicate the basic criticisms made of Lévi-Strauss' work by later structuralists in order to establish that these criticisms are not fundamental.

The main respect in which later structuralists have criticized Lévi-Strauss' work is in relation to his theory of the unconscious foundations of meaning. For Lévi-Strauss, as we shall see, systems of meaning are constituted by an unconscious that emerges on a biological foundation. Later structuralists have criticized two implications of this theory.

Firstly, the unconscious is something external, and prior, to the systems of meaning. Hence Lévi-Strauss in the last analysis resorts to naturalism. For later structuralists this lacuna is removed by Lacan's development of Lévi-Strauss' theory in which the unconscious itself becomes a product of systems of meaning. This development radicalizes structuralism's characteristic cultural idealism, and in eliminating any concept of human nature it radicalizes the structuralists' anti-humanism, but it does not affect the fundamental issues.

Secondly, Lévi-Strauss' unconscious is not only external to the systems of meaning, it is also fixed and so beyond history. This eliminates any source of historical change, for the permanence of the unconscious can only create static structures. Lacan's reformulation of the theory of the unconscious resolves this dilemma too. Since the unconscious is integrated into the systems of meaning the latter no longer have a fixed structure but can be conceptualized as a number of systems engaged in a complex interaction with one another and so subject to change. This idea is developed in Althusser's attempt to integrate a dehumanized version of Sartre's idea of practice into Lévi-Strauss' structuralism, so that structures define practices that themselves change the structures.

Although these more sophisticated versions of structuralism raise new issues in their turn, the developments involved represent no more than variations on a common underlying theme. Essentially they simply represent a further radicalization of Lévi-Strauss' structuralism, providing the means to integrate into the structuralist framework elements that for Lévi-Strauss remained outside it. In this respect, therefore, the fundamental criticisms that are directed at Lévi-Strauss' structuralism in this book apply with equal, or even greater, force to the more sophisticated versions that are now current among the *avant-garde*.

## II. The Crisis in French Philosophy in the 1930s

### 1 THE COMPLEMENTARITY OF STRUCTURALISM AND PHENOMENOLOGY

STRUCTURALISM as a specific approach to the human sciences developed slowly. Lévi-Strauss was born in 1908. He studied Law and then Philosophy at the University of Paris between 1927 and 1931 and taught philosophy in Lycées for two years. His opportunity to become a professional anthropologist came when the Durkheimian sociologist Celestin Bouglé recommended him for a teaching post as a sociologist in Brazil. There he conducted fieldwork, and he published his first ethnographic report in 1936. In 1938–9 he made a more extensive fieldwork trip in Brazil. Following military service in France he fled, as a Jew, to the United States in 1940. There he taught at the New School for Social Research, the Ecole Libre des Hautes Etudes and at Barnard College. He finally returned to France only in 1947, having served for two years as a French cultural attaché in the United States.

On his return to France Lévi-Strauss took up a post as Assistant Director of the Musée de l'Homme in Paris until 1950 when he was appointed Director of Studies and Professor of the Comparative Religion of Non-Literate Peoples at the Ecole Pratique des Hautes Etudes. In 1949 Lévi-Strauss made a short fieldwork trip to Chittagong in Pakistan at the instigation of UNESCO, in which organisation he was very active through the 1950s. In 1959 he was elected to the chair of Social Anthropology at the Collège de France, sponsored by Maurice Merleau-Ponty. In 1967 he was awarded the Gold Medal of the CNRS, and in 1974 received the accolade of election to the Académie Française. His first major work, *The Elementary Structures of Kinship* was published to some acclaim in 1949, but it was only with the publication of *Tristes Tropiques* in 1955, *Structural Anthropology* in 1958 and *The Savage Mind* in 1962 that Lévi-Strauss became a public intellectual figure and structuralism emerged as a major intellectual movement. Lévi-Strauss' work struck a chord in French left-wing culture in the early 1960s as the expression of a philosophy that shared much of the inspiration of the then dominant philosophies of phenomenology and existentialism, while avoiding what had come to be seen as the insoluble problems of the latter. Many of the pioneers of the structuralist movement, such as Lacan, Foucault, and Poulantzas, came to structuralism from phenomenology or existentialism and created new variants of structuralism that sought to integrate structuralism with phenomenology. Many followers of the structuralist movement brought to structuralism the fervour and missionary zeal with which the previous generation had embraced phenomenology and existentialism (and indeed many who entered the 1960s immersed in subjectivity were the same people who entered the 1970s proclaiming the death of the subject).

The ease and speed with which so many intellectuals made the transition from phenomenology to structuralism should warn us against the common belief, held by the proponents of one or the other doctrine, that the two movements are absolutely opposed to one another, a belief that is apparently validated by the antithetical terms in which the debate between the two is conducted.

There is no doubt that between structuralism and existentialism, in particular, there is an unbridgeable gulf, expressed in the by-now standard oppositions of structure to history, object to subject, unconscious to conscious, determinacy to free will, immanence to transcendence. However, this unbridgeable gulf is not a gulf between two absolutely antithetical philosophies, but is one between philosophies that offer complementary, but divergent, solutions to a common set of problems.

Although the structuralist movement emerged in reaction to existentialism, and came to prominence two decades after the heyday of existentialism, the two philosophies have a common origin in the inter-war intellectual crisis in France. Sartre was only three years older than Lévi-Strauss, Simone de Beauvoir and Merleau-Ponty were his exact comtemporaries.

Sartre and Merleau-Ponty were the more precocious, being students at the prestigious and élitist Ecole Normale Superieur, while Lévi-Strauss had a more modest education. Sartre and Merleau-Ponty sought to regenerate philosophy, while Lévi-

Strauss was much more sceptical of the claims of philosophy to provide any kind of knowledge. Sartre and Merleau-Ponty only became seriously involved politically with the Resistance, while Lévi-Strauss' period of political activity was the early 1930s, culminating in his standing as a candidate in the cantonal elections when he was teaching at Mont-de-Marsan in 1932–3. The difference in degree of political involvement in the 1930s is closely associated with the different philosophical concerns of the three. While Sartre and Merleau-Ponty had an introspective concern with the problem of the individual conscience in a society whose values seemed bankrupt, Lévi-Strauss appears to have been more concerned with the exploitation and oppression of the individual in the name of those values, thus with objective social questions rather than subjective moral dilemmas.

This difference in turn is probably related to Lévi-Strauss' Jewish background (although Lévi-Strauss was never a believer) which must have enabled him to distance himself the more from debates whose terms were increasingly being set by the resurgence of Catholic mysticism and the crisis of the moral conscience to which this gave rise among radicals with a Christian background. Hence Lévi-Strauss was protected from the self-indulgence and the nihilistic over-reaction that so often accompanies the adolescent repudiation of an inherited faith, while the resurgence of anti-semitism associated with the rise of the Catholic Right must have given him a more acute political consciousness.

Despite the temperamental and experiential differences between Lévi-Strauss and those who would develop existentialism and phenomenology, they shared more than a place and a date. They all went through the same rigid system of education. They shared a common rejection of the doctrines with which they were confronted as philosophy students, and the grounds for the rejection were remarkably similar in each case. Although their reaction to established doctrines was a negative one, it was still the established doctrines that set the terms of the reaction and imposed on the young radical intellectuals of the late 1920s and early 1930s a common set of problems. It is these common problems, to which Sartre and Lévi-Strauss offered antithetical solutions, that provide the common foundation of structuralism and existentialism, and it is this shared origin that explains the ease with which, thirty years later, a new generation of intellectuals could move from one to the other, or could propose a synthesis of the two.

In this chapter I want to attempt to uncover the intellectual problems in response to which Lévi-Strauss and Sartre developed their contrasting philosophies. I am not concerned with explaining why Sartre and Lévi-Strauss adopted the solutions they chose, but with relating the solutions to one another as alternative possibilities inscribed in a common, and widely-shared, reaction to an acute intellectual crisis.

In following chapters I shall concentrate on the development of Lévi-Strauss' structuralism, but the existentialist theme will continue to run through the book as the ghost that insists on haunting the structuralist enterprise, rudely persisting in pressing the claims of the human subject that structuralism has suppressed, and about whom it would rather remain silent.

## 2 THE INTELLECTUAL ORTHODOXY OF THE THIRD REPUBLIC

To understand the context within which structuralism and existentialism emerged it is necessary to outline the traditions in reaction to which they developed. The close relationship between French academic and political life under the Third Republic means that these traditions, and the reactions to them, also have to be located politically.

In the inter-war years the university was dominated by Durkheimian sociology and by Bergsonian philosophy, two schools of thought that had been closely associated with the pre-war Republic. I shall consider each, briefly, in turn.

The rise of Durkheimian sociology was intimately connected with the rebuilding of France after the Franco-Prussian War. This task fell to the Third Republic, to which the Durkheimians were passionately committed. The Republicans, and the Republic itself, were opposed on the Right by various nationalistic, militantly Catholic, and monarchist, extra-parliamentary groups. On the Left they were opposed by the growing organization of the working-class, which also tended to take an extra-parliamentary, syndicalist, form. The Republicans, whose following was largely petit-bourgeois, were held together by their opposition to the monarchists, and, increasingly, by the anti-clericalism which came to the fore in their attempts to secularize the education system.

To liberal intellectuals the Republic constituted the middle ground between the forces of the Right, dedicated to the overthrow of the Republic, and those of the left, dedicated to the overthrow of the whole society. Particularly after the Dreyfus case the Republic was on the offensive: it represented the new society in the making, it was the force that would subordinate all classes to the overriding good of society as a whole.

This collective social force was seen as a moral force, so the task of the Republic was to develop a secular morality and to forge the institutions that would impose this morality on society. In this way the political reforms of the Republic, and especially the reform of the education system, would overcome the social conflict that was the product of a pathological absence of normative order. The Republican triumph in the Dreyfus affair gave Republicanism the opportunity to implement this programme, and the Durkheimians took it upon themselves to play a leading role in the reform of education by occupying key positions within academic life and educational administration.

It is these political concerns that dominate Durkheim's social philosophy. For Durkheim society is a collective moral force that stands above the individual. Social order depends on the proper integration of the individual into this 'collective conscience'. In Durkheim's earlier writings this integration depends on the existence of a pervasive network of social interactions so that each individual is subject to the moral influence of his or her neighbours. This moral influence imposes norms on the individual that ensure the integration of the personality (which can only find moral guidance through participation in the collective) and that ensure the orderliness of society.

In *The Division of Labour in Society* Durkheim's remedy for economic conflict was to suggest the formation of professional associations that would bring producers and consumers, workers and employers into more intimate contact with one another so as to ensure the cohesion of society by establishing a normative regulation in areas where communication had broken down. Hence in this work society is seen as a moral network of communication through which the collective conscience imposes itself on all members of society.

In his later work, most notably *The Elementary Forms of the Religious Life*, the emphasis changes and the relationship between the individual and the collective is seen as being more direct. The collective conscience consists not only of moral norms but also of collective representations that govern all forms of thought. The collective conscience is the foundation of morality and of science, the source of concepts as well as of norms, thus the seat of reason. Participation in the collective conscience is now seen as the necessary condition for all rationality: the individual isolated from the collective conscience is incapable of rational activity and is guided by pure instinctive emotion. The collective is thus guide and judge of both reason and morality.

The collective conscience imposes itself on the individual through individual participation in collective experiences. In 'primitive' societies these take the form of religious experiences in which individuals come together as collectivities and experience a surge of religious emotion, which is the mystified form taken by their affective reaction to the awesome majesty of the collective conscience.

In a more developed society Durkheim's demystification of religion makes it possible to replace God by a secular authority and recognize the embodiment of the collective conscience in its secular expression, the State. Correspondingly the authority of the collective conscience need no longer rely on irrational emotional reactions to a mystified religious symbol, but can be established through a secular rationalist system of state education.

Durkheim's social philosophy can be summed up in a few words. It is collectivist, asserting the existence of society as an entity distinct from, and standing over, the individual. It is sociologistic, for the reason and morality that distinguish humans from animals derive not from the individual but from society. It is rationalistic, for society is a purely rational sphere, affectivity being a quality of the biological individual that society displaces. It is secular, for religion is the product of an irrational affective reaction to society that is progressively displaced by the advance of society and the concomitant progress of reason. Finally it is positivistic, for social facts are external facts, constraining on the individual, and so amenable to study by the methods of positive science. It was the total commitment of the Durkheimians to the secular rationalism of the Republic that enabled them to maintain such a firm belief in the tangible objective reality of the collective conscience.

The Durkheimian commitment to the Republic was complete. The commitments of the Durkheimians were the commitments of the Republic, their preoccupation with questions of education and of a secular morality were the preoccupations of the Republic. For them the Republic was the embodiment of the collective conscience, the triumph of reason over selfish instinct and blind emotion, the means to an orderly, rational, and so fully human society.

It should not be surprising that the fate of Durkheimian sociology in France was intimately connected with the fate of the Republic, nor should it be surprising that the triumph of Republicanism and the accession of the Durkheimians to the establishment should generate a reaction. The liberalism of the Republican dream was soon undermined by the heavy-handed authoritarianism with which the Republic pursued its anti-clerical crusade. Moreover the Republican reforms that were supposed to usher in the age of reason were patently not having the effect that was expected of them. Far from a harmonious society emerging, opposition to the Republic from Right and Left was growing, and the threat of European war loomed. It was in this context that Bergson's philosophy came to dominance in the decade before World War I.

Bergson was a moderate critic of the Republican ideal who sought in his philosophy a total reconciliation in which everything would have its place, but in which the claims of reason would be limited by their subordination to the ultimate spiritual truths of experience. Bergson recognized the practical claims of reason, but he argued that reason could have no more than a practical value: it could never encompass the wholeness, the richness, the spiritual quality of experience. His philosophy is therefore based on the fundamental opposition between practical reason and spiritual experience.

For Bergson reason imposes an analytic grid on experience in which the data of experience are forced into a network of concepts and of logical relations. Reason, therefore, can only present an image of reality that is static, in which rigid concepts are imposed on a fluid experience. It can give us a form of knowledge, but this is not a direct knowledge of reality, it is mediated by the conceptual framework within which reality is known and this framework necessarily distorts reality. The knowledge gained is therefore only relative. It has a practical validity in enabling us to organize our daily life, to orient ourselves to a world to which we relate instrumentally, but this validity is purely pragmatic. By contrast the task of philosophy is to give us immediate access to true reality, and this can only be achieved through the direct intuitive apprehension of experience.

Whereas reason fragments experience in order to force experience into the mould of its concepts, and so gives a purely external knowledge of reality, intuition penetrates to the inner reality of the world of experience. Intuition is a spiritual experience in which the veil of concepts is torn away and the spiritual unity of the experiencing subject and the experienced object is achieved. It is not a consciousness of self, but a consciousness that dissolves the individuated self into the totality.

This experience is an experience of pure duration, which Bergson contrasts with the scientific concept of time. Science can only conceptualize time by using a spatial analogy and reducing time to a discontinuous sequence of points in space, thus imposing stability and discontinuity on an experience whose essence is continuity and movement. By contrast intuition provides us with a direct and immediate apprehension of the true nature of reality as continuity in which we become part of a spiritual whole which is always in the process of becoming. Thus immediate experience is not the experience of a static present, but of a duration in which the moment is given meaning by its relation to its past and to its future possibilities, an experience of participation in the timeless world of developing and unconstrained spirit: an experience not of things, but of pure movement, not of self, but of the absolute. It is this absolute spiritual principle of purely qualitative, continuous, unpredictable becoming that Bergson called the *élan vital*, the animating principle of the universe.

Bergson's philosophy defies rational formulation since it seeks to go beneath reason. Hence to convey what he wants to say Bergson makes extensive use of metaphor, of imagery, and of allusive formulations to refer to an experience that defies description in the categories embedded in language. Bergson's philosophy was therefore open to a wide range of interpretations. The appeal of Bergson's philosophy lay precisely in this ambiguity. Once the fundamental division between reason and spirit was accepted, then everything and anything could be fitted into the system on one side or the other: everything could either be grasped by reason or escaped it. Moreover, by adjusting the balance between reason and spirit, and interpreting the latter in various ways, the philosophy could be used to support a wide range of interpretations, with a range of political implications.

Bergson's philosophy was institutionalized within the academic system as a rather complacent attempt to reconcile the temporal claims of Republicanism and of positive science with the spiritual values of freedom, progress and absolute creativity. Thus the philosophy recognized the validity of secular rationalism as a moral and cognitive system adapted to the needs of everyday individual and social life, but only as the condensation of one moment in the development of the *élan vital*.

The divorce of reason from immediate spiritual experience introduced a division between the secular state and the eternal spirit, the secular state being a pragmatic requirement of an orderly social existence, the spirit the expression of the moral destiny of society. Just as the appeal of Durkheim's sociology as a positive science of society depended on the identification of the collective conscience with the Republican state, so the initial appeal of Bergsonism depended on the identification of that state as a moment of the *élan vital*.

While the absolutist claims of Durkheimianism meant that its fate was inextricably bound up with that of the Republic, Bergson's philosophy, in dissociating the temporal from the spiritual realm, could be used to curb the ambitions of the Republic. Hence Bergsonism was progressively dissociated from its Republican origins as disillusion with Republicanism grew before and after World War I. The vagueness of the philosophy meant that it was open to a variety of national-patriotic, Catholic or individualist reinterpretations to provide the basis for a series of irrationalist critiques of Republican rationalism. Thus Bergsonism, a philosophy which was originally formulated as a repudiation of metaphysics in the name of immediate experience, became an increasingly metaphysical doctrine and, despite the intentions of its founder, Bergsonism became ever more closely associated with an increasingly reactionary and irrationalist Catholic opposition to the Republic.

Despite their differences Durkheim and Bergson have much in

common. In particular they share classical French philosophy's dualistic formulation of the opposition between reason and emotion. For Durkheim the division between reason and emotion corresponds to the division between culture and nature, or humanity and animality, as two different orders of reality. Reason is the product of collective existence. It is purely objective and external to the individual, and is accessible to the methods of positive science. Emotion, the basis of the illusion of spiritual being, is the expression of an instinctive residue of animality, and so, by implication, of biological processes within the individual psyche. Emotion is therefore derivative: it is vague and confused and so cannot be pinned down by intuition and cannot provide a basis for knowledge.

For Bergson reason and spirit do not correspond to different orders of reality, but to two different aspects of consciousness: mediated and immediate experience. Reason, science and culture are pragmatic mental constructs that individualize humans within the *élan vital*, the life force that pervades all reality. Intuition restores the true unity of culture and nature, reveals culture as an artificial imposition on the flux of nature, an emergent property of nature, residue of the progress of the *élan vital*. Thus for Bergson positivist methods cannot provide true knowledge, which is only amenable to the spiritual, subjective, method of intuition.

This common dualism in which subjectivity and objectivity, reason and emotion, are first separated and then one subordinated to the other is associated in both Bergson and Durkheim with a rejection of the Cartesian ego. For Durkheim the Cartesian ego is replaced by the collective conscience. The empirical ego is the point of intersection of nature, source of instinct and emotion, and culture, source of reason and morality.

For Bergson the Cartesian ego is a construct of reason, an imposition on the flux of experience, thus the empirical ego is the point of intersection of the *élan vital*, eternal and pervasive spirit, and the pragmatic constructs of reason that give the ego the illusion of a fixed location in time and space. Thus for both Bergson and Durkheim the empirical ego is essentially illusory, the contingent point of intersection of two different orders. For Bergson these orders are spiritual, the *élan vital* and the constructs of reason. For Durkheim they are objective, the collective conscience and the biological individual. In each case the empirical ego is subordinated to a higher spiritual (subjective) or secular (objective) reality, the source of a morality that transcends the individual. The 'death of the subject', much vaunted slogan of structuralism, has roots that go back deep into French philosophy. Both Durkheimian sociology and Bergsonian philosophy were prevented from becoming transparently metaphysical doctrines only by the identification of the transcendent objective or subjective principle with the Republic as custodian of the collective conscience or of the *élan vital*. Once the obviousness of this identification was broken by the degeneration of the Republic, the metaphysical character of the doctrines became clear.

The scientific claims of the Durkheimians could only be maintained by an increasing dogmatism that asserted the existence of an orderly collective conscience that, at least in their own society, riven by conflict, they could not identify. Only in the study of 'primitive societies', to which the Durkheimians increasingly turned, or in the study of the tangible realities of law and religion, where they retained some credibility, could the pretence that society is regulated by a harmonizing collective morality be reasonably maintained.

The philosophical validity of Bergsonian dualism came to depend on acceptance of the *élan vital* as a metaphysical and irrational spiritual reality. If the divorce between reason and spirit, at the expense of reason, was rejected, the whole Bergsonian edifice came to be seen as an irrationalist metaphysical ideology that could serve only a discredited Republic or the forces of Catholic reaction. While Durkheimianism was utterly moribund by the late 1920s, Bergsonism had a more menacing appearance.

# 3 THE INTER-WAR INTELLECTUAL CRISIS

World War I and its aftermath left the Third Republic discredited and reduced its historical claims to the level of an hypocritical farce. The glorious war left France with two and a half million dead or permanently disabled, with a huge debt that was the basis of a permanent financial crisis, and with a series of ineffectual governments coming under increasing attack from extra-parliamentary forces on the Left and the Right. The initiative lay firmly with the right-wing Leagues whose militant rhetoric appealed particularly to the young and which came to dominate Catholic intellectuals and writers of the twenties and thirties. Whoever was making history, there was no doubt that it was no longer the Republic.

The degeneration of the Third Republic discredited the liberal philosophies that had been associated with it. Thus there was a fundamental reconstruction of liberal culture in inter-war France, a questioning of received ideology, and the development of new philosophies on the basis of a common rejection of the philosophical heritage of the Republic. Central to this rejection was the critique of the metaphysical character of the pre-war philosophies which had opened those philosophies up to increasingly conservative or reactionary interpretations.

This was not simply a philosophical rejection, but was fundamentally an ideological and political one. The principles that had been presented as eternal moral truths, the culmination of an infinite and continuous evolutionary progress, were now seen as no more than the hypocritical alibi of a morally bankrupt social class. This social class, still nominally clinging to its archaic bourgeois morality, had presided over the degeneration of the Republican ideals, over the destruction of millions of young lives in World War I, over the post-war economic decline and over growing social conflict, and it now sought to abdicate from its responsibility for the economic, political and moral collapse of the society it had created by retreating into the world of spirit, dissociating its absurd morality from the chaos it had created.

A morality that could patently no longer be preserved by appealing to any substantive concern with justice, freedom and equality, was preserved by appealing to the historical evolution of empty moral categories in the self-development of a detached metaphysical world of spirit. Thus Brunschvig, who was Professor of Philosophy at the Sorbonne between the wars, was, with Bergson, the prime object of revulsion. Brunschvig was a critical idealist for whom philosophy was the philosophy of knowledge. The task of philosophy was to grasp the mind 'in its own movement . . . intellectual activity coming to consciousness of itself, this is the integral study of integral knowledge, this is philosophy'.[1] This activity is ceaseless, progressive, and continuous. Lévi-Strauss well expressed a common reaction to this philosophy:

'Philosophy was . . . a kind of aesthetic contemplation of consciousness by itself. It was seen as having evolved, in the course of the centuries, ever higher and bolder structures, as having solved problems of balance or support and as having invented logical refinements, and the result was held to be valid, in proportion to its technical perfection or internal coherence. . . . The signifier did not relate to any signified; there was no referent. Expertise replaced the truth.'[2]

To the young radical intellectuals of the inter-war generation the elaborate philosophies of their teachers were not simply unsatisfactory, they were totally unacceptable. The received philosophies belonged to a bygone age. For many the reaction was a violent one, a reaction of total revulsion with the intellectual and moral bankruptcy, with the utter hypocrisy, of the older generation. Initially the reaction had little political content, and the older generation were confronted not so much with sustained intellectual argument as with ridicule and abuse. Surrealism formulated the reaction of the 1920s. The core of surrealism was the negation of all received doctrines, the denial of all absolutes, its slogan was '*tabula rasa*'. Closely associated with the Surrealists was the 'Philosophies' group that emerged in 1924 and included Henri Lefebvre, Georges Politzer and Georges Friedmann.

The reaction of the 1920s was a largely negative one, an often brutal assertion of objectivity against the subjective fantasies of philosophy, an assertion of the value of action as opposed to speculation, involving the scandalous violation of the norms so dear to the older generation in an attempt to counterpose a brutal reality to the illusions of received philosophy. At first the response was very confused, and it often retained a strong spiritual component which gave it much in common with the extreme right-wing reaction to the decadence of the Republic.

Towards the end of the 1920s the Philosophies group, along with many of the Surrealists, embraced Marxism and joined the Communist Party. But even this did not really provide the movement with a solid foundation, for the appeal of communism to the group was the fact that its rejection of capitalist society and of all compromise with that society was total, this being the period of 'ultra-leftism' in the Comintern, and the appeal of Marxism was the appeal of the young Marx's account of capitalist society as pure negation and of philosophy as the ultimate development of this negation. This Marxism did not offer a new philosophy, but proclaimed the death of all philosophy.

It was only at the end of the decade that a more positive orientation began to emerge, and Simone de Beauvoir has described the renewal of optimism at the end of the decade as the crash of 1929 brought home the fragility of the capitalist edifice.[3] It was from the generation who were students in 1929 that the most important new intellectuals were to emerge: Claude Lévi-Strauss, Jean-Paul Sartre, Raymond Aron, Maurice Merleau-Ponty, Simone de Beauvoir, Paul Nizan and many more.

Nizan, an exact contemporary of Sartre and the man who suggested to Lévi-Strauss that he take up anthropology, was the man who bridged the two decades. Initially attracted by the extreme Right, then on the fringes of the Philosophies group, then a Communist militant, Nizan was serious in a way that many of his contemporaries were not. *Aden-Arabie* (1931) is an account of his trip to Aden in 1926–7 which is both a savage attack on the hypocritical pretensions of bourgeois morality and a denunciation of the various forms of escapism that were offered to the youth of the 1920s, with his trip to Aden revealing the illusory character of the final escape through travel, the last refuge of his generation (and one that is still a central theme in the emerging culture of the 1930s).

In its negative and destructive aspects *Aden-Arabie* is a product of the 1920s, but it also marks a break with the idealist solutions of the 1920s and tentatively offers a way forward. To the illusions in which the bourgeoisie and the rebellious youth of the 1920s are immersed Nizan contrasts the human experience of empirical individuals, and especially of the oppressed, which provides him with a privileged reality from which to launch his attack. In many respects *Aden-Arabie* anticipates the central theme of Lévi-Strauss' account of his stay in Brazil in the 1930s, *Tristes Tropiques* (1955). Lévi-Strauss' book too is about the illusions of travel, the impossibility of escape from a bourgeois culture that has encompassed the globe, and it too offers as the only hope of salvation the human experience of the oppressed that it contrasts with the pretensions of the oppressors. For Lévi-Strauss, writing in 1955, this hope has become a vain one, and humanity is doomed to extinction, whereas Nizan believed through the 1930s that the oppressed could liberate society and committed himself wholeheartedly to the Communist movement.

In *Les Chiens de Garde* (1932) Nizan directed his polemic more directly at the high priests of philosophy, and especially at Bergson, Brunschvig and the Durkheimians, whom he denounced as the official philosophers of a despotic bourgeoisie, whose writings he contrasted with reports of the barbarous reality of oppression and exploitation that the official philosophy sanctified in the name of its absolute morality. Nizan denounces the attempts of this philosophy to mystify the new generation by drawing them into metaphysical diversions, into the cult of the mind. To established philosophy Nizan counterposed everyday experience, to the bourgeois humanist concept of man he counterposed the existence of real men and women whom philosophers, while proclaiming themselves humanists, despise.

Nizan's polemic was passionate, committed and extreme. While many of his generation would reject the tone of Nizan's critique, and many would not have endorsed his decision to commit himself to the Communist Party, his work nevertheless expressed the sentiments of his generation. Most importantly it expressed a commitment to a return to reality, to the reality of the day-to-day experience of individual human beings, and it was this counterposition of mundane human existence to lofty metaphysical constructions that provided both a critique of established philosophy and a way forward: the study of the concept of Man would be displaced by the study of real men and women (although the study of women was left entirely to Simone de Beauvoir). The limits of knowledge, of meaning and of truth would be the limits of real everyday existence. Hence the new generation of thinkers, including Lévi-Strauss, had a profoundly humanistic inspiration, seeking to recover real human beings from the mystifications of bourgeois humanism. They were preoccupied with grasping the true meaning of human existence as an empirical question amenable to rational philosophical or scientific investigation.

This new humanism was the basis of the rejection of the received philosophies, and the basis on which a new approach could be constructed. Firstly, the metaphysical appeal to absolutes of morality was rejected in the name of concrete human existence. Thus a new morality had to be rooted in experience and not imposed on the individual (whence the fundamental slogan of existentialism, 'existence precedes essence', that could be taken, in different interpretations, as the slogan of the age).

Secondly, the rejection of the metaphysical in the name of the individual was associated with a rejection of irrationalism in the name of rationality. This rationality could not be an absolute and eternal reality, but had rather to be rooted in experience, the rationality of everyday existence, to be discovered through a philosophical or a sociological investigation of everyday life.

Thirdly, the rejection of the metaphysical entailed the rejection of all forms of historicism, rejection of the subordination of the individual to externally imposed historical laws of development (whether spiritual or material) and so the rejection of any belief in the necessarily progressive and continuous character of history. Such a belief could hardly be reconciled with the experience of inter-war France in which continuity signified degeneration and decay, in which only a radical break could arrest the continuous logic of decline. Thus 'all our teachers were obsessed with the historical approach', yet 'our teachers were ignorant of History'.[4] Brunschvig's continuous progress of reason and morality, Bergson's creative evolution, the Durkheimian genetic morphology, in which social structures evolved harmoniously from the simple to the complex, were all equally unacceptable, and all contrasted sharply with the reality of history. 'Historicism' stood out clearly as an ideology that masked oppression and exploitation. Thus the rejection of historicism raised the problem of the true human meaning of history.

To anyone from an Anglo-Saxon or a German background this turn to the empirical human individual may not appear very startling, for the rejection of metaphysics on the basis of a liberal individualism has long been a commonplace in the Anglo-Saxon world, and was well-established by the end of the nineteenth century in Germany. But in France liberalism had been traditionally associated not with individualism, but with Republicanism, with the defence of the secular state against the personal exercise of monarchical power. The generation of the 1930s could not turn to an established tradition of liberal individualism to find ready-made solutions. Hence it is characteristic of this generation that they had to find inspiration from abroad. Sartre went to Germany to find Husserl and Heidegger, Aron to find Weber, Merleau-Ponty to find Husserl, Lukacs, and Weber, while Lévi-Strauss discovered North American anthropology. In France itself Freud, Gestalt psychology and a humanist interpretation of Hegel and Marx made headway at this time. Yet this generation did not take solutions from abroad ready-made. They were, after all, heirs to the French philosophical tradition which had provided their starting point. Thus we find novel solutions being put forward, solutions which, particularly in the case of Sartre and Lévi-Strauss, retain a strong metaphysical core and close links with the philosophical tradition they both rejected.

The turn to the empirical individual was not as unproblematic as it might appear. While the idea of the empirical individual is a good polemical device with which to combat an out-dated metaphysics, the real thing is rather difficult to pin down. What, after all, is the empirical individual, shorn of all preconceptions? The Cartesian individual is very different from the individual of English utilitarianism or the individual of American behaviourism or the Kantian individual.

Although both Sartre and Lévi-Strauss try to go behind all such metaphysical constructs to find the pure human individual immersed in the reality of daily life the individual they come up with is not so concrete after all. For Sartre the individual is to be found in a radical phenomenological reduction in which all preconceptions are swept away, all abstractions are abolished, and the truly human individual is found, free and unconstrained, in the immediacy of pure existence. For Lévi-Strauss, by contrast, Sartre's approach to the individual through introspection can only produce another, rather banal, metaphysic. For Lévi-Strauss it is science that can reveal the truly human individual, a purely objective approach to individuals in society that equally rejects all supra-human abstractions but that finds the individual in the objective study of the varieties of human existence.

In neither case is the concern really with individuals as they live their daily lives, for both seek to found a critique of the vanity and illusions of daily life. Both seek a moral theory that can provide a theory of the truth of humanity against which to measure the conceits of everyday life. Thus both seek the fundamental meaning of human existence rather than its mundane reality, and it is this that determines their particular conceptions of the individual, conceptions that are in each case prior to the deceptive reality of everyday experience. Thus both Sartre and Lévi-Strauss seek a privileged human reality in a new metaphysical theory of humanity.

In this respect Sartre and Lévi-Strauss remain more firmly

within the French philosophical tradition than, for example, Aron and Merleau-Ponty, whose concerns were less moralistic. This is reflected in the fact that neither Sartre nor Lévi-Strauss make such a radical break with the traditions they rejected than might seem at first sight, and for both Bergson remains an essential, though always implicit, point of reference.

Sartre adopts the Bergsonian framework lock, stock and barrel, and retains the Bergsonian starting point of the immediate apprehension of experience as the apprehension of an unconstrained holistic becoming, using this apprehension as the basis for a critique of the absolutist claims of analytic reason. Where Sartre breaks with Bergson is in the conception of experience as an experience of participation in a whole that transcends individual existence. For Sartre there is nothing beyond the existence of the individual, no truths to be found in a higher realm of spirit. Thus Sartre's philosophy, to characterize it crudely, seeks to establish the Bergsonian philosophy on a rigorous foundation by abolishing the mystical transcendentalism of the *élan vital*, and by finding meaning exclusively in existence.

In this context Lévi-Strauss can be seen as offering a more radical, but essentially Durkheimian and positivistic, critique of Bergson. For Lévi-Strauss it is only the reason and the intellect that can give us access to anything worthy of being called truth. The emotional and aesthetic 'truths' of immediate experience are simply mystical, vague and misleading sensations that have no objective status. Thus Lévi-Strauss inverts the Bergsonian relation between reason and experience to find the truth of humanity in the emergence of the intellect, and the true meaning of human existence in the subordination of emotion to reason. This essentially Durkheimian critique of Bergsonism is tempered by a rejection of the metaphysical dimension of the Durkheimian identification of reason and intellect, and so of human truth, with the social and the divorce that this introduces between the individual and his, or her, humanity.

Behind the immediate continuity with Bergsonism one can also detect a more fundamental continuity still in the work of Sartre and Lévi-Strauss, and see them as reasserting the traditions of classical French philosophy by offering, on the one hand, a Cartesian and, on the other hand, a Rousseauean critique of Bergsonism. To develop this theme would take us too far from the task in hand, which is to draw out the originality of the contributions of Sartre and Lévi-Strauss. The important lesson to draw is that Sartre and Lévi-Strauss both produce a critique of metaphysics that is itself from the very beginning metaphysical. This is very important to an understanding of Lévi-Strauss' work, and of the subsequent development of structuralism, for it will be one of my central arguments in this book that in Lévi-Strauss' work the metaphysic takes over and, in the attempt to preserve the metaphysical theory of humanity, the fundamental humanist inspiration is progressively eroded as the empirical individual is subordinated to the concept of humanity.

# 4 REACTION TO THE CRISIS—THE EXISTENTIALIST PHILOSOPHY OF SARTRE

The new generation were critics of their society and of the philosophy that, for them, gave this society ideological support. They were seeking a rational basis on which to establish the meaning of individual existence in an irrational world, a standpoint from which to criticize their own society as the deformation of the rationality of individual existence. Thus they were preoccupied with the search for a rational foundation for human existence, and for the conditions for a rational society. Established philosophy and sociology could not provide them with any solutions, indeed it was established philosophy and sociology that was the problem. Sociology offered a supra-individual society as the measure of rationality, philosophy offered subordination to a metaphysical realm of spirit. Nor could established psychology provide any answers, divided as it was between a metaphysical intuitionist psychology and a positivist assimilation of psychology to physiology. Hence established psychology reproduced the deficiences of established philosophy, as Politzer had argued in his very influential *Critique des fondements de la psychologie* (1928).

There were two theories becoming available in France during the 1920s that, for some, provided a ready-made solution to the philosophical problems they confronted: Marxism and psychoanalysis. Both Marxism and psychoanalysis provide a way of integrating the rational and the irrational in a single synthesis. Both provided the means of giving history a new meaning, apparently not based on the continuous progress of some abstract metaphysical principle.

Marxism, especially in the humanistic interpretations of Marx's early works that made headway in France in the early 1930s, restored meaning to history by seeing the irrationality of history as an expression of the alienation of human existence in a class society, to which it counterposed the recovery of the human essence, and the creation of a rational society, in a revolutionary transformation. History is therefore seen as contradictory, yet progressive, given meaning by the positive moment of the dialectic in which the irrational is transcended in the development towards the final goal.

Freudianism restores meaning to human existence in an irrational world not through history, but through the unconscious. The key to the apparently irrational formulations of conscious life, the fantastic mythologies of racism, religious mysticism, blind national-patriotism, is to be found in the unconscious, which provides both an explanation and a critique of the illusions of conscious existence.

A few embraced Marx or Freud enthusiastically. But there were barriers to the acceptance of either thinker even for the more radical young intellectuals, quite apart from the fact that their works were neither widely available nor well understood in France at the time.

Before 1934 the Communist Party adopted an 'ultra-leftist' position, denouncing all other political organizations of the working class as agents of the bourgeoisie, or even as objectively fascist. This gave Marxism an appeal to some, expressing as it did a philosophy of total negativity, but even this appeal was weakened with the expulsion of Trotsky, who had particularly appealed to the Surrealists, from the Soviet Union in 1929. Hence it was not until 1934, and the turn to a Popular Front policy, that the Communist Party became more generally acceptable to intellectuals.

Freudianism was also not wholly acceptable, for Freud's ultimate reliance on instinctive mechanisms to explain the workings of the unconscious smacked too much of the irrationalism against which the new generation was reacting. The Freudian unconscious seemed to Sartre to oscillate between a physiological mechanism and another consciousness.[5] Thus, although Marxism and psychoanalysis provided a vague and diffuse inspiration to many, they were actually espoused by only a few.

Although the young intellectuals who came of age at the end of the 1920s shared a common rejection of established philosophy and of the society that it expressed, the alternatives they adopted varied considerably. While Nizan turned to Marxism to provide a revolutionary critique of his own society, Aron turned to Weber for a liberal critique. The philosophies of Sartre and Lévi-Strauss, by contrast, expressed a more radical rejection.

Sartre and Lévi-Strauss each developed a critique which addressed itself to society and to philosophy *per se*. For both this critique implied the adoption of the individual as the foundation of meaning and of morality, and so of the critique of society and of its pretensions. But this individual was not an historically located individual, living in a particular society, as it was for Nizan or for Aron (or, for that matter, for Merleau-Ponty). For Sartre and Lévi-Strauss society, and the rhetoric that accompanies it, is confronted by a desocialized individual; both seek the foundation of society in the nature of individual existence, and so in the generic individual. Hence both seek philosophical, rather than sociological, solutions, that are based on the radical dichotomization of subject and object, of for-itself and in-itself, with the assimilation of society to one pole, and its critique in terms of the individual to the other.

Sartre and Lévi-Strauss differ fundamentally in their conception of the individual, and this difference establishes both the distinctiveness and the complementarity of their philosophies. For Sartre the individual is Cartesian, in the sense that he or she is defined by the purity and freedom of his or her consciousness. It is the conscious mind that imposes meaning on experience by integrating experience into a meaningful whole. This consciousness is transcendent, unconstrained by any physical or moral absolutes, capable of refusing any obligation imposed by nature or by society. The Bergsonian experience of freedom and of creativity is not the passive experience of an external *élan vital*, it is the immediate consciousness of the self. The Sartrean ego is therefore pure unconstrained subjectivity. For Sartre society with its formidable apparatus of moral constraint, is assimilated to the pole of the object and is criticized from the pole of the transcendent subject.

For Lévi-Strauss the individual is Freudian, though purged of all irrationalism by the reduction of the unconscious to a purely formal structuring capacity, defined by the universal unconscious, an absolute object in which is inscribed the full range of human possibilities. The unconscious is the true foundation of human existence and the necessary foundation of any orderly human social life. Consciousness, and especially consciousness of the subject, is therefore illusory, contrasted with the objectivity of the unconscious as an insubstantial and ineffectual subjectivity. The pretensions of society, expressed in its dominant humanist ideology, are assimilated to the subject as the projection of the vain illusions of a conceited humanity.

Sartre's philosophy is set out in *Being and Nothingness*, a work completed in 1942. Although Sartre has modified it subsequently, the fundamentals remain unchanged. Sartre remains within the Cartesian tradition of French philosophy, reinterpreting the Cartesian Cogito along lines suggested by Husserl. This reinterpretation involves a rejection of the dualistic Bergsonian separation of reason, ruled by eternal and immutable categories progressively revealed in the continuous advance of science and philosophy, and experience, ruled by the irrational and elusive *élan vital*. This Bergsonian separation proposes as the only alternatives a pragmatic, but irrational, subordination of the individual to the dictates of reason, or a mystical, and equally irrational, subordination of the individual to the eternal spirit of creation. Sartre sought to abolish this dualism by reintegrating Bergson's reason and experience not in the eternal spirit, but rather in the individual existence.

Sartre sought to sweep away all the metaphysical dressing in a return to the brute reality of *existence*, the experience of which is an experience of freedom. Direct experience reveals the world to us not as a brute objective fact, but as *our* world, object of our desires, our ambitions, our aspirations. Our relation to the world is not, therefore, determined by the world, but by our own choice of the way in which we, as conscious beings, relate to the world.

Experience is not imposed by the world, nor by an irrational Bergsonian *élan* or Freudian unconscious. It is consciously created by us as a part of the project which defines our being in the world. To believe otherwise, to refuse to recognize our own responsibility for our own actions, is simply 'bad faith'. The world itself is absurd and without meaning: the experience of the transcendence of human existence is the sole basis of meaning, and so the only basis of morality. The moral duty of the individual is simply to assert his or her existence as a human individual in the face of the world, to refuse to submit to any external moral or physical determination. The continuity of meaning and of history, the permanence of cultural values are all undermined. Life is for the moment, consciousness is of the moment, unconstrained and unpredictable.

Sartre offers a philosophy of defiance, a philosophy which holds society at arm's length, refusing to recognize the subordination of the individual to a society dominated by hypocrisy, dishonesty and evasion. Social relations become the struggles between naked individuals in which each tries to assert his or her own freedom. The absolute freedom of the individual includes the freedom to treat the other as an object, but it also implies an absolute obligation on the individual not to permit him or herself to be reduced to an object by the other, so that social life becomes a struggle to reduce others to objects in one's own world and to avoid one's own reduction to an object in theirs. Life is nothing but a struggle for authenticity, a struggle against 'bad faith' in which individuals are ceaselessly pitted against one another. There is no other moral principle, life has no ultimate meaning, in the last analysis it is meaningless and absurd. Since there are no rational grounds for defending one course of action rather than another, the course adopted is ultimately arbitrary, the only obligation being to *choose*.

Society is condemned by being reduced to a mirage, an expression of the abdication to inauthenticity, of the bad faith which pervades society. It is not norms and values which induce people to act, but rather they ascribe courses of action which they have freely chosen, for which they will not assume responsibility, to norms and values. The latter are therefore a myth, an alibi invented to justify the unjustifiable. Certainly exploitation and domination exist, but they do not force people to behave in certain ways, for even the exploited and dominated continue to be human, to have the power to say no, to refuse to submit to the other.

This philosophy gives history a meaning, but that meaning is ascribed to history by the individual who lives that history, and does not exist beyond the individual. The meaning of history is not given to the present by the past from which it came, but by the future towards which the individual projects it in his or her imagination. History is not, therefore, continuous and progressive, nor does it have any absolute meaning. Its meaning is exhausted by the sum of meanings it has for individual participants, and this meaning is fundamentally discontinuous, for it is subject to doubt at every moment in its trajectory.

Sartre's early human philosophy offers a rigorous and coherent rationalization of the position of a radical-liberal intellectual in the thirties, expressing his isolation from a society which he could condemn but not change and providing a basis on which he could live out this isolation by immersing himself in his personal salvation, giving a supreme moral value to the most meaningless actions, to the most futile protests and even to pointless self-sacrifice. As a human philosophy Sartre's existentialism expressed the tragedy of so many of his generation, but for that very reason it could not provide the basis for an understanding of society. Society is simply an absence in Sartre's scheme, an expression of all that humanity is not. It is a tacit pact between people to deny their humanity and to attribute their human capacities to an alien force. People enter into this pact because of their individual moral failings, because of the awesome responsibility which their humanity gives them and which they are too weak to assume. The point is not to understand society, but to abolish it by an individual act of moral heroism, itself quite arbitrary and motiveless, which renounces what is for what might be.

For the intellectual of independent means this view of society could seem quite plausible, but it ignores the reality which society has for those less able to imagine themselves as monads, for those who depend on others, in one way or another, for their day-to-day existence, and particularly for those who cannot afford to ignore the realities of exploitation and domination. For these people it is clear that society is more than a phantom, is more than a collective alibi, but that it is actually constraining and is actually systematic. Moreover for these people individual resistance to society, even when aided by existential psychoanalysis, is futile, while there do exist possibilities of common action to change society.

In Sartre's later work he has attempted to reconcile his early philosophy, and particularly his insistence on the absolute character of human freedom, with the density and systematic organization of society and with the possibilities of common action which can effectively challenge the existing organization of society. Few critics believe that this reconciliation has been successful, for any recognition of the power of external constraint or of the validity of subordination to the collective compromises the absolute freedom on which the philosophy as a whole is founded.

## 5 LÉVI-STRAUSS' REJECTION OF PHENOMENOLOGY

Lévi-Strauss was trained, like Sartre, as a philosopher. However he went further than Sartre in his rejection of the orthodox philosophy of his teachers, abandoning philosophy as the basis on which one can know humanity for anthropology. Nevertheless

'I was brought up a philosopher, and like many in France I came to sociology and ethnology from philosophy. I had in mind to answer philosophical questions.'[8]

Like Sartre, Lévi-Strauss was looking for a base on which to build a rationalist human philosophy, but he rejected phenomenology and existentialism, believing that their immersion in the problems of the individual prevented them from having any possibility of discovering truths about humanity. Lévi-Strauss was not concerned with immersing himself in the experience of a particular individual in a particular society at a particular time, and then proclaiming the results of such self-indulgence as eternal truths. Lévi-Strauss was concerned with the most general properties of the human being, those which are expressed in every society. He sought those characteristics which 'have a meaning for all men', rather than those which concerned only one society, and it was anthropology that could reveal this to him:

'A philosopher by profession I threw myself into ethnology to discover a nature still untouched by man'

Ethnology is nothing less than an effort to explain the complete man by means of studying the whole social experience of man . . . the aim is to isolate, from the mass of customs, creeds and institutions, a precipitate which often is infinitesimal but contains in itself the very meaning of man.'[9]

Thus, while the phenomenologists analyzed meaning by reference to the intentionality of the subject, Lévi-Strauss sought meaning through a scientific analysis in which the conscious meaning is to be explained by reference to a more fundamental, objective, meaning:

'to reach reality one has first to reject experience, and then subsequently to reintegrate it into an objective synthesis devoid of any sentimentality.'[10]

Lévi-Strauss' fundamental objection to existentialism and phenomenology was that they resolve the problem of the Bergsonian dualistic separation of subjective experience and objective reality by reducing reality to subjective experience. For Lévi-Strauss knowledge can never be based on subjective experience, it must have an objective foundation, hence Lévi-Strauss sought to achieve an 'objective' synthesis of experience and reality. His ambition was to reconcile the Bergsonian opposition of rational and irrational, intellectual and emotional, logical and prelogical within a higher objective synthesis whose foundation would be not consciousness but the unconscious.

In explaining his scientific orientation Lévi-Strauss refers to both personal and intellectual influences: a predilection for a 'kind of rationalistic monism'; an early interest in geology, which for Lévi-Strauss provides the 'most majestic meaning' of a landscape, 'that which precedes, commands, and, to a large extent explains the others'; and teenage contact with Marxism, that again sought a deeper reality beneath the level of appearances. These early influences in turn prepared Lévi-Strauss for the impact of psychoanalysis, and coloured his interpretation of it. All these influences combined to reveal to Lévi-Strauss that:

'understanding consists in reducing one type of reality to another; that the true reality is never the most obvious; and that the nature of truth is already indicated by the care it takes to remain elusive. For all cases, the same problem arises, the problem of the relationship between feeling and reason, and the aim is the same: to achieve a kind of *superrationalism*, which will integrate the first with the second, without sacrificing any of its properties.'[11]

Psychoanalysis immediately appealed to Lévi-Strauss as a critical weapon. It restores meaning to the human being through the unconscious, introducing, like geology, an order into apparent incoherence by referring the latter to 'certain basic characteristics of the physical or mental universe' so 'interpreting each action as the unfolding in time of certain eternal truths'.[12] Psychoanalysis overcame the static antinomies of Bergsonism by revealing a deeper meaning, the meaning of the unconscious, in which all aspects of mental life are integrated into a single synthesis that can encompass the whole of human existence.

For Lévi-Strauss knowledge of humanity is possible not because humanity participates in the Bergsonian spiritual 'state of mush',[13] nor because of some empathic or intuitive participation in the consciousness of others, but because of the universality of human nature expressed in the generic unconscious. This unconscious is thus the foundation of the possibility of objective knowledge of human nature, and it is only a scientific approach to humanity that can reveal the true and objective foundation of human existence.

The task that Lévi-Strauss sought to accomplish was precisely that of his phenomenologist and existentialist contemporaries. In a sense it was a very conservative task, for they each sought to reassert the rationalistic values of classical French humanist philosophy, to preserve the principles of the Enlightenment in the face of the onslaught of irrationalism. They therefore sought to integrate the whole of human experience in a rational synthesis rooted in the individual mind: to restore the unity of reason and emotion, intellect and experience as the basis of human existence.

It is this rational synthesis that provides the only true and objective meaning for human existence, for it is only reason that can provide a meaning that does not rely on a metaphysical authority. While phenomenology accomplishes this synthesis in consciousness, and tries to find the certain rational foundation for human existence in the philosophical examination of consciousness, Lévi-Strauss accomplishes the synthesis in the unconscious, and tries to find this rational foundation through the scientific study of humanity.

# NOTES

1 L. Brunschvig, *L'idéalisme Contemporain*, 1905, p. 5, quoted F. Copleston, *History of Philosophy*, 9, Burns Oates, 1975, p. 151.
2 *TT*, p. 52.
3 S. de Beauvoir, *The Prime of Life*, Penguin, Harmondsworth, 1965, p. 15.
4 *TT*, p. 52; J. P. Sartre, *Situations*, Hamish Hamilton, London, 1965, p. 229.
5 Sartre, *Between Existentialism and Marxism*, NLB, London, 1974, pp. 37–8.
6 *Ibid.*, pp. 33, 35.

7   *Ibid.*, pp. 52, 54.
8   1966a, p. 33.
9   1974c, p. 26; 1953c, p. 70.
10  *TT*, p. 58.
11  *TT*, pp. 57–8.
12  *TT*, p. 57.
13  *TT*, p. 55.

## III. The Origins of Structuralism

PSYCHOANALYSIS provided Lévi-Strauss with the idea of the unconscious on which to base his distinctive human philosophy and with which to approach the human sciences. But psychoanalysis was not Lévi-Strauss' chosen discipline. It could provide a concept which made it possible to achieve an objective knowledge of humanity, but the practice of psychoanalysis was not the way to achieve this knowledge, for it involved the study of selected individuals, not of humanity as a whole. It is anthropology that is the science of humanity that Lévi-Strauss sought:

'Anthropology affords me intellectual satisfaction: as a form of history, linking up at opposite ends with world history and my own history, it thus reveals the rationale common to both. In proposing the study of mankind, anthropology frees me from doubt, since it examines those differences and changes in mankind which have a meaning for all men, and excludes those peculiar to a single civilization, which dissolve into nothingness under the gaze of the outside observer.'[1]

Lévi-Strauss did not espouse anthropology immediately. At the University anthropology was dominated by the Durkheimians. Lévy-Bruhl eulogized the positivist tradition of Comte and Durkheim and had developed, with his theory of 'primitive mentality', a doctrine that potentially had strong racist overtones. Bouglé, Assistant Director of the Ecole Normale, had achievements behind him, but had become self-appointed, and rather dogmatic, defender of the Durkheimian orthodoxy. It was Bouglé who recommended Lévi-Strauss for his post in Brazil, but Lévi-Strauss did not belong to Bouglé's 'stable'. Only Marcel Mauss, Durkheim's nephew, manifested any originality and flexibility, distancing himself from the Durkheimian legacy. But Mauss did not hold a doctorate, and so was confined to teaching postgraduate students. Lévi-Strauss never attended Mauss' courses, though he read Mauss' works and conducted his fieldwork along

Maussian lines, studying artefacts and their methods of production rather than beliefs and social institutions.[2]

All the Durkheimians, who wrote so much about the nature of humanity, of primitive mentality, of the positivist method, and of exotic institutions were in fact armchair anthropologists whose contact with the societies they explored was second-hand. For Lévi-Strauss it was the reading of Robert Lowie's *Primitive Society* in 1933–4 that provided the 'revelation':

'Instead of providing one with ideas taken from books and immediately changed into philosophical concepts, it described the writer's actual experience of native societies, and presented the significance of that experience through his involvement. My mind was able to escape from the claustrophobic, Turkish-bath atmosphere in which it was being imprisoned by the practice of philosophical reflection.'[3]

Here was the key with which Lévi-Strauss could unlock the storehouse of knowledge not of the *idea* of humanity, but of real living people. But it is important not to overemphasize the impact of North American anthropology on Lévi-Strauss. Lévi-Strauss has made it abundantly clear that, whatever his debts to North American anthropology in relation to specifically anthropological questions, the latter provided more an inspiration than an intellectual tradition. Although as a student the Durkheimian tradition made no positive impact on him, and he arrived in Brazil in 'open revolt against Durkheim and against any attempt to use sociology for metaphysical purposes', his work is situated very firmly within the Durkheimian tradition.[4]

Simone de Beauvoir, who read *The Elementary Structures* in proof while writing the articles that would become *The Second Sex*, fully appreciated the relation between the French and the North American traditions in Lévi-Strauss' work:

'Heir to the French tradition, but starting with American methods, Lévi-Strauss wanted to resume the project of his masters while guarding against their failings.'[5]

Even in his fieldwork Lévi-Strauss remained within the French tradition: he had little training in fieldwork methods and his reports are, by Anglo-Saxon standards, very limited. In almost fifty years as an anthropologist Lévi-Strauss has made two brief fieldwork trips in Brazil and Pakistan and one longer expedition of several months in Brazil—probably no more in his total career, and with less preparation, than a British or American graduate student would complete in preparation for a doctorate: 'I am not ashamed to confess, my time in the field was spent less in working than in learning how to work'.[6]

# 1 LÉVI-STRAUSS AND DURKHEIMIAN PHILOSOPHY

The offer of an appointment in Brazil forced Lévi-Strauss to confront the Durkheimian tradition. In turning to anthropology Lévi-Strauss was not turning his back on his own society, nor was he leaving his philosophical background behind. His early ambition was to understand not other societies, but his own, and it was to answer philosophical questions that he turned to anthropology.[7] Thus his confrontation with the Durkheimian tradition was a philosophical confrontation.

Durkheim, as we have seen, introduced a fundamental division between the individual and society, locating the specifically human qualities of morality and of cognition in society as a constraining force standing over, and imposing itself on, the individual. For Lévi-Strauss this theory is an abdication of sociology for metaphysics: his task is to recover for the individual the humanity that Durkheim had ascribed to the collective conscience. The nature of human beings as social beings is to be revealed through the investigation of what it is about human beings that makes society possible by making people, in their interaction, create social relations in which they commit themselves to living in society.

Lévi-Strauss sought to remake Durkheim's sociology by putting the social nature of humanity back into the individual. Merleau-Ponty, in a sympathetic commentary on Lévi-Strauss' work that sought to assimilate the latter to his own phenomenology, put this point well:

'This social fact, which is no longer a massive reality but an efficacious system of symbols or a network of symbolic values, is going to be inserted in the depths of the individual. But the regulation which circumvents the individual does not eliminate him. It is no longer necessary to choose between the individual and the collective.'[8]

Thus Lévi-Strauss' philosophical objections to Durkheim's sociology can be summed up as a rejection of the metaphysical concept of the collective conscience and of the sociologistic positivism associated with it. Durkheim's positivism, by dictating that he did not look behind the appearance of social constraint, prevented him from finding its true individual foundation.

While Durkheim saw society as a *sui generis* reality, Lévi-Strauss had to establish the conditions of possibility of society on an individual foundation. This gives Lévi-Strauss' project a marked Kantian flavour, and Lévi-Strauss, like Durkheim before him, recognizes Kant as a forbear.

Kant was concerned to establish the basis of a rational morality, the condition of possibility of a harmonious society. For Kant human action should be ruled by moral imperatives that could be logically derived from the 'general concept of a rational being as such'.[9] This 'categorical imperative' would then provide the basis of an absolute and universal morality. In the just society the laws established in accordance with the categorical imperative, although constraining, would be recognized to be the conditions for the full realization of the individual, and so would be consented to spontaneously. A harmonious society depended, therefore, on the implementation of a rational morality.

Durkheim developed his sociology a century later in an age when the powers of reason seemed insufficient to ensure social order. Durkheim sought to sociologize his interpretation of Kant, making of society not a formal principle which is accessible only to reason, but a substantial reality which has phenomenal effects, experienced by individuals as something existing beyond themselves and constraining them. The study of society could thus, for Durkheim, become an empirical, and not a metaphysical, discipline.

Durkheim's sociologizing of Kant fundamentally alters the significance of Kantian morality. Durkheim fails to make the distinction, fundamental to Kant and to German neo-Kantianism, between fact and value. For Kant the rational morality is purely formal and it is universal, it is not based in any way on what happens to be the current state of affairs. Hence Kant's moral theory provides a basis for criticizing what is in terms of what ought to be: the universal claims of a rational morality are opposed to the particularistic imposition of selfish moral standards.

Durkheim, by contrast, identifies the normative with the objective: the collective conscience is an objective fact and a moral imperative. Lévi-Strauss is well aware of the dangers inherent in this conception, for the consequence is the glorification of the collective:

'Obviously any social order could take pretense of such a doctrine to crush individual thought and spontaneity. Every moral, social, or intellectual progress made its first appearance as a revolt of the individual against the group.'[10]

In criticizing Durkheim's metaphysics Lévi-Strauss is endorsing Kantian individualism and restoring the critical dimension of Kant's philosophy. However Lévi-Strauss does not go so far as to reject Durkheim's identification of fact and value. What Lévi-Strauss rejects is the identification of the collective conscience as a fact. Thus Lévi-Strauss rejects any appeal to a moral authority above the individual, whether it be Kantian reason or Durkheimian society. For Lévi-Strauss the Kantian imperative must be located in the human mind. Thus, while Kant looked to the concept of the rational individual for the condition of possibility of a rational morality and a harmonious social life, Lévi-Strauss looks instead to supposedly empirical properties of the human mind. Thus Lévi-Strauss enthusiastically endorses Ricouer's description of his anthropology as a 'Kantianism without a transcendental subject'.[11] The nature of the mind is established through a deductive argument, as the condition of possibility of society, of culture, of humanity. Thus the source of reason is relocated in the individual, not in a consciousness that is prey for vanity and selfishness, but in the unconscious that is both an empirical and a moral fact.

## 2 LÉVI-STRAUSS AND DURKHEIMIAN SOCIOLOGY

Lévi-Strauss sought to remake Durkheim's sociology by putting the social nature of human beings, inadequately conceptualized by Durkheim as the collective conscience, back into the individual. Lévi-Strauss argues that Durkheim was forced to invent the concept of the collective conscience because he did not have available to him an adequate concept of the unconscious.

The concept of the collective conscience was introduced by Durkheim to reconcile the moral quality of social facts with their objective and constraining character. Social facts were both 'things' and 'representations', both objective and subjective, they were psychic, but they were resistant to the individual will. Without an adequate concept of the unconscious, Lévi-Strauss argues, which is precisely a psychic entity resistant to the will, Durkheim has to invent a 'mind' which existed outside the individual and constrained him or her. Lacking the concept of the unconscious, Durkheim was led to explain social facts not by reference to their human, individual, origin, but by resorting ultimately to evolutionism (in which the collective conscience is explained by reference to an evolutionary chain) and to irrationalism (in which the origin of the collective conscience in the distant past is explained as an irrational, emotional, response rooted in the natural, pre-social, individual).

With the concept of the unconscious we can recognize that the meaning of the social fact is not imposed on the individual but is his or her own creation. But that meaning is not purely subjective, since its objectivity is founded in the unconscious:

'The solution of Durkheim's antinomy lies in the awareness that these objectivated systems of ideas are unconscious, or that unconscious psychical structures underlie them and make them possible. Hence their character of "things"; and at the same time the dialectic—I mean un-mechanical—character of their explanation.'[12]

It is therefore the nature of the unconscious that makes society possible, and it is because the social is located in the unconscious that it seems to experience to be external. Lévi-Strauss thus has a dual task: to develop a theory of the unconscious mind as the condition of possibility of society, and to reformulate Durkheim's sociology on the basis of this concept of the unconscious. It is this double imperative that leads to the two dimensions of structuralism: on the one hand a theory of mind, on the other a theory of culture and society.

The task Lévi-Strauss set himself was to provide a functional underpinning for the social structure in the individual unconscious and so to eliminate Durkheim's appeal to a metaphysical logic of evolution. In this way the social structure, and the representations that correspond to it, would be relocated in the individual. In this way:

'We shall have the hope of overcoming the opposition between the collective nature of culture and its manifestations in the individual, since the so-called "collective consciousness" would, in the final analysis, be no more than the expression on the level of individual thought and behaviour, of certain time and space modalities of the universal laws which make up the unconscious activity of the mind.'[13]

Lévi-Strauss' objection to Durkheimian sociology was clearly an objection from within the Durkheimian tradition. It is to the solutions offered that he objects, not to the problems that Durkheim posed for sociology. Thus Lévi-Strauss rejects Durkheim's claim that society is an emergent whole that has its own laws and that transcends the individual members of society. For Lévi-Strauss society cannot exist other than in the individual members of society and in the relations between these individuals, relations the individuals enter on the basis of an unconscious motivation and not under the constraint of some external entity. However, once we have allowed for this development of Durkheimianism, Lévi-Strauss' conception of the tasks of sociology, and of the nature of society, is thoroughly Durkheimian.

Firstly, Lévi-Strauss concurs entirely with the Durkheimian insistence on the psychic, symbolic, character of social facts, and with the corresponding conception of sociology. Social facts are moral facts, and sociology is the positive moral science which seeks to acquire objective knowledge of systems of meaning.

Secondly, while Lévi-Strauss rejects Durkheim's over-reliance on a sociological functionalism, this is not to reject functionalism. In his early work Lévi-Strauss simply argued that a satisfactory functional explanation cannot be complete until the social functions of an institution can be related to its functions for the individual: it is not sufficient to show what the social function of an institution is, it is also necessary to show how the institution can function at all by showing why individuals consent to engage in it. Thus Lévi-Strauss is not *replacing* Durkheim's sociologism with an alternative psychologistic theory of society that would reduce society to the individual mind. Lévi-Strauss seeks to *complement* Durkheim's sociological functionalism by adding to it a rationalist account of the participation of the individual in society.

Thirdly, Lévi-Strauss pushes Durkheimian intellectualism to its limits. For Durkheim collective representations are rigorously intellectual, rational, constructions. Thus Durkheim rejected

Lévy-Bruhl's notion of the 'primitive mentality' insisting that all forms of social thought are rational. However when it came to the moral character of those representations Durkheim had recourse to the irrational, explaining the moral force of society as an irrational affective response to the majesty of the collective. In replacing this irrational, and wholly passive, individual psychology by a psychological functionalism that provides the rational, though unconscious, grounds for the consent of the individual to participation in society, Lévi-Strauss purges Durkheimian sociology of its residual irrationalism. Society is now rational not because it is a transcendent order standing above the individual, but because it has its roots in the individual reason of the unconscious. The supremacy of reason does not depend on the irrational awe with which the individual regards the collective, but on an accordance of the social with the nature of the individual.

Finally, Lévi-Strauss has a thoroughly Durkheimian understanding of the method of the human sciences. Anthropology seeks not a subjective immersion in other cultures, but objective external understanding. The method of research is the comparative method based on the establishment of functional typologies. The aim of social morphology is to establish a typology of social structures or of social institutions, the different types corresponding to different ways of effecting the fundamental social or psychological function to which society responds. Thus the basis of knowledge of society is the extensive study of different social forms, and not the intensive study of particular societies.

Lévi-Strauss' originality does not consist in his attempt to develop an objective scientific analysis of meaningful cultural phenomena, nor even in his finding the meaning of such phenomena through analysis of their structure, which is already present in the studies of primitive classifications by Durkheim and such of his followers as Mauss, Bouglé, Hertz and Granet. Lévi-Strauss' originality consists in the attempt to give such a structural analysis a psychological foundation and in the insistence that this foundation be provided by a rigorously rational, intellectualist, unconscious. This attempt purges Durkheimian sociology and philosophy of its unacceptable metaphysical and irrationalist implications. It remains to be seen whether the structuralism to which it ultimately gives rise is any more satisfactory.

# 3 TOWARDS A SOLUTION: LÉVI-STRAUSS, MAUSS AND THE THEORY OF RECIPROCITY

Lévi-Strauss was seeking the most general properties of society in order to uncover the origin of the social in the individual. At the same time he was seeking to root this general conception in the concrete, in the mind of the individual member of this or that society. He believed he saw such a conception, at least in embryo, in the work of Mauss, whom Lévi-Strauss acknowledged in his early work as his 'master',[14] and to whom he later dedicated *Structural Anthropology*.

Mauss' insistence on the systematic nature of social phenomena is expressed in the concept of the 'total social fact': 'He studies each type as a whole, always considering it as an integrative cultural complex.'[15] But Mauss ties himself much more closely to the concrete than does Durkheim. The concept of the 'total social fact' leads towards a greater respect for the integrity and specificity of each particular society, and so a lesser readiness to resort to the reductionism of the evolutionary argument to which Durkheim so readily had recourse. Moreover, despite his retention of the concept of a collective psyche, Mauss is much more aware than was Durkheim of the need to relate this to the individual psychology. It is on the basis of a critical reading of Mauss' theory of reciprocity that Lévi-Strauss developed his theory of the social, and it is to the development of this theory that I would now like to turn.

Lévi-Strauss' theory of reciprocity was developed in a number of theoretical articles which he published in 1943 and 1944, which were based largely on those societies he had visited in Brazil.[16]

One problem which is prominent in these articles, and indeed which dominates Lévi-Strauss' later work as well, is the problem of diffusion. The problem was one of explaining apparently remarkable similarities between institutions found in societies as far apart as North and South America, Asia and Oceania. Lévi-Strauss was opposed to all kinds of evolutionary argument, such as those to which Durkheim had recourse, unless there was very good independent evidence for these arguments. Explanation in terms of 'anterior forms' is only acceptable as a last resort, when functional explanation has failed. In the case of one of the societies which concerned Lévi-Strauss, the Bororo, their dualistic social organization could not be explained in evolutionary terms, as a primitive form, because there was clear evidence that this organization derived from a more complex culture. Lévi-Strauss was attracted to diffusionism, which he saw as being complementary to functional explanation. However he argued that, even where there was evidence to support diffusionist hypotheses, these were insufficient. The question of the principle underlying an institution is a different question from that of its origins, as Durkheim himself had clearly argued. Where we find an institution which is general, we must explain that generality by reference to the generality of its function. This function will be revealed by analysis of the fundamental principles of the institution:

'If history, when it is called upon unremittingly (and it must be called upon first) cannot yield an answer, then let us appeal to psychology, or the structural analysis of forms; let us ask ourselves if internal connections, whether of a psychological or a logical nature, will allow us to understand parallel recurrences whose frequency and cohesion cannot possibly be the result of chance. . . . External connections can explain transmission, but only internal connections can account for persistence.'[17]

The common principle which was emerging from the analysis of a number of apparently very different institutions was the principle of *reciprocity*. In the articles of 1943 to 1945 Lévi-Strauss finds reciprocity to be the foundation of power, of dual organization, of war and commerce, and of kinship.

Marcel Mauss had already put forward a theory of reciprocity in his essay *The Gift*. For Lévi-Strauss it is this essay which inaugurates 'a new era for the social sciences'.[18] Mauss found beneath the many different forms of the gift relationship, a common factor. The gift relationship is something other than the immediate giving of the gift, for one object can be replaced by another without the relationship being affected. The gift relationship is also more than the simple sum of its parts, for the giving of a gift institutes an obligation to reciprocate. Mauss saw the key to the relationship in this obligation to reciprocate, and sought to explain this obligation.

Mauss observed that the gift was imbued with symbolic significance. He noted that the real properties of the gift were unimportant, all sorts of quite different items could constitute gifts. He concluded that the gift was very much more than a simple object transferred. It was a total social fact which instituted a social relation between individuals or groups and had religious, legal, moral, economic, and aesthetic significance. It was, furthermore, a binding social relation which had the nature of a contract by virtue of the obligation to reciprocate on the part of the recipient. Thus Mauss saw in the relation of gift exchange the origin of the social contract and so the foundation of the relation between individual and society. Though he made no claim to universality for the institution, as Lévi-Strauss was to do, Mauss' conclusion could be that of Lévi-Strauss too:

'It is by opposing reason to emotion. . . that people succeed in substituting alliance, gift and commerce for war, isolation and stagnation. . . . Societies have progressed in the measure in which they have been able to stabilize their contracts to give, receive and repay'.[19]

According to Lévi-Strauss, Mauss made a serious error, which has its origin in his characteristic empiricism. Lévi-Strauss argues that Mauss isolates the gift-giving relation from the system in which it is inserted. Mauss believed that the giving of a gift *instituted* a system of reciprocity, rather than seeing it as being *inserted* in such a system. He could not see beyond the concrete reality of the relation to the system which lay behind. This led him to see the obligation to reciprocate as being something inherent in the gift, failing to see that the idea of exchange precedes the initial giving of the gift. The gift is given *in order to secure an exchange*, exchange is not the result of the thwarted attempt to give.

Thus Mauss explained exchange in ultimately irrational terms, the giving of the gift setting up a psychological tension which could only be resolved in an exchange. This theory was unacceptable to Lévi-Strauss, seeking as he was a 'super-rationalism'. Lévi-Strauss' own theory, however, was still in the course of development.

Lévi-Strauss was, nevertheless, convinced of the centrality of the institution of reciprocity. His theoretical appreciation was endorsed by his own experience. While living with the Nambikwara he experienced an encounter between two bands. The meeting was accompanied by an elaborate ritual of exchange which lasted for a number of days and which served to reconcile the initially hostile bands to one another. These exchanges were not purely symbolic for, as Lévi-Strauss tells us in some detail, the bands depend on this sort of contact for important goods. This meeting is described in *Tristes Tropiques*, and referred to in many other works. This incident provided the material for one of Lévi-Strauss' first theoretical articles. In this article Lévi-Strauss argued that there is an essential continuity between war and trade, which are not 'two types of coexisting relation, but rather two opposed and indissoluble aspects of one and the same social process'. The groups which meet both fear and need one another. When they meet an elaborate ritual is necessary, involving symbolic conflict, in order to dissipate the fears and make trade possible. This trade may even go so far as an exchange of women between the groups, so that the two groups come to be permanently related by marriage. Lévi-Strauss concludes the article in thoroughly Maussian terms: 'War, commerce, the system of kinship and the social structure must thus be studied in intimate correlation'.[20]

In another article Lévi-Strauss argued that reciprocity underlies dual organization, where the society is organized into two moieties, even where there are relations of subordination, for 'subordination itself is reciprocal: the priority which is gained by one moiety at one level is lost to the opposite moiety on the other'.[21]

This idea was developed as the basis of an exchange theory of power, first published in 1944 in the form of an analysis of chieftainship in Nambikwara society, and, by extension, in other primitive societies. When reprinted in 1947 it appeared as a general theory of power, with the term 'chieftainship' replaced by the term 'power' throughout. Much of this article reappears in *Tristes Tropiques*.[22]

The theory of power is, essentially, a functionalist theory. However, Lévi-Strauss again objects to that sort of functional analysis which imposes a function on an institution instead of discovering that function within it. The function can 'be reached only through analysis of the underlying principle of the institution' (a typically *Gestaltist* formulation of the concept of function). The reason for looking at power in Nambikwara society is that 'precisely on account of its extreme impoverishment, Nambikwara political structure lays bare some basic functions which may remain hidden in more complex and elaborate systems of government'. This, of course, is to take it for granted that the 'function is always and everywhere the same, and can be better studied, and more fully understood where it exists under a simple form'. This identity of function is founded in the identity of the human mind.

The group needs a leader to organize their travels, to decide on expeditions, to deal with neighbouring bands, to supervise the gardens. But the leader does not emerge as a direct response to this need of the group, the leader is not moulded by the group. The group, rather, is moulded by the leader and takes its character from him. If the leader is inadequate the group will disperse and find new leaders. There is no collective conscience to mould the individual.

Although there is a functional need for a leader, this need does not make itself felt directly. Chiefs do not arise because they are needed, they arise 'because there are, in any human group, men who . . . enjoy prestige for its own sake, feel a strong appeal to responsibility, and to whom the burden of public affairs brings its own reward. These individual differences are . . . part of those psychological raw materials out of which any given culture is made.' There is a function, but the fulfilment of this function must be explained in terms of individual, not collective, psychology. The contrast with Durkheim seems clear and deliberate.

The relation of power is a relation of reciprocity. In exchange for the burden of his office the Nambikwara chief is provided by the group with a number of wives. Polygamy is 'the moral and sentimental reward for his heavy duties'. But on top of this real exchange of valuables, there is a symbolic exchange:

'Consent . . . is at the same time the origin and the limit of leadership. . . . Consent is the psychological basis of leadership, but in daily life it expresses itself in, and is measured by a game of give-and-take played by the chief and his followers, and which brings forth, as a basic attribute of leadership, the notion of reciprocity.'[23]

This theory of reciprocity was clearly informed not only by his experience among the Nambikwara, but also in the United States. Lévi-Strauss was struck by the democratic character of United States society, that contrasted sharply with the society he had left behind. For Lévi-Strauss it was the principle of reciprocity that was the key to the liberal democracy of the United States. This idea is developed in an article written in 1944 in which Lévi-Strauss reported back to the recently-liberated French on the virtues of their new masters.[24] In this article Lévi-Strauss makes it clear that the principle of reciprocity is not only of use to an understanding of 'primitive' societies, but it is also the key for the reform of our own society, the model of which is the United States. In the United States, argues Lévi-Strauss, the problem of the relation between individual and collective is solved through the establishment of a relation of reciprocity between 'mass' and 'elite' which contrasts markedly with the relation of subordination between individual and society that characterized his own society. This moment of heady optimism did not last long as an authoritarian nationalism soon prospered on both sides of the Atlantic.

In these early articles we can see a theory developing. Lévi-Strauss is not turning his back on functional analysis of a Durkheimian kind. Trade, co-operation, leadership are all required if society is to be able to satisfy the material needs of its members. These societal functions are all fulfilled by different modalities of the institution, the fundamental social relation, of reciprocity. But the argument so far is incomplete. For Lévi-Strauss the functional argument cannot stand on its own. Society exists not, as Durkheim might have argued, because it creates its own conditions of existence, but because these are part of the 'psychological raw materials out of which any given culture is made'.[25] The functional analysis must be rooted in the individual psychology.

Although the starting point of the analysis is the material needs of the society, the reciprocity which emerges does not take the form of a utilitarian contract, for the psychological roots of reciprocity give the relation a symbolic dimension. Hence the relation of reciprocity is a total social fact, encompassing both material and symbolic interdependence between the members of society, and rooted, in the last analysis, in the unconscious mind.

Taken individually these early articles treat of different institutions as expressions of a common principle, the principle of reciprocity. When we take the articles together, however, it seems clear that Lévi-Strauss does not see reciprocity as one principle among others, but rather as the key to society, as its condition of existence. It is the relation of reciprocity which integrates the individual into society, which makes the human a social animal. In seeking the psychological origins of particular expressions of reciprocity Lévi-Strauss is seeking those properties of the mind which make society possible and which define humans as social beings. It is the nature of the mind which lies at the root of reciprocity, and not an obligation imposed from without. The conditions of possibility of reciprocity, which are the conditions of existence of society itself, take the form of psychological *a prioris*. These psychological properties cannot, therefore, be explained genetically, as Durkheim sought to explain them, as emergent properties which belong to society, for they are the starting point from which sociology must begin.

This theory, outlined in the early articles, is more fully developed in *The Elementary Structures of Kinship*. As we shall see in the next chapter, *The Elementary Structures* is based on a conception of reciprocity as a relational, or structural, principle, which is prior to any institutionalization of reciprocity and prior to the elements which are related by reciprocity. Reciprocity exemplifies the immanence of *relation*, for it is from the beginning a relational principle. This relation is prior to the concrete material on which it is imposed and so its immanence is founded in the mind which imposes it. Thus the notion of reciprocity, for Lévi-Strauss, makes it possible to explain the social relation, and more generally the social structure, by reference, not to a collective conscience, but to the individual unconscious.

# 4  FROM THE THEORY OF RECIPROCITY TO THE ELEMENTARY STRUCTURES

In his earliest theoretical writings Lévi-Strauss used the principle of reciprocity, derived from Mauss, to explain a series of social institutions which had apparently diverse origins, diverse social functions and diverse institutional forms. The principle of reciprocity played a dual role in these early articles. As a principle of anthropological explanation the principle of reciprocity provided a way of explaining these different social institutions without having recourse to sociological or evolutionary reductionism.

We have seen the problems of a sociological reductionism: by making the structural framework of society strictly prior to the existence of social individuals it is unable to explain the origins and development of this structure in the activity of human beings. The structure is thus a self-regulating metaphysical reality. This is why sociologism is so often associated with evolutionism: since it cannot explain the origins of the social structure by reference to the activity of human individuals, it explains the existing social structure in terms of previous states of the social structure in an infinite historical regression, so arranging all societies in an evolutionary series that is invented in order to conceal the gaps in the theory. Because this evolutionary series unfolds without any human intervention its development will supposedly be governed by universal historical laws of succession. This kind of historicist explanation therefore replaces the spatial diversity of societies by a temporal succession in which the simpler societies are merely anterior forms of the more complex.

For Lévi-Strauss the principle of reciprocity overcomes these problems, with their unfortunate ideological consequences, because it is located in the individual mind. But the principle of reciprocity also avoids the dangers of psychologism. The problem with a psychological reductionism is that it is unable to recognize that social institutions have objective structural properties that are logically prior to the activities of individual psychological subjects: for example, the exchange of goods takes place within a social framework that is prior to the individual act of exchange. Just as evolutionism reduces the diversity of social forms by assimilating them to a single historical sequence, so psychologism reduces that diversity by explaining all societies as expressions of the same psychology.

Already in 1945, in an article devoted to the work of Westermarck, Lévi-Strauss had distinguished a psychological reductionism, which he roundly condemned, from a concern with 'permanent humanity', the belief in a 'psychological constant' which is 'both the foundation and the great originality of the work of Westermarck'. The psychological constant is that capacity which makes us human, and so which we all have in common. On this basis humanity has built a diversity of institutions which is irreducible, whether by a crude psychologism or by a crude functionalism.[26] In recognizing the diversity of human societies, therefore, Lévi-Strauss insists that he fully recognizes the autonomy of society. The social and the psychological are, for Lévi-Strauss, inseparable. The individual can only exist in society, but society only has any effective reality in the individual psyche.

The foundation of the principle of reciprocity in the generic unconscious enables Lévi-Strauss to steer a middle course that avoids the dangers of both psychologism and sociologism in recognizing the psychological, but objective, foundation of social institutions. This in turn means that Lévi-Strauss does not have to introduce gratuitous evolutionary hypotheses to account for the origins of social structures.

In terms of the philosophical problems that confronted Lévi-Strauss the early articles, taken together, show us that the principle of reciprocity had much more than a technical anthropological significance for Lévi-Strauss. The principle of reciprocity was a principle that provided the key to the hidden, unconscious, and objective meaning of a range of social institutions. It was a principle that made possible an orderly and harmonious social existence by resolving conflicts at all levels of society. It was, moreover, a principle that was conspicuously lacking in Lévi-Strauss' natal society, a principle whose absence was the source of the conflict and intolerance endemic in that society.

The principle of reciprocity provides the true meaning of all social institutions, it is the ideal against which all institutions should be measured, but it is a meaning that is not necessarily consciously experienced by the participants in those institutions, nor one that is immediately apparent to the anthropologists who study them. It is an objective and unconscious meaning that can only be found if we look behind the subjective and apparent meaning. The theory of reciprocity is therefore also a theory of the objective meaning of social institutions, it is a critical philosophical theory that looks behind appearances to find a truer reality.

The principle of reciprocity ties together Lévi-Strauss' fundamental philosophical concerns and his particular anthropological studies. In both cases he is seeking to show that the foundation of society, or at least of an orderly and harmonious society in which human beings can be true to their own nature, is to be found in the unconscious principle of reciprocity that gives to social existence its truly human meaning.

It is this dual concern that motivates *The Elementary Structures of Kinship*, for it is kinship that provides the basic principles of social organization in so-called 'primitive', non-literate, or classless societies. *The Elementary Structures* represents the realization of the ambition of the theory of reciprocity to provide a general theory of society. Whereas in the earlier articles Lévi-Strauss introduced the principle to explain particular institutions in particular societies, in *The Elementary Structures* he develops the principle into a theory of the possibility of society itself: reciprocity is not simply at the foundation of a particular institution, the institution of the kinship system, reciprocity is the very condition of possibility of society, the condition without which society could not exist, the condition whose emergence marks the emergence of society out of nature.

*The Elementary Structures of Kinship* is a work that can be read on a number of different levels. Superficially it is a technical anthropological study of the kinship systems of a range of non-literate societies, specifically of those societies that regulate marriage positively, through a rule that tells members of the society which categories of people they must marry (as opposed to societies like our own that regulate marriage negatively by proscribing marriage with certain categories of people, such as near kin). The principle of reciprocity is the basis of this study since Lévi-Strauss' argument is that the whole complex of institutions of kinship and marriage can be explained as a functional apparatus designed (unconsciously) to regulate marriage systematically as an exchange of women between social groups.

However, the exchange of women is not, for Lévi-Strauss, simply one exchange among others, and the institutions of kinship are not simply one set of institutions among others. The exchange of women is the most fundamental expression of the principle of reciprocity without which society is impossible. Thus the motivation for the theory of kinship is not simply anthropological, for the principle of reciprocity, universal principle of systems of kinship, is also, and more fundamentally, the condition of possibility of society. The principle of reciprocity is universal, that universality being indicated by the supposed universality of the incest prohibition that marks the dividing line between nature and culture. This universality is an expression of the universal function that reciprocity fulfils. Hence the study of kinship phenomena is the means to discover scientifically the foundation of human society and the true meaning of human social existence.

# NOTES

1  *TT*, p. 58.
2  *TT*, p. 47; 1971n, p. 46; T. Clark *Prophets and Patrons*, Harvard University Press, Cambridge, Mass., 1973, p. 233.
3  *TT*, p. 59.

4 *TT*, p. 59.
5 S. de Beauvoir, 'Les structures élémentaires de la parenté', *Temps Modernes*, vol. 49, 1949, p. 943.
6 1974c, p. 26.
7 1973a, p. 35; 1966e, p. 33.
8 M. Merleau-Ponty, *Signs*, Northwestern University Press, 1964, p. 115.
9 I. Kant, *The Moral Law* (H. J. Paton trans.), Hutchinson, London, 1948, p. 79.
10 *FS*, pp. 529–30.
11 1970b, p. 61.
12 *FS*, p. 228.
13 *SA*, p. 65.
14 1943c, p. 178.
15 *FS*, p. 528.
16 1943a; 1943b; 1944a; 1944b; 1944c; 1946c was written in 1944.
17 *SA*, pp. 248, 258.
18 *IM*, p. xxxv.
19 M. Mauss, *The Gift*, Cohen and West, London, 1966, p. 80.
20 1943a, pp. 138–9.
21 1944c, pp. 267–8.
22 1944b; 1947a; *TT*, Chapter 29.
23 1944b, pp. 28–9.
24 1946c.
25 1944b, p. 31.
26 1945a, pp. 96, 98.

# IV. *The Elementary Structures of Kinship*

*The Elementary Structures of Kinship* marks the full development of Lévi-Strauss' theory of reciprocity and the point of transition to his specifically 'structuralist' human philosophy and theory of culture and society. The philosophical, methodological, and theoretical implications of *The Elementary Structures* are not brought out explicitly in that work, but it is nevertheless the insights that Lévi-Strauss believed that he had achieved in the study of kinship that are the foundation of his structuralism and of those that he has inspired. *The Elementary Structures* therefore merits our close attention.

Lévi-Strauss' structuralism is a philosophy, a theory and a method that offers itself to the human sciences not only on the basis of a philosophical claim to have achieved a privileged insight into the nature of humanity, but more fundamentally on the basis of its scientific achievements. In order to evaluate Lévi-Strauss' structuralism it is, therefore, necessary to come to grips with the anthropological investigations that it has inspired, most notably Lévi-Strauss' very detailed explorations of kinship systems and of the mythology of non-literate peoples.

The study of kinship, as of myth, is a very specialized field and many of the issues raised by Lévi-Strauss' work are very technical, often hanging on the precise interpretation of ambiguous ethnographic data. In a book such as this it would be trying the reader's patience to enter into these technicalities, and yet Lévi-Strauss constantly insists that his theories be subjected to only one test: the test of the evidence. Fortunately for the reader it is possible to outline an evaluation of Lévi-Strauss' theory of kinship without confronting the ethnographic data. On the one hand, a naive interpretation of Lévi-Strauss' theory is so patently and un-ambiguously falsified by the ethnographic data that it is unnecessary to consider the latter in detail. On the other hand, in order to reconcile his theory with data that appears to contradict it Lévi-

Strauss introduces a series of methodological and conceptual devices that deprive the theory of any substantive content, and so make it strictly unfalsifiable.

In arguing that Lévi-Strauss' analyses are unsatisfactory because they are unfalsifiable I do not want to identify myself with the Popperian philosophy of science, according to which a theory is only allowed to claim scientific status if it is able to generate empirical predictions that can be falsified experimentally. This philosophy has been widely criticized on a number of grounds. Firstly, on the philosophical grounds that it is not possible to define in any absolute sense either what is an empirical prediction or what could constitute the falsification of such a prediction. Secondly, on the more pragmatic grounds that it imposes unduly restrictive conditions on the kinds of theory that it will permit.

In condemning Lévi-Strauss' theory as unfalsifiable I use the term much more loosely than does Popper, both in the criteria for falsifiability and in the rigidity with which they are applied. I do not believe it is necessary to espouse a Popperian prescriptive positivism to believe that a theory that has scientific pretensions must either have some empirical content or have an intuitive appeal that might lead us to expect that it can ultimately be given some empirical content. In this chapter I shall argue that Lévi-Strauss' theory of kinship has no significant empirical content, and, moreover, is counter-intuitive so that there is no reason to believe that it could ever be given any content.

If a theory is to have any empirical content it must tell us something about the world. In telling us what the world is like the theory must also tell us what the world is not like, and so to have any empirical content the theory must be inconsistent with at least some states of the world, in other words it must be falsifiable, at least in principle. Lévi-Strauss' theory of kinship is not falsifiable because it is consistent with any possible set of data. Lévi-Strauss' theories do not tell us anything about the form or the operation of the kinship systems that we can find in actually existing societies, what they do is to reduce these systems to abstract models that are supposedly located in the unconscious and supposedly underlie and give meaning to the systems that are observed on the ground. Thus his theories tell us not about the world, but about the meanings imposed on the world by an unconscious.

There is nothing objectionable in itself about the introduction of the concept of the unconscious. There is no doubt that a theory of the unconscious can be given significant empirical content either if the unconscious provides a link between an ascertainable past and the present so that typical unconscious formations that underlie contemporary forms of behaviour are associated with typical past experiences, or if that which is at one moment unconscious can, through analysis, become conscious so that the unconscious is merely a submerged consciousness.

Although the practical evaluation of psychoanalytic theories poses enormous methodological and conceptual problems, there is no doubt that when properly formulated such theories do have empirical content because they provide direct or indirect access to the unconscious. However Lévi-Strauss' use of the concept does not provide for this possibility. On the one hand, the unconscious is preformed and so cannot be related to any experiential past. On the other hand, the meanings that Lévi-Strauss attributes to the unconscious do not coincide with, and in some cases flatly contradict, the conscious meanings that participants attribute to their systems of kinship.

For Lévi-Strauss the unconscious has a neurological foundation, it is the concept that mediates between mind and matter (which is why it can perform all its Cartesian tricks), but since the practical and conceptual problems involved in identifying the neurological substratum of thought are, to say the least, immense, even reference to neurology cannot realistically be expected to provide the theory with any empirical content. Thus there is no evidence, and no possible evidence, that would lead us to believe that Levi-Strauss' theory has in fact uncovered an objective unconscious meaning.

A theory that is without empirical content, or even one that is systematically falsified, is not necessarily without scientific value. It may be that the theory can be modified and developed in order to provide a much more fruitful account. Although Lévi-Strauss' theory of kinship is counter-intuitive, in the sense that it claims that the true meaning of systems of kinship is quite different from the meaning such systems have for their participants, it may be that his theory could be developed to provide a coherent analysis of an objective meaning of kinship systems that does not involve gratuitous reference to an inaccessible unconscious, but rather that finds the 'objective' meaning of kinship systems immanent in the systems themselves. This is the direction in which Lévi-Strauss' work has been developed by anthropological structuralism. It is, however, a development that has proved no more fruitful than has Lévi-Strauss' own theory.

In this chapter I intend to examine Lévi-Strauss' theory of kinship before moving on in the next chapter to consider the later developments inspired by Lévi-Strauss' work.

## 1. THE GENERAL THEORY OF RECIPROCITY

### a) *The general theory of reciprocity and the prohibition of incest*

*The Elementary Structures of Kinship* offers us two different theories which, although related, can be distinguished from one another. The *general theory of reciprocity* seeks to establish that the principle of reciprocity is the condition of possibility of society and so must have a universal, and unconscious, psychological origin. The *theory of kinship* seeks to show that a range of institutions of kinship and marriage express this principle of reciprocity and so, at least in non-literate societies, provide the framework of society. In this part of the chapter I shall look at the general theory of reciprocity before moving on to the theory of kinship in the next part.

In order to establish the status of the principle of reciprocity Lévi-Strauss has to establish *empirically* that reciprocity is indeed universal, and he has to establish *theoretically* that no society could exist without reciprocity. Lévi-Strauss tries to establish the universality of reciprocity by relating it to the supposed universality of the prohibition of incest. Lévi-Strauss then proceeds to try to establish the *necessity* of reciprocity by referring initially to the sociological requirement that society regulate the distribution of scarce resources, and later by referring to the psychological function of symbolic exchange as a way of responding to a psychological need for security. It is from the latter argument about the psychological function of reciprocity that Lévi-Strauss proceeds to establish his theory of the unconscious as condition of possibility of reciprocity, and so of society.

Lévi-Strauss attempts to establish the universality of reciprocity by relating it to the supposedly universal incest prohibition that marks the dividing line between nature and culture. This argument is of some significance because it provides a close link backwards to Freud, whose *Totem and Taboo* undoubtedly inspired the argument, and a link forwards to Lacan, who reintegrated Lévi-Strauss' version of the theory into psychoanalysis. For Lévi-Strauss the prohibition of incest is the 'fundamental step because of which, by which, but above all in which, the transition from nature to culture is accomplished'.[1]

Lévi-Strauss criticizes existing theories of the prohibition of incest for their failure to account for this dual character of the prohibition. It is neither purely natural, nor purely cultural, nor a bit of nature and a bit of culture, it is the point of transition from one to the other.

Lévi-Strauss then introduces his own interpretation. The prohibition of incest is the rule which asserts the primacy of culture in sexual matters. The importance of the rule is not what it *forbids*, but what it *compels*:

'The prohibition on the sexual use of a daughter or a sister compels them to be given in marriage to another man, and at the same time it establishes a right to the daughter or sister of this other man. . . . Like exogamy, which is its widened social application, *the prohibition of incest is a rule of reciprocity. . . . The content of the prohibition is not exhausted by the fact of the prohibition: the latter is instituted only in order to guarantee and establish, directly or indirectly, immediately or mediately, an exchange'.*[2]

So we find that the prohibition of incest is the other side of exchange. If the woman is forbidden to her own group, then she must be offered to another. The universality of the incest prohibition is not significant in itself, it is significant as an index of the universality of reciprocity. However the argument is, to say the least, unconvincing.

In the first place, as many have pointed out, the prohibition of incest is a rule that governs sexual relations while the rule of reciprocity governs marriage. Although these rules may be quite closely related to one another they may be markedly different in extension. Lévi-Strauss' argument is that 'the prohibition of incest establishes mutual dependency between families, compelling them, in order to perpetuate themselves, to give rise to new families',[3] hence at most the prohibition of incest imposes family exogamy, and it is only in the loosest sense that this implies reciprocity.

A second argument questions the universality of the prohibition of incest. It is true that every society has a set of rules that govern sexual relations, but these rules vary enormously from society to society, both in extension and in cultural significance, to the extent that in some societies incest is a misdemeanor barely worth commenting on. What is universal, then, is not the content of the prohibition but rather the fact that there are rules of some kind regulating sexual relations between kin. In this sense the prohibition of incest is no more universal than is, for example, the regulation of table manners. The prohibition of incest is really a red herring, for the regulation of marriage is itself universal, and marriage universally relates individuals and groups.

The most important weakness of Lévi-Strauss' argument is in the attempt to establish the *necessity* of reciprocity on the basis of its supposed *universality*. There is no reason why cultural phenomena should not be universal, hence no justification for identifying the universal with the natural. While it is true that the condition of possibility of society will be universal, it is not necessarily the case that anything which is both universal and a part of culture will be either natural, or a condition of possibility of society. An *a priori* can never be revealed empirically, but only by means of theoretical argument, for only theoretical argument can separate the contingently universal, that without which society does not exist, from the necessarily universal, that without which society cannot exist.

## b) The social function of reciprocity

Lévi-Strauss offers two such theoretical arguments for the necessity of reciprocity. The first, sociological, argument is a hangover from the earlier analyses of reciprocity and need not detain us for long. It is the argument that reciprocity functions to distribute resources, and in particular women, among social groups. It is an argument that refers, therefore, to real exchanges between corporate groups, and not to symbolic exchanges alone, and it is an argument that only appears in the first chapters of *The Elementary Structures*.

Reciprocity is required in order to overcome problems caused by the inequality of distribution of women. Women are valuables, needed to work and to produce valuable children. Problems arise because of 'a deep polygamous tendency, which exists among all men'.[4] Society, therefore, needs to take in hand the distribution of these valuables and not leave the latter to chance or to individual selfishness. Hence reciprocity expresses the supremacy of the group in the distribution of valuables. This argument is not well developed in *The Elementary Structures*. Again the question is that of the *universality* and *necessity* of this function. Its universality is clearly not absolute, for societies can exist with very unequal distributions of women. Moreover, reciprocity is not, in itself, a *distributive* mechanism at all: it is a mechanism of *circulation*, and circulation can only take place once resources have been distributed.

The marriage rules with which Lévi-Strauss is concerned in *The Elementary Structures* do not include any quantitative specification, they simply tell a man where he should go to find a wife. Hence the application of these rules will have no effect on the distribution of women. For example, a man who has more than his share of sons will be able to secure more than his share of daughters-in-law. In general, therefore, the distribution of women is unaffected by the rules of marriage, although it is possible on occasion for there to be redistributive mechanisms, such as a bride-price system, added to the rule of marriage.

It is, therefore, not clear what is universal about the redistributive function, and nor do the rules which Lévi-Strauss studies in fact effect a redistribution. Finally, although every society must have some mechanism for distributing its products, the form of this mechanism will vary from society to society. Moreover, it is quite possible that a society whose survival might otherwise be prejudiced by the existence of inequalities could develop alternative mechanisms to redistributive ones which could maintain social cohesion without affecting inequality (as has our own). Hence there are no grounds for deriving a universal function from a need to regulate distribution for the latter has no substantive universal content.

## c) *Towards a psychological theory of reciprocity*
In the course of *The Elementary Structures* the argument changes. It is no longer its supposed distributive effects which makes reciprocity the condition of possibility of society, but rather its symbolic value. After the first few chapters exchange is seen as an institution whose significance is purely symbolic so that by the end of the book it has become a system of communication rather than a system of distribution of values. Conflict over distribution has

been replaced by a conflict which has a psychological origin and so a symbolic solution. The need for exchange is implicitly given an exclusively psychological and not a sociological foundation. This development follows the introduction of the mind as the foundation of exchange.

Lévi-Strauss argued initially that reciprocity expresses the supremacy of the group in the distribution of valuables. However, the demands of the group do not make themselves immediately effective for Lévi-Strauss, as they do for Durkheim, for the group has no existence independently of its individual members. Hence, although he initially gives a sociological answer to the question of why reciprocity should be the condition of possibility of society, the fact of reciprocity must be explained by reference to the individual psychology. Reciprocity is, therefore, neither imposed by an external authority, nor consciously adopted, it emerges as a spontaneous response of the individual to his coexistence with others:

'If it is objected that such reasoning is too abstract and artificial to have occurred at a very primitive human level, it is sufficient to note that the result, which is all that counts, does not suppose any formal reasoning but simply the spontaneous resolution of those psycho-social pressures which are the immediate facts of collective life.'5

From his very earliest theoretical articles Lévi-Strauss was searching for a satisfactory psychological explanation of reciprocity, and since this is the cornerstone of the entire theory, and ultimately of Lévi-Strauss' structuralism as a whole, his theory could not be regarded as complete until he had achieved such an explanation. The problem was that none of the psychological theories that were available to Lévi-Strauss were at all adequate.

*The Elementary Structures* is often presented as the application of the theories and methods of structural linguistics to systems of kinship. Given the impact which his discovery of linguistics subsequently had on Lévi-Strauss' thought, it is surprising that there are few signs of that impact in *The Elementary Structures*. Lévi-Strauss came into contact with linguistics through Roman Jakobson, whom he met in New York in late 1941, and whose lectures he attended in 1942-3. Lévi-Strauss began writing *The Elementary Structures* in 1943, although much of the research had already been done by then, and completed it at the beginning of 1947. However it was not until 'about 1944' that he became convinced of the similarity of 'rules of marriage and descent' and 'those prevailing in linguistics'.

Lévi-Strauss' first published work to betray the linguistic inspiration, an article in *Word* in 1945 reprinted in *Structural Anthropology*, and much-quoted since, explicitly denies that the method can be applied to terminologies, the subject-matter of *The Elementary Structures*, applying it instead to the system of attitudes, to which a projected third volume of kinship studies was to be devoted. In an article of 1946 on 'French Sociology' linguistics is still not especially privileged, 'philosophy, psychology, history, etc.' being picked out as the complementary disciplines in an appeal for sociology to turn to more concrete studies.[6]

In *The Elementary Structures* the significance of linguistics is only specifically noted in the concluding chapter, where the comparison between women and words is introduced. The only theoretically significant reference to linguistics in the bulk of the book (pp. 93–4) makes a point which has already been introduced by reference to *gestalt* psychology (pp. 89–90). Whatever the 'theoretical inspiration' owed to Jakobson and acknowledged in the Preface, there is very little sign of the influence of linguistics in *The Elementary Structures*.

The obvious source for a psychological theory that could explain the psychic origins of reciprocity would be Freud who had already provided the theory in *Totem and Taboo*. We have already seen that it was contact with Freud's work that drew Lévi-Strauss' attention to the unconscious. But we have also seen that Lévi-Strauss was looking to the unconscious for a rational, intellectualist psychology with which to combat theories that relied on the emotional and the irrational. In this respect Freud's theory was no better than those Lévi-Strauss sought to displace, precisely because it is ultimately irrationalist.

We have seen that both Durkheim and Bergson counterposed, each in his own way, society to the individual as the rational to the irrational, as intellect to emotion, while Lévi-Strauss sought to recover reason and intellect for the individual. In this respect Freud, and especially the Freud of *Totem and Taboo*, is very like Durkheim and Bergson. Moreover *Totem and Taboo* compounds the felony by adding a thoroughly metaphysical (and almost Durkheimian) evolutionary argument in that for Freud the horror of incest that underlies the incest taboo and the social institution of exogamy (marriage outside the group, whether family, clan, moiety, section or whatever) is explained by reference to a real or mythical historical event that is reproduced in succeeding generations. Hence the contemporary existence of the prohibition of incest is explained as the evolutionary residue of an original irrational psychological response.

However much Lévi-Strauss may have been influenced by Freud, the latter's explanation of the incest prohibition is thoroughly unsatisfactory. Firstly, the theory cannot provide an explanation for the contemporary existence of the prohibition of incest because its psychological origins are referred to a distant and mythical past. It cannot be claimed that the persistence of the prohibition of incest expresses the persistence of the psychological impulse that gave birth to it because Lévi-Strauss insists that sentiments are a response to the rational normative order and cannot precede it. Hence the contemporary horror of incest must be explained by its prohibition and not vice versa (thus it is significant that while Freud studies the incest *taboo* Lévi-Strauss studies the incest *prohibition*).

Secondly, the theory reduces culture to an irrational natural response. Thus culture, far from expressing the social nature of the human animal, is for Freud based on the repression of fundamental aspects of human nature: culture, and the reason that it embodies, is essentially foreign to the humans who comprise it. Culture, far from being the means to human self-realization, far from being the means by which humanity raises itself above animality, represents for Freud the alienation of the human being from his or her own nature.

While Lévi-Strauss would not disagree that it is possible for culture to develop alienated forms, this alienation does not represent the imposition of reason upon instinct, but rather the perversion of reason to selfish ends. For Lévi-Strauss Freud, like Bergson and Lévy-Bruhl, must have represented a regression from the positive achievements of Durkheim's sociology, and in particular from Durkheim's insistence that the birth of culture is the birth of reason, and that the achievements of culture are due to the imposition of the intelligence on the instinctual. For Lévi-Strauss the task was not to renounce this insistence, but only to renounce the conception of culture as an external reality that stood over and against the individual and to seek instead its foundation in the individual mind. This is the significance of Lévi-Strauss' rejection of Freud and, as we shall see, of his return to Rousseau.

In fact in *The Elementary Structures* Lévi-Strauss introduces his account of the psychological foundations of reciprocity not with a direct reference to Freud, but by reference to child psychology. He argues that the mind of the child gives us a unique insight into the universal features of the mind because it has been less subject to cultural conditioning but not, as some would have it, because the mind of the child corresponds to a more 'primitive' stage of intellectual development.

We might surmise in view of the reference to child psychology that Piaget might have been an early influence on Lévi-Strauss, and indeed Lévi-Strauss discusses Piaget's work in *The Elementary Structures*, only to dismiss his developmental hypotheses, arguing that different 'mentalities' reflect different circumstances, so that all thought, adult and child, 'civilized' and 'primitive', is rigorously intellectual. On the other hand, in a recent tribute Lévi-Strauss has acclaimed Piaget as the thinker who gave primacy to intellectual activity and to cognitive functions just when psychology was in danger of being 'submerged by confused thought under the double assault of Bergsonism and Freudianism (at least the epigones rather than the founders). Thus psychology and philosophy could extract themselves from the affective swamp into which they were beginning to sink'.[7] However Lévi-Strauss does not acknowledge a direct influence in *The Elementary Structures* and the child psychology he does refer to is that of Susan Isaacs.

Lévi-Strauss quotes research by Susan Isaacs which shows the development of concepts of arbitration among small children. Children find themselves in antagonistic situations because of their desire to possess objects belonging to the other. This gives rise to an antagonistic relation between the self and the other which must be resolved if society is to exist at all. This antagonism is underlain by a psychological need for security. My need for security makes me want the valuables of the other, in case I should need them for myself. This need for security can, however, only be satisfied by co-operation, which is institutionalized as exchange. The institution of the exchange of women is indeed a response to Tylor's injunction 'marry out or be killed out'.

The excursion into child psychology confirms, for Lévi-Strauss, the belief that reciprocity is not something imposed by society in response to social needs, but is something which emerges spontaneously from the 'psycho-social pressures' of collective life. It is, therefore, something which already exists in the mind before it is institutionalized in society.

Lévi-Strauss goes on to specify the 'fundamental structures of the mind' which underlie reciprocity. These structures, which 'are universal', are three:

'the exigency of the rule as a rule; the notion of reciprocity as the most immediate form of integrating the opposition between the self and the others; and finally, the synthetic nature of the gift, i.e., that the agreed transfer of a valuable from one individual to another makes these individuals into partners, and adds a new quality to the valuable transferred.'[8]

These are the fundamental structures of the mind which make society possible. It must be possible to conceive what is involved in a rule. Reciprocity must be seen as a spontaneous response to the experience of opposition between self and other. The mind must have the capacity to endow the object exchanged with significance. This significance derives from the fact that the object is a gift which seals an alliance, and hence is a symbol of that alliance.

A little further on Lévi-Strauss offers a more 'formal' description of the capacities of the mind: 'The transition from nature to culture is determined by man's ability to think of biological relationships as systems of oppositions.'[9] Simonis argues that this capacity itself explains the former three, while Davy regards it as an additional capacity. However, it is surely a capacity which is implied in the three earlier 'structures' without itself explaining them.[10]

The capacities mentioned imply that the mind does more than simply impose a relation, for that relation has a specific character and a specific power. It not only relates, but it also integrates the individual into society through a symbolic gesture. The unconscious, just like reciprocity itself, is not therefore simply a formal capacity at this stage in the development of Lévi-Strauss' thought, it has an active component. Thus the theory of the unconscious in *The Elementary Structures* is not the theory of the purely formal, combinatory, unconscious that Lévi-Strauss was later to take from structural linguistics.

In fact the theory of the mental foundations of reciprocity offered in *The Elementary Structures* is not really a psychological theory at all. The 'structures' just described do not refer directly to properties of the mind. They describe capacities which the mind must have rather than the properties of the mind that endow it with these capacities. Hence what they describe is not the mind but the 'concept' of reciprocity—a rule which effects the integration of individuals into society by means of a symbolic transaction. The exercise that Lévi-Strauss is engaged in is at the moment a logical rather than a psychological one, as he elaborates the logical preconditions for his concept of reciprocity. Thus the underpinnings of reciprocity are true *a prioris*. These 'structures' do not themselves provide an explanation of reciprocity: it is these 'structures' that an adequate psychology must explain.

There seems to be little doubt that the theory that Lévi-Strauss initially believed could provide the psychological foundations for the theory of reciprocity was not that of structural linguistics, nor of Freud, nor of Piaget but that of *gestalt* psychology, which has just the teleological conception of structure he required. The *Gestalt* approach was well-adapted to Lévi-Strauss' concerns. As Piaget has noted:

'The psychological *Gestalt* represents a type of structure that appeals to those who, whether they acknowledge it or not, are really looking for structures that may be thought "pure", unpolluted by history or genesis, functionless and detached from the subject'.[11]

In the Preface to *The Elementary Structures* the book is assimilated to the *gestaltist* movement, and Lévi-Strauss has subsequently affirmed the roots of his concept of structure in the *Gestalt*, as well as asserting the common *gestaltist* origins of both linguistics and anthropology, the latter by reference to Benedict and Kroeber as well as his own work. Within the book the primacy of relations over terms is referred to as a lesson of psychology, not of linguistics, and the concept of structure itself derived from *gestalt* psychology when Lévi-Strauss stresses the unconscious, and so anti-metaphysical, teleology which is precisely what *gestalt* psychology introduced.[12]

The concept of structure in play is *gestaltist* rather than linguistic in more significant ways: the regulating principle, the principle of reciprocity, is substantive, and not purely formal, the basis of a synchronic *functional* whole which itself has a physiological foundation. However the relation between form and its physiological foundation is not a reductionist one, it is a relation of isomorphism. The functional principle that explains the structure the principle of reciprocity, is explained as the result of the attempt to restore equilibrium, which is the central principle of the *Gestalt*.

The *gestaltist* foundation of *The Elementary Structures* is extremely important, for it gives that work an openness that is lost with hindsight. In particular it means that *The Elementary Structures* is very open to phenomenological interpretations, despite Lévi-Strauss' declared antipathy to phenomenology. This openness, or ambiguity, is really inherent in *gestalt* psychology, for the problem with this psychology is that the *Gestalt* itself remains a very mysterious phenomenon: where does it come from, how is it directed? In order to avoid some kind of vitalist metaphysics (shades of Bergson again) it seems that *gestalt* psychology has in the end to decide between a form of behaviourism in which the *Gestalt* expresses biological processes that integrate sense-data, and a form of phenomenology in which the *Gestalt* expresses the intentionality of the perceiving subject. Merleau-Ponty (who explained the subtleties of phenomenology to Lévi-Strauss when the latter returned to France at the end of the war and who remained a close friend and colleague) and Simone de Beauvoir both interpreted *The Elementary Structures* in the latter sense, and indeed Lévi-Strauss' own discussion of Isaacs work has strong phenomenological resonances.

Simone de Beauvoir acclaimed *The Elementary Structures* as a humanist masterpiece when it first appeared:

'Lévi-Strauss . . . assumes that human institutions are endowed with meaning: but he seeks their key in their humanity alone; he abjures the spectres of metaphysics, but he does not accept for all that that this world should be mere contingence, disorder, absurdity; his secret would be to try to *think the given* without allowing the intervention of a thought that would be foreign to it. Thus he restores to us the image of a universe which has no need of reflecting the heavens to be a human universe . . . his thinking is clearly part of the great humanist current which considers that human existence bears within itself its own justification. . . . This book . . . often seemed to reconcile felicitously Engels and Hegel: for man originally appears to us as anti-physis, and what his intervention achieves is the concrete position of confrontation of myself with another self without which the first cannot define itself. I also found singularly striking the agreement of certain descriptions with the theses put forward by existentialism: existence, in establishing itself, at the same time establishes its laws; it is not governed by any internal necessity, and yet it escapes contingency by assuming the conditions of its own springing forth.'[13]

In *The Second Sex*, her analysis of the condition of women, de Beauvoir borrowed Lévi-Strauss' theory of reciprocity and formulated it in terms of the existentialist antagonism of self and other.

The example of Merleau-Ponty is even more instructive. Merleau-Ponty, like the existentialists and even, in his own way, Lévi-Strauss, posed the problem of the relation between the self and the other as a problem of meaning and communication. For Merleau-Ponty the problem of intersubjectivity is the problem of meaning, and it is meaning which ultimately gives us access to the other. We cannot grasp meanings without such access to the other because it is the essense of meaning that it is intentional, so that to reconstitute a meaning is to reconstitute an intention, the intention of the person who meant. Merleau-Ponty developed his analysis of meaning and communication precisely through a critique of *gestalt* psychology.

Merleau-Ponty condemned crude *gestalt* psychology for its formalism. It replaced a behaviourism of the elementary stimulus by a behaviourism of the complex stimulus, the *Gestalt* being something purely formal imposed on the content. Merleau-Ponty therefore reinterpreted the *Gestalt* in terms of the intention of the subject.

Merleau-Ponty fully recognizes the unconscious nature of the code that governs symbolic systems, and even the possibility that the nature of the mind is such as to impose constraints on that code and so to restrict the forms of communication that may exist, but for Merleau-Ponty the *intentional* character of meaning rules out altogether the possibility that the unconscious could constitute the meaning of a communication, for intentions cannot be unconscious.

Lévi-Strauss has explicitly rejected Merleau-Ponty's phenomenological interpretation of his work, but that such an interpretation is possible at all points to the ambiguity inherent in *The Elementary Structures*, an ambiguity that derives from its *gestaltist* foundations. For Lévi-Strauss reference to intentionality in the explanation of structures is insufficient for he wants to argue that reciprocity is present even when it is embodied neither in an intention nor in a consciousness. For Lévi-Strauss the *Gestalt* is the product not of an intention, but of the combinatory activity of the unconscious. Lévi-Strauss does not however, fall back on behaviourism because the particular form of combination is culturally specific, even though the combinatory principle is universal.

It was the encounter with linguistics that gave Lévi-Strauss this model of the unconscious and made it possible for him to go beyond the ambiguities of the *Gestalt*. Thus in *Totemism* Lévi-Strauss espouses a modified form of associationism in which the whole is clearly not emergent, as it is for *gestalt* psychology and for Merleau-Ponty, but is the product of mental activity:

'It is certainly the case that one consequence of modern structuralism (not, however, clearly enunciated) ought to be to rescue associational psychology from the discredit into which it has fallen. Associationism had the great merit of sketching the contours of this elementary logic, which is like the least common denominator of all thought, and its only failure was not to recognize that it was an original logic, a direct expression of the structure of the mind (and behind the mind, probably, of the brain), and not an inert product of the action of the environment on an amorphous consciousness. But . . . it is this logic of oppositions and correlations, exclusions and inclusions, compatibilities and incompatibilities, which explains the laws of association, and not the reverse. A renovated associationism would have to be based on a system of operations which would not be without similarity to Boolean algebra'.[14]

## d) *Reciprocity in systems of kinship and marriage*

The theory of reciprocity relates in two ways to the analysis of systems of kinship and marriage. On the one hand, Lévi-Strauss argues that systems of kinship and marriage universally manifest the principle of reciprocity. On the other hand, in the bulk of *The Elementary Structures*, Lévi-Strauss argues that particular systems of kinship and marriage can be explained as different ways of institutionalizing the principle. It is with the universalist argument that we are concerned in this section.

For Lévi-Strauss the fundamental social relation is the exchange of women, hence it is the study of kinship and marriage that will reveal the unconscious foundations of society. Why is the exchange of women the fundamental social relation? Why is it

'no exaggeration, then, to say that exogamy is the archetype of all other manifestations based upon reciprocity, and that it provides the fundamental and immutable rule ensuring the existence of the group as a group'.[15]

It is because the woman is always and everywhere both a sign and a value. Words and goods are also exchanged, but words have lost their quality of being values, which first, supposedly, led men to communicate with one another, while goods have lost their quality of being signs. Women have an economic value, and in some societies this is important, but it is their sexual desirability which makes them able universally to serve to integrate society. The exchange of women, therefore, is the only exchange which, in every society, can express both a material and a symbolic commitment to society.

It is in giving a sister or daughter in marriage that a man expresses his fundamental commitment to a life in society. This commitment is always, and trivially, an exchange. This exchange need not be institutionalized as a relation which is explicitly recognized as an exchange of women. The rule of marriage, whether this rule is positive or negative, necessarily implies that some individuals give up a right to the woman who is given in marriage. The rule itself institutionalizes the obligation of others to do the same, so that other women are available to those who give up their rights to the particular woman who is daughter, sister, or niece. Hence:

'exchange may be neither explicit nor immediate, but the fact that I can obtain a wife is, in the final analysis, the consequence of the fact that a brother or father has given her up'.[16]

Exchange is 'neither immediate nor explicit', 'this structure is often visible even in systems in which it has not materialized in a concrete form'.[17] Hence all that is meant by 'exchange' is that all social relations are reciprocal in the sense that a man will only give something up to society if society offers him something in return. Such 'reciprocity' must characterize all social relations if the rule is not to be seen as deriving its force from some external constraint such as the collective conscience.

Individuals participate in society spontaneously, and are not compelled to participate either morally or by force. It is the latter belief which gives Durkheim's sociology its 'metaphysical' dimension which Lévi-Strauss found so objectionable. But if people are to engage in society spontaneously, there must be something offered in return for that which they give up: social relations take the form of a 'contract', which for Lévi-Strauss is a contract freely, but unconsciously, entered into, and not one imposed by a supraindividual 'society'. Empirically he owes the insight largely to Mauss, and theoretically it represents merely a restatement of social contract theory. The originality lies in the attempt to found the social contract neither in a *sui generis* social reality, nor in the individual consciousness, but in the unconscious.

We observe that in many societies men are happy to give up women in marriage, even though marriage is not explicitly recognized as an exchange. If men are not aware that the relation is a reciprocal one, then we might ask why they are prepared to give up their women. The answer for Lévi-Strauss is that they are prepared to give up their women because they know 'unconsciously' that this relation is an exchange. Hence every social relation which involves a sacrifice must be, unconsciously if not consciously, underlain by a conception of that relation as a relation of reciprocity.

What is the empirical content of this argument? Lévi-Strauss is not asserting that social relations are conceived of consciously as contractual relations, an assertion that could be falsified empirically without much difficulty, but that they are unconsciously apprehended as such. But how can the anthropologist penetrate to the unconscious meaning of social relations? How can the anthropologist ever discover that the true meaning of the institutions under review is to be found in the principle of reciprocity when that principle is locked in the unconscious of the participants in those institutions?

For a Freudian it is through the analysis that brings what was unconscious to consciousness that the psychoanalyst can reveal the formerly hidden content of the unconscious and find the diagnosis confirmed by the patient. But for Lévi-Strauss there is no such process of analysis, and it is doubtful that he would attribute any significance to the results of such a process. Thus Lévi-Strauss gives us no means of access to the unconscious meanings of the social relations that he describes. There is no way of finding a positive confirmation of Lévi-Strauss' hypothesis.

Nevertheless perhaps it is possible to give negative support to the hypothesis by showing that social relations could be conceived of as reciprocal. Unfortunately this is a claim that is tautologically true, for the concept of a social *relation* implies the existence of more than one related party. Hence the possibility of reciprocity, as understood in Lévi-Strauss' general theory, is already implicit in the concept of social relation. Thus the theory has no empirical content whatever: any relation can be conceived of as reciprocal. Thus Lévi-Strauss has no difficulty in analyzing asymmetrical power relations, the institution of polygamy and the conduct of war as expressions of the reciprocal principle.

Looked at in this way we can see the significance of the unconscious, and of the retreat into the mind, for Lévi-Strauss' theory, and we can see why the foundation of his theory, in the theory of the mind, was the last piece of the jigsaw to fall into place.

It is the unconscious that guarantees that any social relation can be seen as a relation of reciprocity. The 'fundamental structures of the mind' that underlie reciprocity achieve precisely this: they describe the psychological conditions necessary for any social relation to be apprehended as a relation of reciprocity. Consequently there is no conceivable social relation that could not be assimilated to the concept of reciprocity. Thus while on the one hand the claim that social relations *could* be conceived as manifestations of the principle of reciprocity is a pure tautology, the claim that they *are* so conceived unconsciously is strictly unfalsifiable. Lévi-Strauss' general theory of reciprocity is strung between an empty tautology and equally empty speculation.

In the last four sections I have discussed Lévi-Strauss' theory of reciprocity as the condition of possibility of society. In the first section I argued that the prohibition of incest had nothing to do with the regulation of marriage and did not imply, in any significant sense, the necessity for reciprocity. In the second section I argued that marriage systems have nothing to do with the distribution of resources. In the third section I argued that Lévi-Strauss does not have an established psychological theory at his disposal. In this section I have argued that the theory of reciprocity has no substantive sociological content, that it is a purely speculative claim about the nature of the unconscious, a claim that does not derive from a theory of the mind but rather one for which the theory of the mind is invented as a necessary support. The general theory of reciprocity is, therefore, vacuous, and the theory of the unconscious that underlies it is a purely speculative, metaphysical theory that has no empirical content.

However reciprocity is not only the object of a general theory for Lévi-Strauss. It is a concept that has degrees. Hence Lévi-Strauss, in the bulk of *The Elementary Structures*, seeks to establish that different systems of kinship and marriage represent different institutional forms of the principle of reciprocity that correspond to different degrees of 'dissimulation' of reciprocity. If the theory of reciprocity has any empirical content it is in the study of specific systems, and not in the general theory, that it is to be found.

In the analysis of kinship systems Lévi-Strauss appears to be arguing that the principle of reciprocity is not merely an unconscious principle, but that it has an objective existence in social institutions. The substantive content of the theory lies in the claim that these systems are *objectively* systems of exchange, and not only that they can be interpreted, unconsciously by the participants and consciously by the analyst, as systems of exchange:

'The problem of the incest prohibition is to *explain* the particular form of the institution in each particular society. The problem is to discover what profound and omnipresent *causes* could account for the regulation of the relationships between the sexes in every society and age.'[18]

Thus Lévi-Strauss is not seeking to establish that exchange is a possible *result* of these systems, but that it is their *cause*. Hence Lévi-Strauss has to show that the systems that he is studying are *objectively reducible* to the structural principle of exchange. This is the task Lévi-Strauss sets himself in studying the elementary structures of kinship.


## 2. THE ELEMENTARY STRUCTURES OF KINSHIP

### a) Social classification and the regulation of marriage

The bulk of *The Elementary Structures* consists of an attempt to prove that reciprocity does in fact underlie the systems of kinship and marriage of those societies which can be characterized by what Lévi-Strauss calls an 'elementary structure of kinship'. A later work on other societies, those with complex structures, was promised, but has never appeared. The idea behind the distinction between elementary and complex structures is that societies are divided into those which regulate marriage by giving positive instructions about whom to marry and those which regulate marriage negatively by prohibiting marriage with certain categories of person. The former societies are those with elementary structures.

Marriage rules formulated in positive terms instruct the man looking for a wife to take his wife from a particular class or category of women. Hence consideration of the marriage rule cannot be separated from consideration of the forms which societies adopt to classify their members in relation to one another. In the context of *The Elementary Structures* there are two different kinds of classification which are relevant.

The first kind of classification divides the society objectively into a number of different classes, in the simplest case into two 'moieties'. Members of the society are allocated to these classes on the basis of descent. In a matrilineal system class membership is defined through the female line; ego, for example, may be allocated to the class of his or her mother in the simplest such system. In a patrilineal system class membership is defined through the male line, in the simplest system ego being allocated to the class of his or her father.

The situation becomes more complicated if the classification operates 'horizontal' as well as 'vertical' divisions, distinguishing class members by generation as well as by descent line. In a patrilineal system with generation alternation, ego will be allocated to the class of the father's father, in a matrilineal system to that of the mother's mother. Such systems are known as section systems.

This kind of objective classification can be used to regulate marriage negatively, by insisting that classes should be exogamous (i.e. that marriage partners be taken from outside the class), or positively, by specifying the class into which an individual shall marry. However it is important to realize that this kind of classification is not necessarily associated with the regulation of marriage either positively or negatively. It is also very important to understand that we are dealing with a system of social classification and not with a form of social organization. Thus the 'classes' do not necessarily have any corporate existence, they can perfectly well be purely nominal: in our society the surname denotes the class membership of each individual in our society, and membership of the class is defined by descent (patrilineally): the son of M. Dubois is a Dubois, the daughter of Mr Smith is a Smith. However the classes denoted by the names Dubois or Smith have no corporate existence and play no role in the regulation of marriage, they are purely nominal.

The classic form of class systems are those of the aboriginal societies of Australia. Although such systems can be used to regulate marriage, they are not necessarily so used. There has therefore been considerable discussion about the nature of these systems and their relationship to marriage regulation. One view is that these systems are to be explained by reference to principles other than those of kinship and marriage: some, following Durkheim's example, argue that the systems have an essentially ceremonial, religious purpose, others argue that they have an economic purpose in establishing territorial rights. In either case any connection with the regulation of marriage is a secondary characteristic of the system. The other view, proposed by Lévi-Strauss, is that the essential function of these systems is their role in the regulation of marriage.

In our society marriage regulation is not expressed in terms of an objective classification, but in terms of an ego-centred classification, the relationship terminology or 'kinship system'. This classification arranges members of society in categories according to their relationship to ego. Thus in our society the negative rule of marriage is expressed by forbidding us to marry certain categories of relative. In the same way societies with a positive rule of marriage may designate certain categories of relative who should be married, usually some kind of 'cousin'.

Kinship systems do not express biological relationships, they are systems of social classification that differ considerably from one society to another. In our society, for example, kin terms apply primarily only to near kin with whom direct relationships can be traced. In many societies, however, the kinship system has a much broader application, to the extent that every member of the society is designated by one term or another. In our society no distinction is made between paternal and maternal kin, whereas such a distinction is fundamental for other societies. In our society no reference is made to age in the definition of kin terms, but in other societies relative age is a fundamental principle of classification of kin.

In our society the kinship system has a limited role to play in the regulation of social life, whereas in a non-literate society the kinship system will often play a very important role in the regulation of a wide range of social relationships: economic, political, religious as well as personal. The kinship system provides 'a language in which the whole network of rights and obligations is expressed',[19] and so the study of kinship systems plays a central role in the study of such societies. For Lévi-Strauss, and for many anthropologists of different persuasions, it is the kinship system that provides the framework for every kind of social activity. Thus debate about the explanation of kinship systems, that often appears to the non-specialist as an esoteric discussion of exotic institutions, is in fact a debate about the nature of society and of sociological explanation.

The basic relationships used in the construction of kinship terminologies are the relations of consanguinity and of marriage. It is important to be quite clear, however, that these notions are shorn of any necessary biological significance when used by a terminology. Hence the existence of a descent relationship between two people does not imply the existence of a biological relationship, nor does the existence of a biological relationship imply the recognition of a descent relationship.

In the relationship terminology of our own society relationships are traced genealogically. Hence, a relative by marriage is only such if the relationship can be individually traced through a marriage. A relative by descent is only such if the relationship can be individually traced through descent. Thus, for example, the term 'sister' is correctly applied only to the female descendents of ego's parents in ego's own generation, though it may be applied also, and by extension, to other women. Notice that even in our society the institution of adoption means that descent is divorced from its biological foundation.

In many other societies the application of kinship categories is not defined primarily by reference to genealogy. For example, the category which includes the genealogical 'sister' might be applied indiscriminately to all female members of ego's generation in ego's moiety without there being any special term for genealogically traceable relatives.

There has been a long debate about the nature of 'classificatory' terminologies and their relation to 'genealogical' terminologies. Some have argued that the former develop as an extension from the latter, the term 'sister', for example, being extended from the genealogical specification to cover all female members of the sister's group and generation. This argument, however, depends on a view of a genealogical classification as being in some way privileged, a view for which there is no justification, for the genealogically based classification is no more 'natural' than is a 'classificatory' one.

The classificatory principles employed by kinship systems are often very complex. Although the basic principles are those of descent and of marriage other criteria may also be employed in distinguishing categories from one another, most notably sex and generation. Moreover the *application* of the terms to particular individuals may introduce still more criteria that have nothing to do with kinship as such, for example age, residence, membership of corporate groups, political relationships, etc., and where no clear criteria exist assignment to a particular category may be arbitrary, as, for example, when an anthropologist arrives in the society and has to be fitted into the classification. Finally, as I have noted, the system is used to articulate a wide range of social and symbolic relationships: jural relations of rights and obligations, sentimental relations, property relations, residence, marriage, religious relationships etc.

When it comes to the explanation of kinship systems there is a basic division between those who propose 'sociological' explanations, insisting that the kinship system has to be explained as a means of articulating social relationships that are themselves explained by reference to non-kinship principles, and those who propose 'intellectualist' explanations, insisting that the classification must be explained as an intellectual construct independently of, and prior to, the use to which it is put.

For those who take the sociological view the kinship system is derivative, superstructural, kinship principles providing a means of establishing a classificatory framework the *content* of which is determined independently. Thus, for example, Homans and Schneider explain the kinship system as an extensionist development of a genealogical system in which categories express sentimental relations. Coult explains the kinship system as an expression of jural relations. Leach, with a more catholic approach, explains kin terms as denoting sociologically significant categories. Marxist anthropologists have tried to explain the kinship system as an expression of relations of production.[20]

These sociological explanations are all, in one way or another, reductionist explanations in arguing that kinship systems can only be explained as the expression of other social relationships, whether sentimental, political, economic, or a combination of all three.

The 'intellectualist' approach insists that the kinship system is logically prior to any of these non-kinship relationships, for the latter can supposedly only be defined in kinship terms. Hence, for example, it is argued that the distinctive categories of the kinship system cannot be explained as expressions of different sentimental relations, since it is argued that it is the kinship system that alone introduces the distinctions between different kinds of kin with whom different sentimental relations are entertained. In the same way political, legal and economic relations are all regulated in kinship terms and so, it is asserted, cannot be conceived as being independent of or prior to the kinship system. The kinship system is the language that introduces social differentiations that are the basis of all social organization. Thus sentimental, economic, political, juridical and other relationships must express the relationships articulated by the kinship system, and not vice versa.

In *The Elementary Structures* Lévi-Strauss tries to show that kinship systems are intellectual constructs that serve a sociological purpose, namely the regulation of marriage. Thus Lévi-Strauss' theory of reciprocity, and his attempt to set sociology on an intellectualist foundation led him to a thoroughly intellectualist theory of kinship systems that challenged quite fundamentally the sociological theories that had been dominant hitherto. Although Lévi-Strauss was not the first to adopt an intellectualist approach to kinship systems, and he acknowledges Kroeber and Boas as sources of inspiration, *The Elementary Structures* did mark a decisive moment as the first systematic elaboration of the approach and as the prime inspiration for those who developed the approach subsequently. In the last analysis it is the confrontation between intellectualist and sociological approaches, rather than the specific explanations of kinship systems offered, that is the decisive issue raised by *The Elementary Structures*, for this is the issue that concerns the nature of sociological explanation and the very possibility of sociology.

It is only relatively recently that these issues have become clear, with the development of the intellectualist approach, most notably by Needham and Dumont. This is because Lévi-Strauss' own theory, although it is intellectualist, is simultaneously a reductionist theory in treating kinship systems as devices for organizing the regulation of marriage. Lévi-Strauss' own theory was therefore open to sociological reinterpretation, most notably by Leach. It was only when Dumont and Needham removed this sociological dimension from the intellectualist theory that the real significance of Lévi-Strauss' approach became clear. I shall therefore postpone discussion of this confrontation to the next chapter.

## b) The Elementary Structures

Lévi-Strauss' theory of kinship and marriage seeks to reduce class systems, kinship systems and rules of marriage to a single functional principle, the principle of reciprocity. He aims to provide a general theory which will show that

'marriage rules, nomenclature, and the systems of rights and obligations are indissociable aspects of one and the same reality, viz, the structure of the system under consideration'.[20]

The principle of reciprocity, expression of an unconscious need for security, is mobilized in the operation of marriage rules within systems of classification. In order to establish the plausibility of his theory Lévi-Strauss has to show, at the very least, that the regulation of marriage within such systems does in fact lead to systematic exchange in some meaningful sense. Conversely, if it can be shown that exchange is not in general the result of these systems, Lévi-Strauss' theory of kinship and marriage can be regarded as, at best, implausible.

In order to establish empirically that the principle of reciprocity can provide an explanation for systems of kinship and marriage Lévi-Strauss adopts a two-stage approach. Firstly, he defines what he calls 'elementary structures of kinship', which are ideal-typical systems constructed deductively as the different possible ways of implementing the principle of reciprocity with a positive rule of marriage. This deductive exercise reveals that there are only a very limited number of ways of doing this, each associated with a particular marriage rule expressed in relationship terms.

Secondly, Lévi-Strauss seeks to show that these 'ideal-typical' constructs can be used to explain the structural features of the kinship systems and marriage rules that are found in the ethnographic literature. Evaluation of the theory of kinship and marriage thus involves us in asking whether the elementary structures do in fact express the principle of reciprocity, on the one hand, and whether the elementary structures can provide satisfactory explanations of the systems found in the ethnographic literature, on the other.

The 'elementary structures' that play a central role in Lévi-Strauss' study derive directly from the Durkheimian Sinologist Marcel Granet, whose inspiration Lévi-Strauss has fully acknowledged only recently. Granet in turn seems to have derived his ideas from van Wouden, whose work Lévi-Strauss did not discuss.

Granet sought to explain certain Chinese social structures as systems of exchange between social groups based on landownership. These social groups were organized into class systems that Granet explicitly compared with the Australian section systems on which Lévi-Strauss bases his discussion of the elementary structures.

Granet argued that the groups were related by a complex system of exchanges, including the exchange of women in marriage, and he further argued, and herein lies his originality and the source of inspiration for *The Elementary Structures*, that the kinship systems of these societies also expressed this system of exchange between social groups, but from an ego-centred perspective. He then argued that the regulation of marriage within the kinship system guaranteed the exchange of women between land-owning groups. The different social structures that Granet isolated, combining a class system, a kinship system and a rule of marriage were precisely the structures that Lévi-Strauss adopted as his 'elementary structures of kinship'.

Lévi-Strauss adopted from Granet the structural principles on which he built his own analysis, but he rejected sharply Granet's sociologism and his evolutionism. Granet arranged his structures in an evolutionary succession that was, for Lévi-Strauss, based on 'facile conjectures'.[21] Moreover he did not explain exchange as the expression of a psychological principle, nor the kinship systems as classifications established in order to secure an exchange. Rather he argued that exchange is socially enforced and that the kinship systems reflected the social structure of exogamous landholding units related by a complex system of exchanges.

The exchange of women is for Granet only one aspect of these systems, and the regulation of marriage is not the cause of the systems, but rather is an effect necessary to maintain the coherence of the systems of classification, and, behind them, the integrity of the fundamental social groups. Thus the regulation of marriage and the systems of classification were, for Granet, secondary expressions of the social organization of landholding groups, the marriage rule being devised in order that the relations between classes, at the objective level, or kin categories, at the subjective level, be maintained. Thus Granet explicitly rejected any intellectualist explanation of these systems: it is illegitimate 'to transpose a certain arrangement of society into a logical system'.[22]

Although rejecting Granet's explanations, Lévi-Strauss did so by simply inverting Granet's analysis, explaining Granet's systems by their effects, and generalizing the theory to all systems of social classification. To Lévi-Strauss Granet's solutions were unnecessarily complicated, for Granet sought to explain the common phenomenon of the regulation of marriage as an exchange by reference to a variety of different origins. For Lévi-Strauss, by contrast, the universality of marriage regulation meant that the rules under investigation 'must possess some secret and common function',[23] and this function is to be found in their effect, exchange.

We must ask whether the inversion of Granet's solution is possible, and whether the generalization is legitimate: can all systems of kinship and marriage be reduced to the principle of reciprocity?

## c) Systems of Kinship and Marriage

The bulk of *The Elementary Structures* comprises a comprehensive, if sometimes cavalier, survey of the ethnographic record in order to try to establish the central thesis that class systems, kinship systems and marriage rules can all be reduced to expressions of the unconscious principle of reciprocity. The discussion is very detailed and often technical and the issues raised have been clarified only gradually over the three decades since the book was first published. However the conclusion of the debates is clear and almost unanimous on the fundamental point: there is not any necessary relationship between either the form of the kinship system, or the form of objective classification, or the positive or negative rules of marriage current in a society, and either the practice or the representation of marriage. The attempt to generalize Granet's analysis of marriage as an exchange runs into the difficulty that there is not any non-trivial sense in which marriage is in general either practiced or represented as an exchange.

The difficulties for Lévi-Strauss' theory arise at a number of different levels. Firstly, kinship and class systems are forms of classification that do not necessarily have any direct sociological correlates. Thus it is not in general the case that these systems organize relationships between social groups. Lévi-Strauss tends repeatedly to confuse social organization with intellectual classification when the two do not necessarily correspond. There is therefore no justification for Lévi-Strauss' initial belief that his theory was concerned with the sociological explanation of real exchanges between corporate groups. The intellectual systems which he examines, even when they can be said to express exchange at the level of the model of the system, do not necessarily generate such real exchange relations and indeed may prevent the establishment of such exchanges. This difficulty has led Lévi-Strauss subsequently to insist that he has never been concerned with the reality of marriage but only with the 'model' of the system.

Secondly, even at the level of the model of the system formulated in abstract terms as the ideal-typical 'elementary structure' there is no presumption that the system should generate exchange in any non-trivial sense. Lévi-Strauss himself formulates the elementary structures in such a way that exchange will take place, but this formulation is gratuitous.

In particular the 'elementary structure of generalized exchange' is formulated by Lévi-Strauss as marriage in a circle: class A marries into B which marries into C which marries into A. When there are only three categories the system, which is based on the principle that a wife must be taken from a category other than the category to which wives are given, does have such cyclical implications since B cannot marry into A nor C into B nor A into C. However as soon as there are more than three categories this is not in general the case. Thus the model of the system does not imply cyclical exchange, nor do native representations of the system necessarily recognize or privilege such exchange, nor does native practice necessarily produce such cycles. Indeed if the system has a defining structural characteristic it is that it specifically prohibits the direct exchange of women.

Lévi-Strauss' response to these difficulties has been to argue, firstly, that he is not interested in whether or not marriages really do take the form of exchange since he is concerned with exchange as a psychic, symbolic reality. Thus the woman does not acquire her symbolic significance, nor the marriage its symbolic value, by virtue of its results, but by virtue of the mental 'model' it expresses, a model which, moreover, is not a conscious representation, since 'generalized exchange' is not usually represented consciously as such. Thus Lévi-Strauss' theory is concerned with the unconscious models of the system. Hence it is reduced to the unfalsifiable, and so empty claim that even when the system is not in practice a system of exchange, even when it is not consciously represented as an exchange, and even when exchange is not implicit in it, it is still unconsciously apprehended as a system of exchange.

There is no arguing that it would be possible to use Lévi-Strauss' 'elementary structures', even that of 'generalized exchange', to produce marriage by exchange, but only in the most trivial sense is exchange implicit in these structures. Hence to claim that the elementary structures are unconscious models of systems of exchange is to reiterate the trivial claim to which we have already seen the general theory of reciprocity reduce.

A third kind of difficulty arises as soon as we go beyond the models to examine the ethnographic data. Lévi-Strauss' 'elementary structures' are, as we have seen, ideal-typical models in which kinship system, class system and marriage rule coincide in such a way as to regulate marriage. In practice, however, such a coincidence of class systems, kinship systems and marriage regulation is the exception rather than the rule.

In the case of class systems it has long been recognized that these systems do not in general serve to regulate marriage, and do not necessarily correspond to the regulation of marriage. This is why students of such systems have consistently rejected attempts to explain such systems in general as marriage-class systems, and have instead explained them as ceremonial or as legal institutions.

In the case of kinship systems too the regulation of marriage does not necessarily correspond with the relationship terminology. In practice quite different rules of marriage are associated with formally identical kinship systems, and often a number of different marriage rules are associated with a single kinship system. So long as the marriage rule prevents people defined as 'kin' from marrying one another it will not disrupt the classification. If people defined as 'kin' are allowed to marry anomalies can arise but even then these need not compromise the existence of the kinship system. Finally, many of the marriage rules that are examined by Lévi-Strauss are no more than vague preferences for marriage with particular categories of kin that are as often broken as they are observed.

In order to get around the lack of coincidence between the regulation of marriage, kinship systems and class systems Lévi-Strauss introduces a number of expedients that finally deprive his theory of any empirical content. In the case of class systems Lévi-Strauss explains their divergence from the regulation of marriage on the most gratuitous evolutionary grounds: the systems must once have coincided even if they do not now, the divergence being explained by the fact that the societies in question have changed their section system for one reason or another. At other times Lévi-Strauss explains the divergence by referring to the lack of familiarity of the natives with his theory, arguing that they are 'incompletely aware' of the structural implications of their marriage rules so that they institutionalize the system incorrectly.[24]

In the case of the divergence between kinship system and the regulation of marriage Lévi-Strauss abandons any pretence of relating his theory to the ethnographic record. Where the regulation of marriage does not coincide with the existing kinship system Lévi-Strauss simply argues that it expresses the unconscious awareness of the possibilities inherent in the rule if it were associated with another system. In this way he reconciles all manner of anomalies with his theory: the role of the maternal uncle in matrilateral systems and especially those of the Asian systems.

Lévi-Strauss deals with the anomalies in the Asian systems in three ways. Firstly, through the methodological device of the 'reduced model', which comprises only the central terms of the terminology in order to simplify the task of explanation. Secondly, Lévi-Strauss interprets some of the remaining anomalies in diffusionist-evolutionist terms as 'traces and survivals of two systems, which coexisted'.[25] Thirdly, he refers to the unconscious to explain the systems as the result of the coexistence of more than one elementary structure, the elementary structures existing in the unconscious mind.[26]

'Is there any need to emphasize that this book is concerned exclusively with models and not with empirical realities' wrote Lévi-Strauss in the Preface to the Second Edition of *The Elementary Structures of Kinship*. Given Lévi-Strauss' concern with the psychological, symbolic, significance of marriage this preoccupation with the model would be quite unexceptionable if it were to the indigenous model that he referred. However Lévi-Strauss refers to indigenous models only when they happen to accord with his theory. When indigenous institutions do not accord with his theory he immediately shifts the point of reference to a supposedly unconscious model which is accessible only to Lévi-Strauss and which reveals that the systems that are neither in reality nor in the native representations systems of marriage exchange are nevertheless expressions of the unconscious apprehension of the principle of reciprocity. This reference beyond any ethnographic reference to an inaccessible unconscious finally deprives the theory of kinship, like the theory of reciprocity on which it is based, of any empirical content at all. Since any conceivable kinship system, class system and marriage rule could be reconciled with Lévi-Strauss' theory by means of the devices of which he avails himself, the theory has no explanatory value, the supposed need to secure exchange having become a deeply unconscious need that can be unconsciously satisfied within any institutional framework at all.

Although the attempt to explain systems of kinship by reference to their supposed role in regulating marriage as an exchange must be adjudged a resounding failure this does not dispose of the more fundamental aspects of Lévi-Strauss' approach that were discussed earlier. Although it failed, *The Elementary Structures* did set out to destroy reductionist theories of social classification. In *The Elementary Structures* Lévi-Strauss argued that systems of classification could not be explained either in terms of the subjective apprehension of the systems expressed in conscious representations or in terms of some supposedly more fundamental reality, whether economic, political or affective, but could only be explained in terms of their own immanent properties. It is this attempt to show, more generally, that the 'true' or 'objective' meaning of ideological systems is inherent in those systems and cannot be found beyond them that is the distinguishing characteristic of structuralism. The fact that Lévi-Strauss did not discover the immanent meaning of the systems of kinship that he explored does not rule the project out of hand. In the next chapter we shall see how this project was taken up by Lévi-Strauss' followers.

## NOTES

1 *ESK*, p. 24.
2 *ESK*, p. 51, my emphasis.
3 1956a, p. 349.
4 *ESK*, p. 38.
5 *ESK*, p. 42.
6 1972b, p. 78; 1974a; *SA*, pp. 36–7; *FS*, p. 536.
7 1976f.
8 *ESK*, pp. 75, 84.
9 *ESK*, p. 136.
10 Simonis, *Cl. Lévi-Strauss ou la Passion de l'Inceste*, Aubier-Montaigne, Paris 1968, Ch 2, 1.c; G. Davy, 'Les structures élémentaires de la parenté', *Année Sociologique*, 3ᵉ series, 1949, p. 353.
11 J. Piaget, *Structuralism*, Routledge & Kegan Paul, London, 1971, p. 55.
12 *ESK*, pp. 411, 100.
13 S. de Beauvoir, 1949, *op. cit.* pp. 943–4, 948–9.
14 *Tot*, p. 90.
15 *ESK*, p. 481.
16 *ESK*, p. 62.
17 *ESK*, p. 143.
18 *ESK*, p. 23, my emphasis.
19 1971e, p. 63.
20 *ESK*, p. xxiii.
21 *ESK*, p. 251.
22 M. Granet, 'Catégories Matrimoniales et relations de proximité dans la Chine ancienne', *Année Sociologique*, Série B, fasc. 1–3, 1939, p. 83.
23 1971n, p. 46.
24 *ESK*, pp. 102–3, 143.
25 *ESK*, p. 353.
26 e.g. *ESK*, pp. 309, 442, 452–3.

# V. *The Impact of* The Elementary Structures of Kinship

## 1 THE THEORY OF KINSHIP

IN the last chapter I indicated the reasons why Lévi-Strauss' theory of kinship is unacceptable. I have argued, on the one hand, that the models constructed by Lévi-Strauss do not necessarily generate the exchange of women at the level either of the model or of reality and, on the other hand, that kinship systems found in the ethnographic literature cannot be explained in terms of Lévi-Strauss' elementary structures. The attempt to explain institutions of kinship and marriage in terms of the need to exchange must be adjudged a total failure. More detailed technical consideration of Lévi-Strauss' analyses would serve only to reinforce these conclusions.

In this chapter I want to broaden discussion for it is very common, indeed it could almost be said to be the rule, for the most productive theories to be those that are most in error. Lévi-Strauss' theory qualifies on the latter score, and there is no doubt that it has generated a very extensive debate that has gone far beyond Lévi-Strauss' original design, a debate that has had a major impact within anthropology and far beyond.

Evaluations of *The Elementary Structures* by anthropologists have been varied, becoming more unfavourable with the course of time. Thus Hart wrote in an early review 'it is no exaggeration to say that this book does for social organization what *The Origin of the Species* did for biology', while Korn's more recent conclusion is that the book 'arranges some of the most interesting ideas conceived by Lévi-Strauss' predecessors in many decades of social anthropology, but in a rhetorical, ill-ordered and contradictory scheme. It is built upon defective reasoning combined with deficient or mistaken reports of the ethnographic facts'. Needham regarded *The Elementary Structures* as 'a masterpiece, a sociological classic of the first rank' in 1962, but by 1971 had come to endorse the conclusions of his student Korn.

Although Lévi-Strauss continues assiduously to defend his work and insists 'I reject not one part of the theoretical inspiration or of the method, nor any of the principles of interpretation', there is no doubt that in retrospect *The Elementary Structures* can be seen to be theoretically confused, methodologically extremely unsound and empirically, where original, inadequate.[1] For anthropologists *The Elementary Structures* is as much a part of their history as is the work of Morgan or Fraser, an inspiration that has been assimilated and discarded. But despite all its technical and theoretical inadequacies, *The Elementary Structures* has had an enormous impact.

Lévi-Strauss' focus on reciprocity was rejected at an early date, even by his closest followers, for there was no way in which this theory could be rationally sustained. Thus Needham criticized Lévi-Strauss for being concerned with reciprocity when his book was really about conceptual schemes. For Needham 'prescriptive alliance systems are indeed elementary structures—not of kinship, but of classification'.[2] Similarly the work was only really taken seriously as a contribution to the study of particularly systematic classificatory kinship systems, what Needham has come to call 'prescriptive systems'. Thus for anthropologists the general theory of reciprocity and the universalist claims of the analysis were largely ignored. The interest of *The Elementary Structures* for anthropologists was not that it refounded sociology but that it challenged the orthodox interpretations of kinship systems.

The dominant interpretation of kinship systems saw kin terms as expressions of the status relations between ego and other members of his or her society. The ascription of the same term to different people was taken to imply that the status of these people in relation to ego was the same. In general these statuses were seen as originating in the relationships in the nuclear family and between near relatives and then being extended in some way beyond those close relatives to more distant relatives. For example Radcliffe-Brown argued that kinship terms were used to categorize people according to their rights and duties in relation to ego, originating in the nuclear family and being extended on the basis of the assumption of lineage unity. Others have based the categorization on affective considerations or on jural or moral rights, and have introduced other principles in addition to that of lineage unity.

This approach to kinship systems reflected a view of social structure in which the corporate descent group is primary and the relations between the individual and the descent group are mediated through relations within the nuclear family. The system of kinship reflects non-kinship relations, so the theory is a reductionist one, and it corresponds to a particular conception of social structure. This interpretation was one that worked quite well in Africa, where corporate descent groups do indeed play a fundamental role in social organization, but elsewhere it did run into difficulties that led it to proliferate *ad hoc* explanations.

This approach to kinship systems had many weaknesses. Its reductionism tended to be too crude to accommodate the complexity of kinship systems; the priority it attributed to corporate descent groups was too glib; the extensionist hypothesis that privileged genealogically close kin smacked of ethnocentrism. These aspects all came under attack in the debate that followed *The Elementary Structures*, but they were not the focus of Lévi-Strauss' challenge. What Lévi-Strauss did do was to replace one reductionism by another and to challenge the priority given to the principle of descent.

While the starting point of descent theory is the nuclear family, Lévi-Strauss insisted that society only began at the point at which nuclear families entered into relations with one another. Thus the basic unit, the 'atom of kinship', is not the nuclear family, but the interlinking of nuclear families through marriage:

'It was established that it was impossible to derive kinship, even when envisaged at its most elementary level, solely from consideration of the biological order: kinship could not be born simply from the union of sexes and the breeding of children; it implies from the beginning something else, that is the *social alliance* of biological families of which at least one cedes a sister or a daughter to another biological family. That, and that alone, is the universal principle which the text of 1945 (1945c) stated, and which *Les Structures Elémentaires de la Parenté* sought to demonstrate.'[3]

This change of focus seems very simple, but its implications are considerable, since it changes the meaning of the marriage relation. For descent theory the marriage relation is derivative from relations of descent and consanguinity and so has no independent role to play. This is possible because the kinship systems with which we are concerned are closed systems in which a notional connection in terms of descent (strictly speaking 'filiation') and consanguinity can always be traced, without any reference to marriage. Thus the woman who is to be ego's wife is also, notionally, his mother's brother's daughter. For Lévi-Strauss, however, marriage is an original relation, at the centre of explanations of kinship phenomena. Thus for Lévi-Strauss what is significant is not that the woman in question is a mother's brother's daughter but that she is a prospective spouse. Thus the marriage relation comes to play a role in the constitution of kinship systems as central as that of the relations of consanguinity and descent.

For most anthropologists the positive value of *The Elementary Structures* consisted in its drawing attention to the role of marriage as a solidarizing social relation and as a principle of social clasification that had been unduly neglected by descent theorists. Lévi-Strauss was certainly not the only, or even the first, anthropologist to do this, but his book was certainly the most influential challenge to descent theory because it made its claims for the priority of the marriage relation in such radical and provocative terms, claiming not simply that the principle could help sort out some of the anomalies of descent theory, but that it was the basis of all kinship systems. Recognition of the independent importance of the marriage relation does not, however, depend on acceptance of Lévi-Strauss' theory of reciprocity, let alone of the universalistic ambitions of this theory. Thus this lesson can perfectly well be assimilated by other anthropological traditions, and this is essentially what Edmund Leach has done.

Leach emerged from the tradition of Malinovskian functionalism, and his theoretical orientation remains essentially functionalist, bringing to functionalism a new concern with relationships. Leach retains the functionalist concern with society as a system which relates various sub-systems of a single whole. Hence for Leach kinship phenomena are to be understood in terms of economic and political phenomena, and not in relation to the mind.

In *Pul Elija* Leach sees landed property as the basis of the social structure, with the kinship system as a superstructural phenomenon. In his analysis of the kin term *tabu* he explains the term as a category word whose primary meaning derives from outside the kinship context. The term is analyzed by treating the terminology as an ideology which reflects certain aspects of the social organization. For Leach exchange relations are seen as being social relations and not relations between conceptual categories.

He shares with functionalism a concern with social relations as means of securing solidarity, his innovation being the recognition of the marriage relation as a means of securing alliance at least on a par with the descent relation. Hence he has followed Lévi-Strauss in analyzing the relation with the mother's brother as a relation constituted by marriage, and not a relation based on Fortes' principle of 'complementary filiation'.

Although many have regarded Leach as an interpreter of Lévi-Strauss' work, Leach has assimilated some of Lévi-Strauss' claims to a tradition completely alien to Lévi-Strauss' intentions. Lévi-Strauss has, therefore, consistently rejected Leach's interpretation of his work in the most vehement terms, and in particular has rejected Leach's attempt to make Lévi-Strauss' theory into a sociological reductionism. For Lévi-Strauss the kinship system does not reflect marriage relationships, it is a device designed to create and to regulate those relationships. Thus 'the primary function of a kinship system is to define categories from which to set up a certain type of marriage regulation', hence 'a kinship system is an arbitrary system of representations, not the spontaneous development of a real situation'.[4]

Lévi-Strauss rejects any sociological reductionist interpretation for which the kinship system expresses social relations. For Lévi-Strauss it is the social relations that express the kinship system, and the kinship system is fundamental because it is established in order to create the social relations that hold society together, the exchange of women. The kinship system is an intellectual construct, created (unconsciously) by the mind and expressing only kinship principles.

Lévi-Strauss sees his theory as an intellectualist rather than a sociologistic theory, kinship systems being intellectual classifications created by the mind, constrained only by the inherent properties of the mind. For Lévi-Strauss the importance of his theory is not that it modifies existing interpretations of kinship systems, but that it offers a completely different approach to the social.

In his anxiety to defend his original position Lévi-Strauss has not clarified the issues in his subsequent contributions. The result has been that he has fallen between two stools, enraging 'sociologists' with his metaphysical 'intellectualism', but failing to satisfy the more rigorous 'intellectualists' because of his desire to retain sociological points of reference. Lévi-Strauss himself wisely abandoned the study of kinship phenomena after the publication of *The Elementary Structures* and left his work to be developed and clarified by others. There is no doubt, however, that the thrust of Lévi-Strauss' work is intellectualist, as was recognized by Davy, the doyen of the Durkheimian school, in an early review which saw the introduction of sociological argument as 'imprudent' and a dangerous supplement to the intellectualist argument.[5]

This intellectualist approach has been clarified and developed by anthropologists emerging from the Oxford tradition, inspired originally, at least in part, by Lévi-Strauss, but subsequently developing their structuralist approach in opposition to Lévi-Strauss' persistent attempt to sustain his reductionist theory of reciprocity.

## 2 FEMINISM AND THE EXCHANGE OF WOMEN

Before considering the structuralist development of Lévi-Strauss' theory of kinship it is worth looking briefly at another use that has been made of Lévi-Strauss' theory. I have already noted that Lévi-Strauss' theory had an immediate appeal for Simone de Beauvoir, who interpreted the theory of reciprocity in existentialist terms. However it was not only its existentialist resonances that struck Simone de Beauvoir. More importantly Lévi-Strauss was offering a general theory of the subordination of women, of the reduction of the woman to an object of exchange between men, which de Beauvoir immediately absorbed into her classic work *The Second Sex*.

The originality of this theory is that the subordination of women is not at first sight explained in traditional terms by the supposed biological necessity of the functional differentiation of roles within the universal nuclear family: the subordination of women has a social foundation, in the relations between families, and not a biological foundation, in a supposedly natural division of labour within the family. The subordination of women is therefore associated with a particular type of society, a society based on the resolution of the opposition between the self and the other by means of exchange. In this way de Beauvoir interprets the subordination of women as a reflection of a particular resolution of the fundamental existentialist dilemma of the relation between subject and object, self and other. The liberation of women requires that women make the existential choice and refuse to accept their ascription as Others, as objects, and recognize instead that they too are subjects. Subordination is therefore not inscribed in biology, it is the result of 'bad faith', of the denial of the existential self.

More recently Lévi-Strauss' theory has been taken up in a somewhat different theoretical context, as a complement to the psychoanalytic theory of sexuality, and especially to Lacan's interpretation of Freud, that itself leans heavily on Lévi-Strauss. The main exponent of this interpretation is Juliet Mitchell, in her influential book *Psychoanalysis and Feminism* (1974).

Mitchell regards Lévi-Strauss' analysis as being important for two reasons. Firstly, because the theory of reciprocity provides a theory of society that can complement the psychoanalytic theory of the individual, the link being provided by the incest prohibition which is the basis of the Oedipus complex. Secondly, because the theory asserts that it is not the nuclear family, but the many and varied forms of relations of exchange between families that create society. Thus the Oedipus complex is not an expression of the patriarchal bourgeois family, as critics of Freud had charged, but is an expression of the exchange that makes culture possible in every society, an expression that takes a different form within different family structures. In our society, where exchange of kin is of limited significance, the family exists in isolation and the Oedipus complex takes an intense, and contradictory, form. In other societies the Oedipus complex and the Freudian unconscious also exist, but they exist in a different form.

Mitchell's conclusion is that the distinction between the sexes is a universal one, but it is not based on biology, it is an expression of the cultural universal of exchange, mediated through the Oedipus complex and the ideology of 'patriarchy'. Women are not, therefore, oppressed by men, they are oppressed by patriarchy. The conclusion is that the liberation of women depends on the overthrow of patriarchy, and that in our society the conditions for this overthrow exist in the contradiction between patriarchy, internalized in the form of the Oedipus complex, and the nuclear family in which it is embodied.

Although it is not altogether clear what this contradiction is, or why it appears particularly in a capitalist society, it seems that Mitchell's argument is that for some reason the law of exchange, and so patriarchy, has outlived its usefulness and now persists as an ideology that is reproduced through its internalization by means of the Oedipus complex and is perhaps reinforced by other means. It is therefore now possible for women to engage in a political struggle to overthrow patriarchy and so to create a new society in which women will be liberated. For Mitchell this struggle is quite distinct from, and, it seems, unconnected with, a parallel struggle that sets class against class and will result in the overthrow of capitalist society.

Mitchell's account is very eclectic, inspired by both de Beauvoir and Lacan, and the argument is not at all clear, especially at the most critical points: it is not clear why patriarchy is outmoded, so that it persists only as an ideology, nor is it clear why, if this is the case, it does survive as an ideology. It is not clear what the contradiction is between patriarchy and the nuclear family. It is not clear whether patriarchy is merely an ideology in our society, so that the liberation of women requires only that they renounce their stigmata, or whether it continues to express particular social relations, so that fundamental social change is required. It is not clear what form the struggle against patriarchy would take, whether it would be a struggle against the ideology of patriarchy, or against the prohibition of incest that underlies the Oedipus complex, or against the economic or political subordination of women, or whether it would take the form of mass psychoanalysis. However such ambiguities are not surprising since Mitchell's account is admittedly tentative.

Subsequent developments of this approach have relied directly on Lacan to develop a psychoanalytic theory of patriarchy. These developments, and indeed the work of Lacan himself, lean heavily on Lévi-Strauss' theory of reciprocity to justify the universal and non-sexist claims of psychoanalysis, in providing a link between society and the psyche and in giving sexual differentiation a cultural, and so variable, foundation.

Unfortunately, attractive as such formulations may be, there is no justification for using Lévi-Strauss' theory in this way. The previous sections should have established the inadequacy of the theory of reciprocity for present purposes. Firstly, I have shown that there is no justification for the claim that exchange is ubiquitous, let alone primary, even in non-literate societies, nor is there any justification for the presumption that where exchange does take place it is the exchange of women that is primary. The exchange of women in marriage, where marriage is represented as such, is simply one exchange in a complex network of real and symbolic interactions that seal an alliance that more often than not has important, if not fundamental, political, economic, legal or religious dimensions: marriage seals an alliance, it does not motivate or create it.

Secondly, there is no justification for the claim that exchange, or exogamy (which is what 'exchange' reduces to), has a psychological foundation. Exchange is a social institution, where it exists, that relates social groups to one another: families, households, local groups, lineages, clans, sections, moieties or whatever. Exchange is not a relation between individuals, although a number of individuals will have roles to play in a particular network of exchange. There is, therefore, no justification for connecting the institution of exogamy or of exchange with the formation of the individual psyche.

In particular the authority of men over women that underlies the fact that it is women who are given in marriage is not a personal authority, that has a psychological or an ideological foundation, it is a public authority that expresses the fact that it is men who dominate the appropriate social group, and this group is, more often than not, a much wider group than the nuclear family. Thus we are concerned with a public and political authority, which cannot be given a psychological or ideological foundation. There is no justification for using the theory of exchange (exogamy) to establish a link between patriarchal social structures and the Freudian theory of the Oedipus complex.

Thirdly, the last conclusion is reinforced when it is remembered that the incest prohibition is quite distinct from the regulation of marriage. This is not a pedantic point, for the different sets of rules affect different categories of people, different social groups, different authorities. This severance of the link between the two breaks any possible universal link between the Oedipus complex and the regulation of marriage (although, of course, specific connections might be postulated in particular societies).

We must conclude that the more general implications drawn from this kind of analysis are equally without foundation: there are no grounds for regarding the Oedipus complex as the point of intersection of the psychic and the social, the point at which the individual is subordinated to culture while being distinguished from it, so there are no grounds for seeing the Freudian unconscious as the meeting point of the individual psyche and the collective symbolic systems of culture and ideology. Consequently there are no grounds for using Lévi-Strauss' theory of reciprocity as the means of extending the application of Freudian psycho-analytic theories from the psyche to culture and ideology, as has recently been attempted by those who have developed this approach following the inspiration of Mitchell and Lacan. Finally, there is no justification for using Lévi-Strauss' theory of reciprocity to rescue Freud's theory of the psyche from charges of sexism and ethnocentrism. In short, Lévi-Strauss cannot provide Freud with a life-belt.

In fact, if we return to Lévi-Strauss' own theory of reciprocity we can see that, far from rescuing Freud from charges of sexism, Lévi-Strauss' theory is thoroughly sexist. Not in the trivial sense that Lévi-Strauss asserts that it is always men who exchange women (if exchange is an unconscious gloss on the systems there is no reason why they should not be interpreted as systems in which, unconsciously, women exchange men: the subordination of women to men is not inherent in the structures of the systems, which are perfectly symmetrical, but in their application). Lévi-Strauss' theory is sexist in that his explanation of the universality of exchange presupposes the subordination of women in the patriarchal family as a phenomenon that is prior to exchange, and so prior to culture. Thus, contrary to Mitchell's interpretation, Lévi-Strauss does explain the fact that it is men who exchange women in biological terms, and he does regard women as being pre-social beings.

The need for exchange derives for Lévi-Strauss from the tensions set up by the polygamous tendency of all men and the fact that each covets his neighbour's women. Exchange is necessary because women are a symbolic and material asset of men. Thus the necessity for exchange, as well as its possibility, depends on the fact that men already have authority over women.

The counterpart of this is that the needs of women are ignored completely: women feel no deep polygamous tendency, nor do they covet their neighbour's men, nor do they need to exchange men to achieve social integration. Thus, while men are integrated into society through exchange, in which women appear only as objects exchanged, women are integrated into society through their participation in the naturally constituted nuclear family. Men's psychological needs require the establishment of society, while women's can be satisfied within the biological family. Moreover it cannot be claimed that these psychological needs are the *product* of patriarchal society, for the universality of patriarchy is then unexplained. It is these inherent psychological needs that explain the universality of patriarchy. The implication is that if patriarchy responds to universal psychological needs it is necessary.

For Lévi-Strauss, therefore, the argument that it is the relations between families, and not the family, that is the basis of society is not an argument that liberates women, it is one that consigns their subordination to the presocial. The nuclear family pre-exists society, and it is in the family that relations between the sexes are established, based on the natural division of labour. Society only emerges with the creation of relations between families, which are relations in which women do not participate but to which they are subjected. Hence relations between men and men are social, relations between women and men are natural, and relations between women and women ignored. Lévi-Strauss is clear and unambiguous

'exactly in the same way that the principle of sexual division of labour establishes a mutual dependency between the sexes, compelling them thereby to perpetuate themselves and to found a family, the prohibition of incest establishes a mutual dependency between families, compelling them, in order to perpetuate themselves, to give rise to new families'.

'Society belongs to the realm of culture while the family is the emanation, on the social level, of those natural requirements without which there would be no society, and indeed no mankind.'[6]

# 3 FROM STRUCTURES TO STRUCTURALISM

*The Elementary Structures of Kinship* is a very confused and profoundly ambiguous work and this is, at least in part, because it is marked by the uneasy coexistence of both a sociological and an intellectualist interpretation of kinship systems. It is only retrospectively, in the light of the subsequent development of Lévi-

Strauss' thought and of the structuralist movement, that we can see the intellectualist interpretation as dominant, and so see *The Elementary Structures* as a transitional work.

Structuralism is based on the rejection of any kind of 'reductionism' that would explain the meaning of symbolic systems by reference to anything beyond those systems, whether it be by reference to some natural or social foundation or to some prior conscious or unconscious meaning. Structuralism attempts to develop an objective analysis of meaning that refuses to go beyond the immediate data. It therefore seeks the meaning of a symbolic system through a purely immanent analysis that considers only the internal relationships established by that system, and that excludes from consideration any externally defined content.

In order to see how the intellectualism introduced by Lévi-Strauss into *The Elementary Structures* leads us to structuralism it is necessary to return to Lévi-Strauss' conception of society and of the nature of sociology, for this has changed in the development from the early analyses of reciprocity to the later approach of *The Elementary Structures*.

The early analyses of reciprocity, and the first few chapters of *The Elementary Structures*, were concerned with completing Durkheimian social morphology: they were concerned to discover the psychological foundations of the distributive and redistributive mechanisms that made it possible for stable social structures to exist. The structures of reciprocity are the networks of social relations between the constituent corporate groups of the society. Thus by combining Durkheim's *Division of Labour in Society* with Mauss' *The Gift* Lévi-Strauss is able to locate the psychological underpinnings of Durkheim's mechanical solidarity. This is no longer based on the irrational awe that society inspires in the primitive mind, it is based on a perfectly rational appreciation of the material and psychological benefits of living in a society based on reciprocity.

However the bulk of *The Elementary Structures* is not about such real structures of reciprocity at all, it is about the systems of representations of kinship embodied, above all, in the system of terms by which kin address one another. This is because Lévi-Strauss' interest has shifted from the sociological function of distribution to the psychological foundation of kinship systems which is, supposedly, to satisfy a psychological need for security by representing marriage symbolically as an exchange. Once attention has shifted to the symbolic it becomes irrelevant whether or not exchange really takes place. What matters for social solidarity is that the members of society think that their relationships are reciprocal.

From this point of view what is important is not the objective fact of exchange, but the meaning of the act of exchange for the individual engaged in it. What gives the act its meaning as an exchange is not the objective fact of exchange, nor an individual conscious decision to treat the act as an exchange, but the system of social representations within which it is inserted. Study of the system of representations therefore reveals the true and objective meaning of social actions, a meaning that may escape the consciousness of those immersed in the system.

In shifting his attention to the symbolic systems of representations Lévi-Strauss is following the path already trodden by Durkheim, whose work also showed an increasing concern with the moral, as opposed to the material, dimension of society.

Lévi-Strauss rejects a psychologism for which social structures can be explained as the result of the interaction of pre-social individuals. Individuals already exist within society and their actions only have social significance to the extent to which they are integrated into the social order. This social order is a symbolic order, and it is society alone that can provide the symbolic resources that make it possible for individual action to acquire a meaning. Thus individual action expresses the conceptual system which gives it meaning, and is regulated by rules formulated in terms of that system: marriage is prescribed with certain categories of relative.

The individual becomes a social individual only by being socialized into the scheme, and individual action is social to the extent that it is oriented by that scheme. Hence individual action only has sociological significance to the extent that it expresses the system of classification and the associated rules of behaviour current in the society. Deviations of individual behaviour from the constraints of the system do not have any sociological significance, but are merely pathological symptoms of the intrusion of contingent non-social considerations.

In these respects Lévi-Strauss' theory is completely Durkheimian: social action is the result of externally constraining rules that are mobilized within a collective system of representations and that impose themselves on the individual. The task of sociology is to study the collective systems which mediate between the individual and the world by orienting and giving meaning to the actions of the individual. For both Durkheim and Lévi-Strauss this meaning is an objective meaning, inherent in the systems of representations, and quite different from the individual's conscious apprehension of the meaning of the actions in question.

Lévi-Strauss parts company with Durkheim only when it comes to the question of the status of the systems of representations. For Durkheim these systems comprise a *sui generis* reality that stands outside the individual and imposes itself on the individual with an irrational authority. The systems of representations are to be explained not as emanations of the psyche of an empirical or a generic individual, but as aspects of the 'collective conscience', to be explained by reference to the social structure which provides their material substratum and whose preservation they serve to assure. Thus for the Durkheimians social structure and symbolic representations have to be considered in relation to one another as, in Bouglé's phrase, the body and soul of society.

For Lévi-Strauss the systems of representations, although collective, objective and beyond consciousness, can exist only within the individual mind, specifically in the unconscious, and can only have the (rational) authority of the unconscious. This means that the social structure, in the Durkheimian sense of the system of social relations between corporate groups, belongs to a quite different order of reality from the systems of representations and the two cannot be related directly to one another. The relationship between social structure and the systems of representations must for Lévi-Strauss be mediated by the individual mind. The implication is that the social structure is only an expression of the systems of representations, for the social structure is simply the product of a series of individual actions which are oriented and given meaning by the systems of representations. The social structure is thus a projection of the symbolic systems embedded in the individual psyche and has no *sui generis* reality. It is therefore impossible to attempt a sociological explanation of symbolic representations since there is no society outside such representations. Thus sociology becomes the study of systems of representations and Durkheimian social morphology disappears from view.

If society is a symbolic order then there can be no social reality beyond the symbolic systems which give meaning to social existence. This meaning must therefore be inherent in such symbolic systems, an objective meaning that cannot be reduced to anything external to those systems, whether to an external nature or an external social structure, on the one hand, or to a conscious apprehension of those systems, on the other. The meaning of the symbolic order is irreducible. Thus, for example, kinship phenomena cannot be reduced to biological relations of kinship, nor to jural or affective relations. They are meaningful, cultural phenomena in which symbolic relations, which are only constituted in and through a kinship system, replace natural relations. Thus kinship exists only within a kinship system that establishes the culturally meaningful differentiation of kin. It is only on the basis of this symbolic system that kinship can have any objective reality, on the one hand, or subjective meaning, on the other.

The belief that social and cultural phenomena have an objective meaning, independent of any subjective interpretation or of any external environmental, social or cultural context, has fundamental implications.

If symbolic systems exist which have a meaning independent of their context or of their application, then we have isolated an objective order of reality that transcends the individual, but that is irreducible to nature. These symbolic systems mediate between individuals, and between the individual and nature, so it is only through these systems that the individual can relate to others or to nature. In short these symbolic systems constitute society, a society that is prior to, and independent of, the individuals who comprise it, and that alone can give meaning and orientation to the action of biological individuals.

The belief that it is possible to isolate cultural systems that have an objective meaning leads directly to the conception of society, adopted by structuralism, as a series of systems of representations which exist independently of, and prior to, individual actions and beliefs. Any particular society is simply the result of the application of these systems of representations and associated rules of behaviour at a particular time and place. It is a more or less perfect expression of the system of representation, imperfections deriving from contingent failures to apply the system correctly for one reason or another.

These autonomous systems of representations exist quite independently of their application, they can be studied even if they are never applied, they continue to exist even if the societies that practised them have died out. Hence the anthropologist can study the societies even after they have been extinguished, or can study societies from afar on the basis of other people's ethnographic reports (whence the characteristic Durkheimian indifference to fieldwork that so shocks Anglo-Saxon anthropologists).

It is the systems of representation that define the social, they are the only true *social* reality, and in studying them we can study the social undisturbed by the accidental influence of distortions arising out of geographical, demographic, psychological or contingent historical factors. The system of representations provides a constant atemporal system that underlies all the various expressions of that system in particular societies at particular times. Thus society is, in the last analysis, when considered in abstraction from irrelevant influences, made up of a series of conceptual systems, the most fundamental of which in non-literate societies is the classification of kin, and an associated series of rules of behaviour, the most fundamental of which is the rule of reciprocity.

The coherence of this conception of society, and the privilege that it accords to the study of conceptual systems, depends entirely on the belief that such ideal conceptual systems can be isolated and that their objective meaning can be scientifically established. In evaluating the viability of the structuralist enterprise it is this belief that we must put to the test.

The systems of representations that make up society are ideal systems in a double sense. Firstly, they have a purely psychological reality, existing in the unconscious of each individual and directing individual behaviour with the force of an unconscious constraint. They are therefore to be explained as the expression of certain properties of the human mind and, for Lévi-Strauss, the study of these systems provides a way of studying the human mind. Secondly, the systems of representation exist independently of any particular manifestation in the consciousness of particular individuals or the practice of particular societies. Every particular example of the system will in fact be corrupted and distorted by various contingent factors that the analyst must ignore.

This has important methodological implications, for it means that the analyst is not studying particular examples of the systems under investigation, but the ideal-type, the pure form, or the 'model', in Lévi-Strauss' terminology, of the system. Thus a repeated claim of structuralists is that they do not study reality, they study models which are a kind of purified object.

This gives rise to the characteristic epistemology of structuralism, in which it is argued that the object of any science is an ideal object, not to be confused with any particular empirical object. Hence, for example, the theory of kinship does not concern itself with representations of kinship systems reported by particular individuals, for these conscious representations may fail to correspond to the deeper, unconscious, reality of the system. Nor does the theory concern itself with the application of the systems in particular societies, where irrelevant geographical, demographic, psychological or historical factors will have distorted the systems in operation.

This kind of argument has a perfectly respectable pedigree within the philosophy of science. Indeed the idea that theories are based on the deductive elaboration of hypothetical claims is the *credo* of modern positivism. Newton, for example, did not study falling apples. Newton studied the behaviour of point-masses, bodies of zero extension. Not only is the point-mass an ideal object, it is an object which could not possibly exist, for the very concept is self-contradictory. Newton's theory, like any other theory for modern positivism, is therefore a deductive theory that derives the properties of point-masses, an ideal object, from certain fundamental hypothetical postulates. This is not a theory whose *validity* depends on the existence of point-masses, it is a theory that is valid universally and indubitably, for it is a deductive theory that exists independently of any reference to reality.

The application of the theory, and so its scientific usefulness, is a quite different question for positivism. Anybody can elaborate deductive theories of ideal objects *ad infinitum*, but these theories can only be claimed to have any scientific value if they tell us something about the world that we would not know without them. Hence for positivism the problem is one of translating the language of theory into a language of observation that can establish connections between deductive theories and the external world.

The problems raised by this attempt have proved insuperable, and positivism has not managed to formulate any satisfactory criteria by which alternative theories can be evaluated. The central problem is that of establishing criteria that will be strong enough to reject theories considered to have no application, while not being so strong that theories considered to be of scientific value are rejected. The conclusion that many have drawn from the failure of positivism to achieve this is that it is impossible to decide between theories on empirical grounds. The evaluation of theories becomes something completely irrational (Feyerabend), an arbitrary decision of the community of scientists (Kuhn), or the objective result of the rationalist logic of evolution (Popper).

The alternative adopted by structuralism is a relativist rejection of the evaluation of theories by reference to reality, so structuralism has tended to adopt the rationalist slogan 'save the theory' as a counter to the old empiricist slogan 'save the appearances': the task of the scientist is to purify the logic of the theory, to formalize and axiomatize it, to create a closed logical theory of an ideal object and not to worry about the correspondence between this object and a mythical reality. A theory which is adequate is one that can provide a coherent and logical framework for discourse, the task of science is not to create a view of the world that is true, it is to create a view of the world that is without contradiction. Thus positivism is preserved by turning into a form of rationalism.

From this point of view Lévi-Strauss' theory of kinship sets the human sciences on a genuinely scientific foundation by providing them with an object that is untainted by contamination with the prejudices of ideology, or of common sense, or of conscious representations, that inevitably corrupt the purely empirical objects of everyday life.

However, the structuralist methodological separation of the ideal object from reality, although it has a superficial plausibility when seen in the context of the failures of the older positivism, has serious dangers inherent in it. The separation of the model from reality can provide, in the guise of a methodological principle, a device that serves to preserve intact a theory that appears to be overwhelmingly falsified by empirical evidence.

Lévi-Strauss can certainly elaborate models of kinship systems in which marriage can be seen as a systematic exchange. However for most people such models would only qualify as knowledge if they corresponded in some way to an external reality. Lévi-Strauss' models do not enjoy this status, for they are not, in general, consistent with the reality contained in reliable ethno-graphic reports (which is as near as we can get to reality). To protect the models from such contamination they are claimed to exist undetected and undetectable in the unconscious. Althusser's 'symptomatic' reading of Marx enjoys the same status: Althusser did not claim that what Marx wrote corresponded to Althusser's reading of Marx, for Althusser was describing a 'problematic' that Marx was in the course of developing, which he could only express inadequately, and of which he was incompletely aware. As Althusser's work developed Marx's problematic came to have less and less connection with the work of Marx: at first it expressed itself in Marx's writings after the mid-1840s, but later Althusser came to claim that it did not even exist in *Capital*, only appearing in outline in work of the 1880s.

Foucault's 'epistemes' are no different: Foucault does not claim to discuss the thought of particular people or of particular social groups, he discusses a system of thought that is an ideal object, that is only inadequately and incompletely expressed in the work of a particular thinker. Hence Foucault's arguments cannot be countered by claiming that the thought of a particular thinker does not correspond to the ideal object, to the episteme, for this shows not that Foucault has inadequately characterized the episteme, it shows that the thinker in question had inadequately expressed it.

In structuralist hands the rationalist development of positivism is the basis on which it is the theory that is made the judge of the evidence and not vice versa. Indeed for Lévi-Strauss this is a great virtue of structuralism, for structuralism is able to produce new facts and correct old evidence, without ever venturing from the study.[7]

This structuralist methodology is extremely powerful for it makes any theory proposed strictly unfalsifiable for the simple reason that the theory does not claim to be a theory of any identifiable reality, but is a theory of unconscious systems that lie behind reality and that reality expresses only inadequately and imperfectly. The problem that such a methodology constantly confronts us with is a simple one: what is the value of a scientific theory that gives us undubitable knowledge of an object for whose existence and properties there is not, and cannot be, any independent evidence whatever?

We can go further than this and ask to what extent it is possible to discover any objective meaning inherent in any symbolic system, whether real or ideal. The question leads us to consider the privilege accorded by structuralism to the formal structure of symbolic systems, from which the doctrine derives its name and in terms of which it justifies its particular method of analysis.

If the systems that structuralism examines are objective systems of meaning, then that meaning must exist independently of any subjective apprehension of that meaning, and must be inherent in the systems. The meaning cannot, therefore, derive from any particular *content* that the system may have. The implication is that, when we have abstracted from all particular contents, we are left with the formal relations internal to the system. Thus the attempt to discover an objective meaning, if pursued logically, dissolves the systems into their formal structures.

In Lévi-Strauss' theory of kinship this follows from the theory of reciprocity, for reciprocity is essentially a structural principle, and this immediately means that Lévi-Strauss is concerned with the formal, structural, properties of kinship systems, whatever their manifest content. This meaning is objective because it is, supposedly, inherent in the system and independent of any particular interpretation or application of the system.

The search for an objective meaning leads ineluctably to the formal structure of the system. The fundamental question we shall have to ask of the supposedly objective analyses of structure is whether the form can be dissociated in this way from the content of the system, and hypothesized as the basis of an objective meaning, or alternatively whether form and content are inseperable, so that no formal structure exists in isolation from the content of the system.

Despite its sociological integument *The Elementary Structures* already contains all the motifs of structuralism. In *The Elementary Structures* Lévi-Strauss establishes a number of 'elementary structures of kinship', which represent different structural arrangements of kin terms, by deduction from the principle of reciprocity. He then proceeds to attempt to reconcile his models with the empirical data, and indeed he uses his models to assess the data, explaining divergences between his model and the data by reference to contingent historical, demographic and psychological factors.

The systems of kinship and marriage studied by Lévi-Strauss in

*The Elementary Structures* not only provide an object on which to exercise the structural method, they also provide the means of access to the ultimate truth of humanity, and so the basis of the structuralist philosophy. It is the systems of kinship and marriage that are, in non-literate societies at least, the key mediating term between the individual and society, the study of which can at one and the same time reveal to us the deepest and truest meaning of human existence and provide the key to an explanation of social phenomena by revealing those fundamental properties of the human mind that make society possible. Thus it is through the study of kinship and marriage that Lévi-Strauss tries to establish his human philosophy on a scientific foundation, to discover through anthropology the true meaning of human existence. The central themes of the philosophy that emerges are taken up and developed not only in Lévi-Strauss' later work, but throughout the structuralist movement.

For Lévi-Strauss it is the system of classification that unites the subject with objective reality. However the subject and objective reality have no meaningful existence independently of the classificatory framework which alone can give the world meaning for the subject, and assign a place to the subject in the world.

Before the conceptual schemes there is merely an undifferentiated nature of which biological individuals are an undistingished part. Thus the conceptual scheme does not mediate between a pre-existent subject and a reality that is already external. The conceptual scheme alone introduces the distinction between subject and object, between culture and nature.

The birth of culture is the emergence of systems of classification that counterpose subject to object and create a space for the social individual in a world of symbolic representations. The opposition between subject and object, individual and society, culture and nature that has plagued Western philosophy and the emerging human sciences is an imaginary opposition, created by the conceptual scheme, the 'problematic' or the 'episteme', that dominates our systems of thought.

The conceptual scheme, although it has a psychological foundation, exists independently of, and prior to, the subject or subjective consciousness: the social subject exists only in the place assigned to him or her by the conceptual scheme, hence the subject, and the consciousness of subjectivity, is the product of the conceptual scheme, an 'effect of the structure', and is in no sense its creator. The subject is not, therefore, a reality that exists prior to the conceptual scheme: before the conceptual scheme all that exists is the biological individual. The subject is a symbolic construct and as such can only be an expression of an objective system of meaning that is prior to the subject. This is the core of the structuralists' 'death of the subject'. It is the foundation of Lacan's reinterpretation of Freud and of Foucault's and Althusser's consideration of the 'problematic of the subject' that dominates Western, or bourgeois, philosophy. It derives directly from Lévi-Strauss' analysis of kinship, but behind Lévi-Strauss stands, as always, Durkheim, whose *Division of Labour in Society* took as its central theme the emergence of individuality as a social construct.

The conceptual scheme constructs not only the subject, but also a reality defined as external to the subject. The conceptual scheme is therefore neither the construct of a creative subject, nor can it in any sense express an independent reality, for an independent reality only exists within the conceptual scheme. The conceptual scheme is essentially arbitrary, expressing nothing but itself and the mental constraints that alone underlie it. The implication is that the imaginary, ideological, conception of the subject that dominates our thought is not an expression of the reality of subjectivity, of the freedom and independence of the individual in bourgeois society. This freedom and independence is a purely symbolic, mythical, expression of a spurious subjectivity. This myth is a particularly dangerous and misleading way of living in the world because it inverts the true relation between subject and structure.

The structuralist conception of society as a series of symbolic systems, the structuralist method of analysis of ideal objects and of exclusive consideration of internal relations of such objects, and the structuralist philosophy that sees the symbolic systems as prior to both subject and object, and so the symbolic systems as the only true reality, can all be found in embryo in *The Elementary Structures of Kinship*. It is in this sense that *The Elementary Structures* is the work that establishes the foundations of structuralism. In it the structuralist conception of society, the structural method, and the structuralist human philosophy are all developed for the first time.

On the other hand both the originality and the achievements of *The Elementary Structures* are extremely limited. The 'structuralism' of *The Elementary Structures* derives ultimately from the attempt to achieve a rationalistic radicalization of Durkheim's positivistic sociology. The attempt to uncover objective systems of representations and to locate their unconscious meanings is a dismal failure.

At its root structuralism depends entirely on the claim that the systems of representations that it studies are a privileged order of reality whose meaning can be discovered objectively. Society is seen as a system of symbolic representations because these are considered to be prior to, and so more fundamental than, either the object that they represent or the subject to whom it is represented. This privilege accorded to the systems of representations over the individual consciousness and external reality depends on being able to isolate the objective meaning of these systems independently of any reference to either subject or object, on the basis of an immanent analysis.

In *The Elementary Structures of Kinship* Lévi-Strauss tried to do just this. He sought to establish that the systems of kinship and marriage have an objective meaning, as systems of reciprocity, that is more fundamental than the meaning they have for those who practice them, an unconscious meaning that can be established objectively without any reference to native conceptions of the system.

In fact, I have argued, Lévi-Strauss does no such thing. Insofar as he establishes that the principle of reciprocity is immanent in the systems under review the conclusion is trivial because the principle is deprived of any significant content. Insofar as the principle of reciprocity is given any content Lévi-Strauss offers no acceptable evidence to support his claim. Thus the principle of reciprocity is not an objective meaning that Lévi-Strauss discovers in the data, it is a meaning that is imposed on the data and then attributed to an inaccessible unconscious. Thus his claim to provide an objective, scientific, analysis of the meaning of these systems falls down.

For a structuralist the failure of Lévi-Strauss' account is a result of the residual sociologism in *The Elementary Structures*, so that Lévi-Strauss looks beyond the internal relations of the systems to find their meaning. An adequate objective account must divorce the systems altogether from any contingent, externally-imposed, content and must find the true and objective meaning in the internal structural relations established by the system, relations that exist independently of the context or of the subjective interpretation of the native or of the analyst. Any other account will introduce extrinsic criteria, and so will be arbitrary.

This is the direction in which the structuralist analysis of kinship systems has been developed. Since it is in this area that structuralism has the longest history, and that its analyses have been conducted with the greatest degree of rigour, it is very instructive to look at the results that have been achieved.

# 4 ANTHROPOLOGICAL STRUCTURALISM

The structuralist implications of the theory of kinship were fully developed by Louis Dumont and by Rodney Needham, social anthropologists trained in the Oxford tradition established by Evans-Pritchard, and integrating Lévi-Strauss' analysis of kinship into that tradition.

Evans-Pritchard had developed an intellectualist cultural idealism that was more radical than that of Lévi-Strauss in its refusal to countenance any kind of reductionism, the task of anthropology being to describe rather than to seek to explain. In his work on *The Nuer* (1940) Evans-Pritchard had produced a structuralist interpretation of Nuer society in which he saw the structural framework of classification as prior to any particular content that the classification acquired in use, whether religious, political or economic: the search for an *objective* description of an independent system of classification led Evans-Pritchard inexorably to a *structural* description which divorced the form of the system from its content. *The Nuer*, however, did not take full account of the marriage relation as a structural principle complementary to that of descent. Lévi-Strauss' work, therefore, played a part in developing Oxford structuralism by drawing attention to a new structural relation.

The principles of structuralism had already been laid down by Evans-Pritchard:

'The thesis that I have put before you, that social anthropology is a kind of historiography, and therefore ultimately of philosophy or art, implies that it studies societies as moral systems and not as natural systems, that it is interested in design rather than in process, and that it therefore seeks patterns and not scientific laws, and interprets rather than explains. These are conceptual, and not merely verbal, differences'.[8]

Dumont, although French, spent some time in Oxford, and it was he who developed the structural analysis of kinship. Following Evans-Pritchard, Dumont argued very strongly against all forms of reductionism, including Lévi-Strauss' attempt to explain kinship systems in terms of the regulation of marriage. Thus, in a series of analyses, Dumont has shown that there are no necessary connections between the form of the kinship system and either the regulation of marriage or the organization of descent groups in the society, so undermining any simplistic reductionism. Dumont argues instead that social organization and the kinship system must be analyzed quite independently of one another, the kinship system being analyzed as an intellectual classification whose principles are conceptual. The kinship system is a purely intellectual construct that makes use of certain classificatory principles in order to define other individuals in relation to ego, and so it expresses certain ideas about the nature of different kinds of relationship in the society in question.

Dumont has reinterpreted the 'prescriptive' kinship systems that Lévi-Strauss analyzed by arguing that these systems do not organize marriage, but rather that they express certain ideas the particular society has about the difference between consanguines and affines. Systems such as these, that are based on a systematic differentiation between consanguines and affines, express the idea that there is a fundamental difference between 'blood relatives' and 'relatives by marriage', the two categories being themselves conceptual, and not reflecting specific biological or affinal connections. The classification itself says nothing about what this difference is, nor about why these categories are different, nor about how people come to be allocated to the two categories.

Dumont introduces a fundamental, and very radical, distinction between the formal structure of the system of classification and the content that the classification may acquire in any particular society. The system of classification can, and must, be studied independently of its application. Thus in one society the system may be used to organize marriage, in another it may be seen as a framework for economic relations, in another it may express emotional ties. The system cannot be explained by any of these particular functions, for the system is prior to any of these uses. The meaning of the system has to be found in the conceptual distinctions that give rise to the system, and this meaning is independent of, and prior to, any particular content that the system may acquire in a particular society.

Dumont's lead has been followed by other Oxford anthropologists, most notably Rodney Needham who has sought to develop and to defend the intellectualist, structuralist, approach to kinship systems. Needham was originally very close to Lévi-Strauss, although he did not accept the theory of reciprocity, in that he was concerned to see the kinship system in its relation to other aspects of the symbolic classification of society. However he has progressively abandoned the attempt to make substantive connections of this kind and has adopted an increasingly rigorous and formal intellectualism. In the course of doing so he has gone beyond even Dumont's isolation of the kinship system, to reject the interpretation of the system in terms of any kinship principles, whether of descent or alliance, consanguinity or affinity, and to reduce it to a pure form.

This development is interesting because Needham has followed the logic of structuralism through to its limits and, in pursuit of an objective meaning, has found the ground progressively disappearing from under his feet until finally structuralism has nothing left to explain.

The attempt to secure a scientific analysis of meaning depends on the separation of the system of classification from its application in a particular society and its isolation from any particular subjective interpretation of its meaning. The application of the structural method depends on the isolation of such an autonomous object.

The crucial question that we have to pose to structuralism is that of the possibility of isolating such an objective system for study, of separating the system of classification from its particular applications and interpretations. We have seen that Lévi-Strauss' attempt to do so was a failure. Dumont therefore rejects all reductionism and insists that the systems be analyzed solely in terms of kinship principles. But are these principles objective, are they internal to the system?

Dumont rejects Lévi-Strauss' reductionism and deductively establishes models on the basis of the principles of consanguinity (blood relatives) and affinity (relation by marriage). He constructs a system by arranging categories around ego in a structure whose relations are defined by those principles. Ego's relationship to any individual in the structure is then traced by one or other of these connections, or a combination of them, and categories within the structure are distinguished from one another solely on the basis of these two structural principles. The simplest classification of all would simply separate 'blood relatives' from 'relatives by marriage' and so would define two categories according to the relation involved. The model can, however, be elaborated by introducing further distinctive features, such as sex or generation, or by applying the distinctions repeatedly. Thus any particular kinship system can be defined as the structure that results from the application of these distinctive features.

The question we have to ask is: what is the status of this model? There is no doubt that it is independent of any application, for it has been constructed deductively by the analyst, with no reference to ethnographic data, just like Lévi-Strauss' elementary structures. It is, therefore, an ideal object constructed by the analyst. The crucial question is whether it can be claimed coherently that this ideal object corresponds to some reality that is more fundamental than the application of the system or of the native conception of it. If it turns out that native conceptions do not necessarily correspond to the model, or that it is not necessarily applied in the form that it has been constructed, what justification is there for claiming that it is more than a figment of Dumont's imagination?

The problem of the status of the model arises because Dumont offers not a meaning that is inherent in the system, but an interpretation of the system. Dumont specifies certain relations between the categories of the system, and the implication is that these, and no other, relations actually exist. Dumont specifies the distinctive relations to the system as relations of affinity and consanguinity. However this distinction is not inherent in the system, but represents a particular interpretation.

The problem is that the distinction between (notionally biological) kin and (notionally social) allies is not an objective nor an unambiguous one. On the one hand, all relationships within closed systems of kinship can be traced both through marriage and through consanguinity, which is why descent theory can present a quite different interpretation of the system as a classification of kin, without any reference to marriage, that is equally consistent with the data. At the level of the model there is no way of deciding between Dumont's interpretation and that of descent theory.

Only reference to the application of the system can decide between the descent theory interpretation and that of Dumont, for each interpretation can provide a perfectly consistent model that relates the categories according to quite different principles. The validity of Dumont's model therefore depends on the extent to which it corresponds to ethnographic reality. Although constructed deductively it can only have the validity of a generalization from the data, whether of a native model of the system or of the practical application of the system.

If Dumont's model does not correspond in some way to the native reality of the system there is no justification for claiming that the model has any special significance. Thus Dumont's model of the kinship system cannot be claimed to be prior to its particular applications or interpretations, for it depends on a culturally specific definition of the difference between kin and affines.

As soon as we appreciate that the model has no validity independently of its existence in ethnographic reality, we also realize that its status is simply that of an abstraction from a functioning system. Once this is recognized, there is no longer any justification for interpreting the system solely in kinship terms, for the functioning reality of the system is very complex. It is not in practice simply a kinship system, it is a classification that organizes a wide range of social relationships, which differ from society to society. There is no *a priori* reason why kin relations should be arbitrarily abstracted from the other aspects of the social system and made into the 'essence' of the system, its objective meaning as opposed to its contingent application.

In reality there is no distinction between the system of classification and its application. In reality there are people living and working together who refer to each other by using various terms that express their mutual relations to one another. These concrete social relations are multidimensional, and certainly cannot be reduced to relations of kinship or affinity. The application of the terms does not depend on any traceable genealogical connections, and it will frequently depend on principles that have nothing to do with kinship.

Concepts of kinship provide a very powerful and flexible

language within which to articulate an enormous range of social relationships. The distinction between 'our own kind' and 'their kind', that is expressed in Dumont's distinction between consanguinity and affinity or in Evans-Pritchard's lineage structure, or in Lévi-Strauss' distinction between exogamous groups exchanging women, or in the comedian's distinction between mother and mother-in-law, provides an extremely powerful way of conceptualizing social relationships in a relatively simple society. It should not be surprising, therefore, to find that these conceptual distinctions, in various forms, are used to conceptualize very different relationships in different societies.

There is no justification for isolating the language of kinship from the social relations it expresses. Thus it is no more justifiable to claim that the system of kinship provides an independent framework within which other social relations can be expressed, than it is to argue that the kinship system is the simple expression of non-kinship relations. Although it is certainly true that in non-literate societies the definition and regulation of social relations is conducted in kinship terms, so that economic, political or legal relationships cannot be examined independently of kinship categories, it is also true that kinship categories cannot be defined independently of the social relations that those categories regulate, for even though kinship terms have conceptual connotations of specific genealogical relationships of kinship or affinity, the application of those terms cannot be determined only by reference to genealogical principles. Thus it is not possible to define either the kinship system or the social relations that it expresses independently of one another, so it is not possible, on logical or any other grounds, to assign absolute primacy to one or to the other. The question of the relation between kinship principles and other features of social organization and social consciousness can only be posed as a question of the interdependence of the parts of a complex whole.

The language of kinship is not a universal language. Kinship concepts differ from one society to another, and the kinds of relationships expressed in kin terms also vary widely. Thus it seems that there is no possibility of developing a general theory of kinship, because once we have abstracted from the particular there is nothing of substance left to explain.

For this reason Needham has recently argued that there is not really any such thing as kinship, that kinship systems are purely formal systems that arrange the categories in a particular structure, the relations of which are purely formal. It seems that by retreating into the formalism of a pure structure structuralism can finally locate an absolute and objective meaning, a meaning independent of any content and so of any particular application or interpretation.

But the problem with this ultimate retreat is that if we abstract altogether from the content of the system, the structure also disappears, for the structure is ineradicably the structure of a system of kinship, and it corresponds to a particular interpretation. A different interpretation of the system, for example in terms of descent theory, would involve different structural relations. Thus once we have abstracted from all content, the structure disappears as well and there is nothing left to explain. The 'ideal object' becomes a pure, disembodied, meaningless form. Needham, to his credit, seems belatedly to have recognized this and to have disappeared up his naval into a Wittgensteinian void.

These developments in the structural analysis of kinship bring out very vividly the dilemma of structuralism. Structuralism aims to isolate a cultural system whose objective meaning can then be subjected to a scientific analysis. In order to do this it is necessary to establish the pure objectivity of the system. But to establish the pure objectivity of the system it is necessary to abstract from every particular content that the system might have and every particular interpretation that might be placed on it. At each stage the objectivity of the analysis is compromised as it becomes apparent that the interpretation proposed does not have any absolute validity, is not inherent in the absolute objectivity of the ideal system, but is a construct of the analyst whose validity must depend on its empirical evaluation.

The attempt to separate the system from its context leads to a progressive retreat into formalism, and ultimately to complete defeat. The conclusion, that we will find recurring, is that the attempt to locate autonomous cultural systems, whether linguistic, conceptual or symbolic, whose meaning is objective, independent of and prior to their particular application, is a vain one.

The conclusion should hardly be surprising, for the structuralist project implies that there is a world of meanings beyond the human apprehension of particular meanings, that meaning can exist without being meaning for somebody. It used to be believed that such an objective world of meaning existed, and the apparent contradiction implicit in the claim was resolved by inventing an absolute Being for whom the world was meaningful, God. The study of these meanings was called theology, and it is to theological questions, and theological solutions, that structuralism leads, as it too invents a God, the great Scientist in the sky, who can guarantee the objectivity of its systems of meaning. For those, like Lévi-Strauss, for whom God has no meaning, the retreat into formalism ultimately yields the conclusion that foredoomed the project: the world is declared to be inherently meaningless, all meaning is therefore subjective, arbitrary, vain.

# NOTES

1 C. Hart, 'Review of Les structures élémentaires de la parenté', *American Anthropologist*, 52, 1950, p. 393; F. Korn, *Elementary Structures Reconsidered*, Routledge & Kegan Paul, London, 1973, pp. 141–2; R. Needham, *Structure and Sentiment*, University of Chicago Press, Chicago, 1962, p. 2; R. Needham, *Rethinking Kinship and Marriage*, Tavistock, London, 1971, p. xciv.

2 R. Needham, 'A Structural Analysis of Aimol Society', *Bijdragen tot de Taal-, Land- en Volkenkunde*, 116, 1960, p. 102.

3 1972d, p. 334.

4 *FKS*, pp. 13, 14; *SA*, p. 50.

5 Davy, *op. cit.*, pp. 351–2.

6 1956a, pp. 273, 284.

7 1970c, p. 302.

8 E. Evans-Pritchard, *Social Anthropology and Other Essays*, Free Press, Glencoe, 1962.

# VI. *Structuralism in Linguistics*

IN the last two chapters I have shown how Lévi-Strauss' fundamental philosophical inspiration drove him to develop a distinctive theory of society and method of analysis in the attempt to discover the objective meaning of human culture. In particular Lévi-Strauss sought to isolate kinship systems as objective systems of meaning that existed, and could be analyzed, independently of their particular application or of their meaning for particular individuals. These objective systems of meaning Lévi-Strauss located in the unconscious mind which determined not only that they would be objective, but also that they would be more fundamental than any subjective interpretation of them. The structural method, and the corresponding emphasis on the formal properties of the systems under review, followed from this attempt to isolate the objective, universal, meaning of the systems.

In the last chapter I argued that it is this view of the human world as a world of objective, unconscious or collective, cultural systems within which individuals are inserted, that is the fundamental inspiration of structuralism. It results from the search for the objective meaning of culture, and it results in the isolation of objective cultural systems that are amenable to study by the methods of the positive sciences.

Structuralism, therefore, appears to make possible the establishment of autonomous and objective human sciences, because it provides those sciences with their own independent and objective fields of study: the particular cultural systems which are their concern, whether art, literature, music, myth, or, as in the case already studied, systems of kinship.

The viability of structuralism depends entirely on its ability to isolate genuinely autonomous and objective systems of meaning. The scientific claims of structuralism, as well as the cultural idealism on which these are based, depend on the validity of its attempt to isolate such cultural systems. In the case of the theory of

117

kinship I argued that such systems could not in fact be isolated, for once kinship systems had been abstracted from their ethnographic context, there was nothing left to explain.

In Lévi-Strauss' case the failure of the ethnographic data to correspond to the ideal object that he had constructed led him to retreat into the unconscious and postulate a purely metaphysical existence for this object, with the result that he offered knowledge of an object for whose existence there was no evidence, while he reduced ethnographic reality, which departed from this object, to the status of a massive distortion of this fundamental, but inaccessible, reality, produced by subjective illusion and contingent historical events.

In the case of the structuralism of Needham and Dumont the failure to locate any objective universal properties of kinship systems led first to an empty formalism and, ultimately, to the abandonment of any attempt to generalize beyond the specific ethnographic context in which particular systems are found.

Although Lévi-Strauss' work, and particularly *The Elementary Structures of Kinship*, has been the main stimulus to the development of structuralism as an intellectual movement, this stimulus has owed much of its force to the fact that Lévi-Strauss' work reproduces an approach that had been developed quite independently within linguistics. It was above all this convergence that suggested that the structuralist approach might have a more general applicability than the particular fields of linguistics and kinship studies in which it was developed.

Linguistics is important to structuralism for several reasons. Firstly, although Lévi-Strauss' structuralism was formed quite independently it was only with his encounter with linguistics that he became fully aware of the theoretical, methodological and philosophical implications of his approach, and it was only this encounter that gave him the confidence to generalize his findings and to offer structuralism as a method for all the human sciences. Linguistics, moreover, filled the last gap in Lévi-Strauss' theory by providing him with a purely intellectual theory of the unconscious, and it was this that enabled him to elaborate his human philosophy.

Secondly, it is the human linguistic capacity that more than anything else distinguishes humans from other animals, and it is language that is the most powerful and the most complete means of symbolic communication available to humans. Thus for structuralism, which is concerned precisely with the question of the objective foundation of culture, and with the analysis of culture as a series of symbolic systems, linguistics must have strong claims as the fundamental human science.

Thirdly, the structuralist approach within linguistics (using the term in the European rather than the North American sense) has considerable achievements to its credit in advancing our understanding and our knowledge of language. It was, therefore, the achievements of structuralism within linguistics, at least as much as within anthropology, that gave structuralism an apparent scientific authority.

Fourthly, linguistics has provided a direct inspiration to the development of modern structuralism, quite independently of Lévi-Strauss. This is particularly the case with the rise of 'semiology' which represents an extension of the methods of linguistics to non-linguistic symbolic systems. Thus Roland Barthes and the *Tel Quel* group developed a structuralist semiology independently of any contact with Lévi-Strauss, although their work was subsequently influenced by Lévi-Strauss.

In this chapter I want to look at structuralism in linguistics. Structuralism in linguistics has been based on exactly the same foundations as those developed independently by Lévi-Strauss in *The Elementary Structures*. It too has supposedly established linguistics as a positive science by isolating objective systems of linguistic meaning, independent of any particular application or of any particular subjective interpretation, which it has located in the unconscious mind. In this chapter I want to look at linguistic structuralism to ask whether it has successfully isolated language as such an objective system.

# 1 SAUSSURE AND THE OBJECTIVITY OF LANGUAGE

Saussure is hailed as the founder of the modern science of linguistics because it was he who isolated language as an autonomous object amenable to scientific investigation. His aim was, as far as possible, to isolate language from psychological, sociological and physiological considerations, and so to explain the facts of language by reference to 'linguistic' constraints alone. He did this by the application of three contrasts. Saussure distinguishes between *langue* and *parole*, between form and substance, and between synchrony and diachrony. The application of these contrasts defines a closed corpus of scientific facts, an objective system of language supposedly divorced from any particular application of the system or from any particular interpretation of it.

The distinction between *langue* and *parole* derived in part from Durkheim, but mainly, it seems, from Meillet, Naville and Whitney. The aim of the distinction was to separate a system lying behind the linguistic act from the act itself, and so to separate purely linguistic questions from those which would introduce psychological, physiological or sociological considerations. *Langue*, for Saussure, represents the social and the essential, while *parole* represents the accessory and accidental. *Langue* is, therefore, strictly comparable with Durkheim's collective conscience as an objective system that is external to the individual and resistant to the individual will. Linguistics confines its attention to the facts of *langue*, and so is provided with an object that is free of interference arising in the use of *langue*.

Although *langue* is an ideal-object, constructed by the analyst by abstraction from the actual sentences used by native speakers, Saussure believed that *langue* was a specific reality which has its 'seat in the brain'. Saussure, therefore, retained the mentalism of his contemporaries, seeking 'to explain the facts of language by facts of thought, taken as established'. Hence, for Saussure, the linguistic sign is a 'psychological entity', uniting a 'concept' and a 'sound-image', and linguistics is a specialized branch of psychology.[1]

The second fundamental contrast introduced by Saussure is that between form and substance: '*Language is a form and not a substance*'.[2] For Saussure the relation between the concept and the sound-image that make up the sign is an *arbitrary* relation. There is nothing in the concept 'tree' which makes the sound 'tree' especially appropriate, nor does the sound 'tree' in itself contain anything of its concept. Hence each language uses a different bit of sound to signify a different bit of thought, and the assignment of concept to sound-image is arbitrary. In this respect spoken language differs from other symbolic systems in which the relation between *signifier* and *signified* (the two faces of the sign) is not arbitrary. Idiographic writing is an obvious example, where the concept 'tree' may be represented by a picture of a tree.

For Saussure thought and sound represent two continua, in the absence of language:

'Without language thought is a vague uncharted nebula. . . . Phonic substance is neither more fixed nor more rigid than thought. . . . Not only are the two domains that are linked by the linguistic fact shapeless and confused, but the choice of a given slice of sound to name a given idea is completely arbitrary'.[3]

The linguistic sign does not, therefore, take pre-existing ideas and pre-existing sounds and then associate them one by one in an atomistic way. Instead language relates two systems to one another, the system of sounds and the system of thoughts, dividing up each continuum in a particular way. It is this conception of meaning that for Lévi-Strauss contrasts so sharply with Bergson's metaphysics.[4]

It is this conception that underlies the separation of *form* from *substance*. The difference between different languages is a difference of *form*, a difference in the way in which the common substances, continua of sound and of thought, are divided up in different languages. Hence linguistics concerns itself only with the form, and not with the substance of language, the latter being a matter of indifference for the linguist. The system of sounds, for example, is created solely by the relations between sounds, the physical reality of the sound being irrelevant. From the linguistic point of view all that is important is that distinctions between sounds are introduced into what is naturally a continuum.

This emphasis on form follows directly from the isolation of the system of language from its material and its conceptual substratum. By abstracting altogether from substance linguistics acquires its autonomy from physiology and psychology. Thus phonemics, which studies the sound system of language as a formal system, is distinguished from phonetics, which studies the substance of linguistic sounds and is a branch of physiology and psychology. Hence it is the isolation of the system of language that gives rise to the structural method of analysis, for in abstraction from content language is pure form. The crucial critical question is whether form can be dissociated from content in this way.

The conception of the sign also makes it possible for Saussure to separate sound and thought from one another and to study the system of sounds and the system of thoughts independently of one another. This means that linguistics can analyze language as a combination of sounds without making any reference to meaning. Correlatively meaning can be analyzed independently of sound, so phonology and semantics are distinct branches of linguistics.

Saussure's third contrast completes the isolation of a closed system which can become the object of a specifically linguistic analysis. Saussure distinguishes the synchronic, or static, perspective, from the diachronic, or evolutionary, perspective, according primacy to the synchronic. The synchronic perspective focusses exclusively on the relations between the parts of the system of *langue* at a particular point in time. The diachronic perspective studies the historical relationship between linguistic facts. Saussure gives several different reasons for according priority to the synchronic, and his opposition to historicism, which had personal as well as ideological and scientific origins, certainly predisposed him to seek the laws of the system. His two main arguments are very different in kind.

Firstly, Saussure offers a mentalist argument. His psychologism means that he is interested essentially in establishing 'logical and psychological connections'. The synchronic viewpoint, therefore, 'predominates, for it is the true and only reality to the community of speakers', while the historical connections have no psychological reality.[5] This argument clearly depends on the mentalist assumption that linguistics is a branch of psychology.

Secondly, Saussure offers a methodological argument. It is the character of the object of linguistics which makes it amenable to synchronic analysis: 'Because the sign is arbitrary it follows no law other than that of tradition.' Saussure argues by analogy with marginalist economics, which to a considerable extent offered him a model for his own systematic linguistics. From marginalism he borrows the notion of value as an arbitrary relation between a thing and a price, which he then applies to the linguistic relation between signifier and signified. In each case the value is determined by the insertion of the element in an equilibrium system and so depends solely on the interrelations between the elements, and not on past states of the system.[6]

The fact that Saussure offers two arguments for the priority of the synchronic is very important, for these arguments are mutually exclusive. Saussure's work is riven by a contradiction between two quite different views of language and of linguistics. The dominant view is the mentalist one according to which language is a psychological reality, seated in the brain, and the linguist explores psychological connections. Linguistics is then an autonomous branch of psychology. The other view is that language is a collective institution, and so a social reality, and the linguist therefore explores functional connections. In the former case the linguist is concerned to discover psychological relations between the elements of language, in the latter case the linguist is concerned to discover linguistic relations. The two are by no means the same: while linguistic relations need have no psychological reality, psychological relations need have no linguistic significance.

The mentalist argument in favour of the priority of the synchronic clearly only applies to the mentalist view of linguistics. The methodological argument, on the other hand, does not apply if linguistics is concerned with 'psychological and logical connections', for the sign is not arbitrary from a psychological point of view. The meaning of the sound 'tree' for a particular individual is not determined only by its relations with other linguistic sounds: its contrasts with 'bush', 'house', 'sky', 'pole', etc. It is also determined by all the previous uses of the sign that the individual has encountered: the trees to which it has been applied, the contexts within which it has been uttered. Thus if I hear a word the psychological connections it establishes contemporaneously refer to a whole series of past linguistic events. Thus if language is looked at as a mental reality the sign is by no means arbitrary and its meaning is by no means defined by its relations with contemporaneous elements of the language.

Linguistics has been plagued by a confusion of the psychological and the linguistic viewpoints ever since Saussure. Both viewpoints are legitimate, but they are mutually exclusive in that they not only provide different explanations, they are also explaining quite different things. The linguistic approach is concerned with the language as a functioning system. The psychological approach is concerned with the way in which the individual learns and uses a language. A language exists at the intersection of these two approaches: it must function as a language, and it must be possible for people to learn and to use it.

Because Saussure regards language as a mental phenomenon he makes the synchronic and the diachronic approaches mutually exclusive. There is no panchronic viewpoint, he insists, so language cannot be seen as a *developing* system, because the synchronic perspective seeks internal, psychological and systematic connections, while the diachronic viewpoint relates not *systems* but *terms*. History for Saussure is therefore the integration of contingent events into a stable system, and linguistic change becomes inexplicable.

The application of the three contrasts provides linguistics with an object. That object consists in a synchronic and stable system of signs between which the linguist can seek 'logical and psychological connections'. This system is not an object *presented to* the linguist, but has been analytically isolated from discourse on the basis of a number of assumptions about the nature of language. The effect is to isolate language as a scientific object from the speaker, from the hearer, and from the context in which language is used. Hence an ideal-object is constructed which constitutes a closed system whose relations can be established purely objectively.

Saussure's discovery of a system immanent in the relations between the terms apparently made it possible to establish a scientific linguistics. Even meaning, within Saussure's theory, could be given a rigorously objective and systematic definition. It is the system of differences, imposed on the continuum of experience, that introduces precision to the Bergsonian 'state of mush'. The convergence between the achievements of Saussure and those of Lévi-Strauss seems startling, a vindication of the theories of each.

However it is important to be very clear that Saussure's linguistics is no more an achievement of science than is Lévi-Strauss' anthropology. Saussure never managed to embody his philosophy of language in systematic analyses of particular linguistic systems, and so it remained programmatic. It is, moreover, an extremely confused programme in many respects, which is one reason why Saussure can be claimed as a forbear by very different schools of linguistics. The convergence arises not because Saussure and Lévi-Strauss independently discovered something about reality, but because they independently set themselves the same task.

This task was the development of a positive science of human culture based on a conception of cultural phenomena as objective systems of forms dissociated from the individual subject, with their own immanent and specific laws, imposing themselves on the individual with the force of the unconscious. In the case of Saussure, as much as in that of Lévi-Strauss, it is this ideological programme that gives rise to the structural approach, and it gives rise to comparable theoretical problems.

# 2 POSITIVISM AND PHENOMENOLOGY IN THE STUDY OF LANGUAGE

Saussure proposed a scientific linguistics that would be based on the isolation of *langue* as a stable, well-defined, objective system whose internal relations linguistics could analyze with the methods of positive science. Saussure's programme begged many questions that would have to be confronted before a systematic linguistics could develop, but his insistence on the priority of form over content was vital in making possible the emergence of linguistics as an autonomous discipline. The phonic and psychological substance of language could be studied by acoustics, physiology and psychology. The form of language, however, could not be studied by other disciplines, the form was the responsibility of linguistics and of linguistics alone: it was the form, the systematic relations between the parts, that made the phonic and psychological substratum function as a language.

Saussure's work is one small moment in an intellectual and ideological upheaval of global dimensions, in which attention came to be focussed on the systematic relations between the parts of wholes which nineteenth century positivism had tried to disaggregate into their component atoms. In this sense structuralism in linguistics is simply a part of the global movement and has no special significance. As Jakobson wrote in 1929:

'Were we to comprise the leading idea of present-day science in its most various manifestations, we could hardly find a more appropriate designation than *structuralism*. Any set of phenomena examined by contemporary science is treated not as a mechanical agglomeration but as a structural whole, and the basic task is to reveal the inner, whether static or developmental, laws of this system. What appears to be the focus of scientific preoccupations is no longer the outer stimulus, but the internal premises of the development; now the mechanical conception of processes yields to the question of their functions.'[7]

Within linguistics Saussure introduced a new way of looking at language as a system. Instead of regarding language as an organism in which the wholeness of language derived from some transcendent spiritual quality, he looked on language as a system whose wholeness derived from the internal, formal, connections between its parts. Thus Saussure's conception of language as a system made it possible to steer a course between the reefs of 'atomism' and 'transcendentalism': the whole is more than the *sum* of its parts, but it is no more than the sum of the *relations between* the parts.

However, before the new linguistics could develop it had to specify more clearly than had Saussure what precisely is the new object of linguistics, *langue*. For Saussure *langue* remained a psychological reality and the relations he sought were psychological relations to be discovered by an intuitionist psychology. Thus the basic unit of sound is the auditory impression. Two different sounds express a single auditory impression if they are experienced as the same sound, and they are different if speaking subjects are conscious of a difference. This led to a conception of the sound units of language as discrete substantive elements, defined independently of the relations between the elements, a conception that proved quite inadequate. Thus linguistics could not advance on the basis of Saussure's mentalism. The relations of language could not be the conscious psychological connections between discrete substantive elements that Saussure postulated, but must be more abstract in character.

If *langue* is not immediately identified as a psychological reality the question arises of the status of the object of linguistics. How is *langue* to be isolated from the data of *parole*? What relations make up the form of *langue*? What are the elements of *langue* united by those relations? What is the status of the relations uncovered— do they correspond to real psychological or even organic connections, or do they have some other status?

There are two distinct approaches to these questions to be found within linguistics, which can be broadly characterized as positivist and phenomenological. The positivist view is that the ideal-object, *langue*, that is isolated by the linguist corresponds to a substantial psychological or behavioural reality, thus *langue* exists independently of, and prior to, *parole*. This means that the terms of the linguistic theory can be translated into observational terms that describe a reality that is the mechanism that people use when they speak. Linguistics is therefore, as it was for Saussure, an autonomous branch of psychology. The study of language therefore reveals facts about the biological or psychological human organism.

The phenomenological view is that there is no such thing as a *langue* dissociated from the context in which language is used. Once abstraction has been made from the context, so that language is divorced from the speaker or the hearer whose interaction it articulates, it ceases to be language and becomes a meaningless jumble of sounds. To discover what is linguistic about language, to discover the systematic relations that make it possible for language to be the means by which meaning can be communicated, we have to refer not to 'objective' relations existing between the parts of an inert object, but rather to the *intentions* of the speaker of the language that impose meaning on language. Language thus has to be seen as a functional system and the internal relations of a language have to be related to the functions of the language as the instrument by which communicative intentions are realized.

For the phenomenological approach *langue* is an abstraction and the relations that make up the system of *langue* are abstract relations, not inherent in the object, but imposed on the object by the intention of the speaker and recovered by the hearer. Language is not an objective reality, but nor is it purely subjective, it is the intersubjective expression of a subjective intention. Linguistics is concerned with the study of the way in which language as a conventional reality makes it possible for mere sounds to give a subjective intention an intersubjective reality. Since language does not express physiological or psychological mechanisms, linguistics cannot tell us anything directly about the mind or the brain.

Both these approaches can be used to legitimate the structural analysis of language, but the two approaches legitimate the analysis in different ways, understand the relations that emerge quite differently, and draw very different conclusions from the findings of linguistics.

Saussure's linguistics was based on an intuitionist psychology for which the internal relations of language were to be discovered by introspection. At the time Saussure was writing this was the dominant approach advocated by positivist philosophy, and exemplified by the psychology of Wundt or Titchener (whose task was not to discover structures, but to decompose them into their elements). At the time it was felt that the only certain truths were those revealed by introspection and so introspection provided the only basis for a genuinely objective science. However, it soon became clear, in linguistics as in psychology, that the truths of introspection were far from secure. From this point the divergence between positivism and phenomenology emerges.

Phenomenology, developed by Husserl on the basis of work by Brentano, sought to establish intuitive truths that were secure and indubitable, while positivism, developed by Russell, Wittgenstein and above all by the Vienna Circle, sought to re-establish a secure science on the basis of a total renunciation of the point of view of the subject, rejecting any appeal to evidence that was based on subjective reports.

Within psychology a corresponding divergence developed between a phenomenological psychology that came to rely on the intuitive recovery of meaning, and a behaviourist psychology that renounced any appeal to introspection and abolished any reference to the mind or to a mental reality as hopelessly metaphysical.

The basis of the divergence in each case was the search for certainty, for a meaning of human existence that is indubitably true. For phenomenological approaches the true meaning of human existence is irreducibly subjective, to be discovered in the human intentions that it expresses. For behaviourism the subjective meaning is pure epiphenomenon, a conceited illusion, reducible to the only true reality which is the reality of the organic processes that underlie the connections between stimuli and responses. Thus behaviourism deduces an objective structure of the organism from the properties of human behaviour.

The divergence is strictly parallel to that between Sartre and Lévi-Strauss already examined: both sought the true meaning of human existence behind the deceit and hypocrisy of contemporary society, one believing it to be a subjective meaning to be found through the philosophical critique of subjective experience, the other believing it to be an objective meaning, embedded in human nature, expressed in the objectivity of human cultural achievements. Language is, of course, pre-eminent among such achievements. Thus the study of language has both reflected and stimulated the fundamental philosophical debate between positivism and phenomenology.

## 3 POSITIVISM AND FORMALISM: FROM BLOOMFIELD TO CHOMSKY

With the positivist rejection of intuitionist psychology linguistics took an increasingly formal direction. The linguists rejected the search for psychological connections between the elements of language in favour of the search for purely 'objective' connections whose discovery did not depend on any particular interpretation. Such objective connections could only be connections divorced from all substantive content, connections that could be reduced to relations of identity and difference, of succession and of combination. In Europe the most extreme formalization of linguistics was mapped out by Hjelmslev's 'glossematics'. In the United States it was achieved by the behaviourist 'structuralism' of Bloomfield and Harris that dominated US linguistics until the arrival of Chomsky in the mid-1950s.

American structuralism was based on as complete a rejection of mentalistic concepts as possible. Its programme was to analyze language on the basis of a minimal intervention of the analyst. Thus it rejected the distinction between *langue* and *parole*, identifying the object of linguistics as the corpus of utterances of the language under investigation collected by fieldwork. It sought to eliminate any reference to meaning in the analysis of language, treating the corpus as a set of purely formal, inert sequences of sounds. It sought to analyze this corpus mechanically, by means of an inductive logic, that could ideally be undertaken by a computer. Thus it sought to establish by purely inductive means the formal phonemic and syntactic features of language, leaving questions of 'meaning' to a behaviourist psychology that was concerned with language use: with the connections between linguistic and other behavioural stimuli and corresponding responses.

In this way, it was believed, linguistics would at last become a positive science, for the structural description that emerged would owe nothing to the linguist and everything to the mechanical application of the logic of induction to an objective corpus of utterances. No reference would have to be made to a subjective interpretation, by either the analyst or the native speaker, of the meaning of the utterance, of the function of language, or of the connection between the parts of the language. All the connections that were discovered would be connections that indubitably existed in the corpus.

This positivist approach, although it dominated North American linguistics in the immediate post-war period, was both linguistically and philosophically inadequate. Its major weaknesses were those of the crude positivism that it sought to apply. This positivism assumes, firstly, that the object (in this case language) presents itself ready-made to the analyst and, secondly, that a logic of induction can produce a satisfactory account of this object. Both of these assumptions are false.

Firstly, language does not simply present itself to the analyst. In any science what is to be explained is defined by the science itself. This point was realized early in the development of Vienna positivism. No theory seeks to explain everything, so every theory is a theory about a part of the whole that is the world that we daily confront. The theory, therefore, is always based on an initial abstraction from that whole that defines which aspects of the whole the theory will explain, and which aspects it will ignore.

When the theory is evaluated empirically it can only be evaluated against the task it initially set itself. Thus, for example, the theory of relativity revealed that the ambition of classical mechanics was too grandiose. However it did not change the use of classical mechanics by engineers into the application of a theory that was wrong. It led to a redefinition of the object of classical mechanics: a redefinition of the limits within which classical mechanics could be justified empirically (and a corresponding conceptual re-evaluation of classical theories).

If a theory is to have any explanatory value it must be possible, in principle, to falsify the claims made by that theory empirically. Such falsification can only be achieved within the terms of the theory, and so can never be absolute. However if it is to be possible at all the theory must define its object independently of its explanations. In other words if the theory expressed in the claim that 'all women are biologically inferior to men' is held to apply only to those women who are biologically inferior to particular men, the theory has no explanatory value since it becomes a tautology.

The realization that the object of every theory is ideal, in the sense that the theory defines its own object, does not mean that sciences are not empirical. What it does mean is that the science, or the particular theory where agreed scientific procedures have not been established, has to define the conditions under which it would be empirically falsified. This it does by defining in advance the object to which it is held to apply, and this definition must be independent of the particular theory under review.

If we apply this idea to language we can see that the corpus with which Bloomfieldian structuralism confronts the linguist is not given but is constructed by the analyst. The corpus is a list of sound sequences that have been selected from a complex network of human behaviour. Although each sound sequence is different and was uttered in a different context the analyst will claim that some sequences or parts of sequences are identical. It is only on the basis of the identification of repeated occurrences of the same event that the logic of induction can be applied, and yet it is only on the basis of a particular abstraction that utterances can be identified, for they were made by different people at different times for different reasons.

Thus the linguist has to use a particular definition of language to abstract the corpus of utterances from the mass of behavioural and psychological data that is potentially available. For the Bloomfieldian language is defined within the framework of a behaviourist psychology. Thus no reference is made to the understanding or intentions of the native speaker in identifying the corpus, nor is any reference made to sounds that do not have a linguistic significance, defined implicitly in behavioural terms, such as grunts, coughs, sneezes. Thus in establishing the corpus the analyst filters out aspects of behaviour or thought considered to be non-linguistic, and this can only be done on the basis of a definition of language.

Even the linguistic corpus so produced will be inadequate because it will be degenerate: many utterances will be incomplete or will include errors, ellipses, etc. Thus the linguist will have to filter the data again to separate utterances that are correct and complete from those that are degenerate. If this distinction is not made any analysis can be falsified immediately by a native speaker producing an utterance which the grammar has formally excluded. Thus the distinction between *langue* and *parole* cannot be avoided in some form, and the Bloomfieldians did not avoid it in practice.

The crucial issue is how *langue* is to be distinguished from *parole* in such a way as to define an object in terms of which the theory can make claims which have a substantive empirical content.

Not only is it impossible to define language independently of a theory of language, it is also impossible to analyze language inductively. There are two major problems with a logic of induction in this context. Firstly, induction can only establish regular relationships between elements that can be defined independently. Saussure's achievement was to show that the elements of language could not be defined independently, for it was the system that defined the elements.

If the parts cannot be defined independently of the whole, then the whole cannot be discovered inductively as the relations between the parts. Thus, for example, the identity of a given sound element in different environments is not a substantive identity that can be defined acoustically, it is a functional identity that can be defined only by the constancy of its contrast with other sound elements. Hence the element cannot be identified until the relations have been defined, but the relations cannot be established by induction if we don't know in advance what is being related.

The second problem is that a logic of induction operates on a finite corpus and this means that it cannot establish the bounds which restrict the applicability of a particular relation. Logically this means that induction cannot establish from the fact that A has always been followed by B that next time A occurs B will occur. In linguistics the importance of this is that the potential corpus is infinite, for language is creative and there is no upper-bound on the number of sentences that comprise the language. Thus language must have means for generating an infinite number of sentences, and these means cannot be discovered by induction. It was Chomsky who applied this philosophical critique of inductivism to Bloomfieldian linguistics.

Chomsky was trained in mathematics and mathematical logic, as well as in linguistics, and this brought him into contact with the more sophisticated variants of positivism that had developed in response to the problems of the crude inductivist positivism of the Bloomfieldians. Chomsky reintroduced, and redefined, the distinction between *langue* and *parole*, recognizing that the object of linguistics was not given but had to be constructed. He also rejected the emphasis on induction and adopted the neo-positivist hypothetico-deductive model of scientific explanation, according to which the scientist formulates certain hypotheses, deduces the empirical consequences of these hypotheses, and then tests these consequences against the evidence. An adequate theory, according to this model, is one which can generate deductively those and only those empirical statements that make up its domain: it will generate all true statements and no false ones.

Chomsky argued, firstly, that the Bloomfieldian behaviourist definition of language, which implicitly underlay its definition of the corpus, was unacceptable. Chomsky's critique of behaviourism is devastating and has been enormously influential within both linguistics and psychology. For a behaviourist the utterance 'that bull is mad' is a conditioned response to an encounter with a mad bull, and nothing more. It does not express the 'idea' of a mad bull, nor does it represent the application of some unconscious rules of language. Its relation to the stimulus that calls it forth requires no reference to 'mental' reality.

Chomsky argued that this view of language is, at best, incoherent. He argues in a review of the work of Skinner[8] that outside the laboratory there is no clear way of identifying stimuli and responses, and in particular the stimulus cannot be identified independently of the response: the stimulus is only a stimulus because it has elicited a response. Hence the behaviourist only 'discovers' that the stimulus of a mad bull operates because of the response 'that bull is mad'. Correspondingly the knowledge that there is a mad bull around cannot lead to the prediction that there will be a response 'that bull is mad'. The response might be to ignore the bull, to scream and run, to misdiagnose the bull's condition etc. This circularity at the heart of behaviourism leads to even greater difficulties in its attempt to explain language learning, for when the child learns a language it acquires the capacity not only to reproduce the appropriate response to a repeated stimulus, it acquires the capacity to react in new ways to new situations.

Chomsky's critique of behaviourism led him to reassert the mentalist claim that language could only be understood as a mental phenomenon. This means that the object of linguistics cannot be defined without reference to the mind.

For Chomsky the object of linguistics is not a corpus of utterances that have been identified as verbal behavioural stimuli and responses. The object of linguistics is linguistic *competence*, defined as the native speaker's knowledge of the rules that he or she applies in speaking the language correctly. It is only these rules that can identify a particular sentence as belonging to the language, thus it is these rules that are the object of linguistics. By formulating the concept of a language in this way Chomsky gives linguistics a finite object, the rules that generate all and only the sentences of the language, instead of the infinite object that definition of *langue* in terms of a corpus provides. However, as we shall see, Chomsky's definition of language does introduce a dangerous circularity into linguistics.

Having defined linguistic competence as the finite set of rules that can generate the infinite set of sentences of the language Chomsky goes on to argue that these rules cannot be generated by induction. The philosophical reasons for this have already been discussed.

Linguistically the kinds of grammars produced by induction are inadequate not only because they ignore the creativity of language, but also because they are in some sense complex, *ad hoc* and do not uncover relations that correspond to our intuitive understanding of the grammar of a language. A favourite example is the two sentences 'John is easy to please' and 'John is eager to please'. If we consider these sentences with reference to nothing but their form we are led into extreme contortions. For example we know that we can reformulate the first sentence as 'John is easily pleased'. By inductive generalization we will therefore know that we can reformulate the second sentence as 'John is eagerly pleased'. Unfortunately this reformulation changed the meaning of the sentence while the first, formally identical, transformation, does not. Thus the generalization fails and an *ad hoc* qualification would have to be introduced to allow for this. Chomsky argues that a much simpler grammar can be produced if we recognize that there are more fundamental grammatical differences between the two sentences than can be revealed by a grammar developed inductively.

Thus Chomsky argues that a grammar must be established deductively, and the task of the linguist must be seen in the light of the hypothetico-deductive model of scientific explanation and not the outdated model of inductive generalization. The starting point of linguistics is not a mass of empirical data waiting to be fed into a word-crunching computer, it is a theory of language which expresses, in hypothetical form, assertions about the nature of language from which we can establish deductively the form of grammar, and within which we can formulate grammars of particular languages.

Chomsky takes as his starting point a 'theory of natural language as such' which provides him with a series of *linguistic universals*. These universals define both the basic categories and the basic relations of linguistic description. *Organizational universals* are intended to specify, 'the abstract structure of the subcomponents of a grammar, as well as the relations between the subcomponents'. These universals dictate that the grammar shall consist of a syntactic component which generates a surface structure by the application of transformations to a deep structure, a semantic component which provides an interpretation of the deep structure, and a phonological component which provides a phonetic interpretation of the surface structure. *Formal universals* define the character of the types of rules in the grammar, as for example the requirement that certain phonological rules be applied cyclically. *Substantive universals* 'define the sets of elements that may figure in particular grammars'.[9]

The linguist will seek to construct a description of a language in terms of the abstract elements defined by the substantive universals, making use of the kinds of relations specified by the formal and organizational universals. The construction of grammars for particular languages will obviously lead to the modification of the theory of natural language in the light of the particular analyses. The task of linguistics is primarily that of developing and improving the theory of natural language, particular analyses are the means of doing this.

Chomsky's approach to language was extremely important in overthrowing the crude behaviouristic positivism of post-war American structuralism. However Chomsky does not renounce positivism, although in practice he stretches it beyond its limits. Chomsky replaces an inadequate and outdated positivism by a more sophisticated and up-to-date, but no less inadequate, version. Chomsky, no less than Bloomfield, seeks to isolate language as an object from meaning and from context and his linguistics, no less than that of Bloomfield, leads to a completely arbitrary formalism that purports to tell us about both language and the mind, but in fact tells us about neither. The problem in each case is the same, it is the problem of *justifying* the formal linguistic descriptions that are produced. This is the fundamental problem of positivism.

Chomsky's fundamental objection to Bloomfieldian linguistics was that it could not justify either its observational basis or the generalizations that it produced by induction. Chomsky's solution is to adopt the more sophisticated hypothetico-deductive model of scientific theories developed by Vienna positivism on the basis of precisely the same objections to inductivism.

Chomsky's grammar is structured just like the neo-positivists' theories, indeed the grammar is a theory of language. A universal grammar is a theory that with suitable specifications will generate the grammars of all particular (and indeed all possible) languages. Within the grammars the syntactic component is a purely formal system that relates strings of symbols to one another, while the semantic and phonological components interpret the terminal strings generated by the syntax, i.e. map these strings of symbols onto the observational reality of sound and meaning. Thus Chomsky's linguistics reproduces the radical positivist separation of form and content, syntax and semantics.

The adoption of the hypothetico-deductive model frees Chomsky's linguistics from the constraints of behaviourist inductivism, but it does not solve the fundamental problem of theoretical and observational justification. The problems are those of neo-positivism, and not simply of Chomsky's linguistics.

Neo-positivism has faced two fundamental, and insoluble, problems. Firstly, since there is no such thing as a pure observation statement it has proved impossible to provide any non-arbitrary demarcation between observational and theoretical statements. Every observation statement abstracts elements from a particular context and subsumes them under general concepts: every observation statement rests on theoretical assumptions.

The problem, therefore, is that logical connections can never take us outside language to a world of untheorized observations. If scientific theories are to be given any empirical content the distinction between theoretical and observational statements breaks down. Thus there is no way in which theories can be evaluated against a reality that is defined independently of the theory. This means that there are grave dangers of circularity in the formulation of any scientific theory.

Secondly, and more importantly, if a scientific theory is a purely formal construct there is no way of justifying the adoption of one theory rather than another. It is unfortunately the case that any finite set of observation statements can be generated by an infinite number of different theories, thus we have to have some way of deciding which theory is the best. If theories are supposed to be purely formal systems we can only assess them in relation to one another on formal grounds: the best theory is that which is simplest, most elegant, has the smallest number of axioms, the greatest power, or whatever.

Which theory is adopted will depend on the formal criteria of evaluation selected, and this selection is, from the scientific point of view, arbitrary. It will be determined, for example, by the constraints of exposition or manipulation of the theory and not by any consideration of how adequate the theory is to the world. The isolation of the theory from the world of observation means that the theory has no purchase on reality: it is not legitimate to claim that the theory can tell us anything about the world since it is constructed according to purely formal criteria.

Thus the advantages of the hypothetico-deductive model over the inductivist model are purely formal: it admits more elegant theories that are able to avoid recourse to the *ad hoc* because their power is not restricted by the constraints of inductivism. In substantive terms, however, the hypothetico-deductive model produces theories that have no greater power than those produced by the inductivist model. Both models limit knowledge to the observational content of the system under review.

These problems are not simply of philosophical significance, they undermine Chomsky's linguistics altogether. The first problem is that the corpus of sentences to be generated by the grammar cannot be defined independently of the grammar.

For Chomsky linguistics does not seek to explain all the sentences uttered by native speakers, nor all the meaningful sentences uttered by native speakers, but all, and only, the *grammatical* sentences uttered by a native speaker. Any grammar is evaluated by its ability to generate these sentences. However to say that a sentence is grammatical is to say that it has been generated in accordance with the rules of grammar. Hence it is only the grammar that defines which sentences are grammatical. The danger of circularity should be apparent, for if the grammar defines which sentences are to count as grammatical there is no independent corpus with which to evaluate the grammar: any grammar will do.

Chomsky avoids such a devastating conclusion by defining grammaticality very loosely. He appeals to the 'native speaker's intuition' to define which sentences are grammatical, and in practice the 'native speaker' in question is Chomsky or one of his associates.

The implicit assumption is that the 'native speaker's intuition' is the expression of some objective standards of grammaticality inherent in the native speaker's linguistic competence. However native speakers' judgements of the acceptability of sentences, and particularly of the distinction between sentences that are semantically and syntactically unacceptable, will express not only their 'competence' but also the theories of grammar that they have learnt in the past. Thus Chomsky's criterion avoids circularity at the expense of evaluating one theory of grammar in terms of its concordance with another. It should not be surprising that the latter turns out to be very like the prescriptive schoolbook grammar, so that Chomsky's linguistic revolution actually produces some very conventional results.

The definition of the corpus is a very serious problem, and especially so if linguistics tries to go beyond the explanation of a corpus of grammatical sentences towards the explanation of language as it is used in everyday speech. Even more serious, however, is the problem of the justification of the linguistic theory that generates this corpus. This is the second major problem faced by neo-positivism. Since the theory of language and the grammars that it produces are purely formal, only formal criteria can legitimately be used to evaluate alternative theories. The problem then becomes one of justifying the particular criteria of evaluation that are adopted.

In Chomsky's case the theory of language specifies the organizational, formal and substantive universals of language which define in advance the character of any particular grammar. The details vary in different versions of the theory, but basically Chomsky's theory tells us that the grammar of any natural language can be written in the form dictated by his theory of language—as three components, with base and transformations, using such elements as Nouns, Verbs, Sentences, etc., which are established independently of the relations between these categories in any particular language, but which are hypothesized as universals. On the basis of this theory of language the linguist can construct a description of the language in terms of these abstract elements making use of the kinds of relations specified in the formal and organizational universals.

Despite certain ambiguities, it seems clear enough that Chomsky does not regard his grammar as offering simply one possible description of language among an infinite number of possible descriptions. The grammar is supposed to provide a model of the speaker's competence, that competence being the speaker's tacit 'knowledge' of a language, that knowledge having been learned and providing the basic mental apparatus which enables the speaker to perform. Hence Chomsky follows Saussure in seeing the object of linguistics as a system whose constitutive relations are 'psychological and logical connections', the aim of linguistics being to describe how the mind works when learning to speak and when speaking.

Problems of justification strike Chomsky's grammar at two levels. Firstly, if we accept Chomsky's universal grammar, there is the problem of establishing a unique description of any particular language. Secondly, there is the problem of justifying the postulates of the universal grammar. The first problem is itself serious. It has been established that for any conceivable recursively enumerable natural language

'there is a version of the theory of transformational grammar in which there is a fixed base grammar B which will serve as the base component of a grammar of any natural language'.[10]

This applies for any B we care to choose. In other words the weakness of the constraints on the transformational component is such that, because excessive power is given to the transformation rules, any language can be represented in transformational form on the basis of any fixed base grammar whatever. This means that if we arbitrarily write a grammar for the base, we can then turn this base into any language we choose, even an invented one, by applying enough transformations. Simple English, for example, can be turned into Chinese by applying enough transformation rules. Hence there are an infinite number of grammars which will satisfy Chomsky's theory of language for any particular language, while there is no conceivable language that cannot be represented in transformational form. Hence there is no way of knowing which of all possible grammars is the correct one for a particular language, on the one hand, and no conceivable language could falsify the theory of language on the other.

Chomsky gets around this awkward fact by establishing an evaluation rule to decide which grammar is appropriate. The evaluation rule tells us to select that grammar which is simplest while accounting for all the facts. Simplicity is defined as a measure of the degree of 'linguistically significant generalization' achieved by a grammar.

Chomsky therefore establishes a unique grammar for a language by applying two sets of criteria. On the one hand, the grammar must accord with his theory of language—it must be written in transformational form, with Nouns, Verbs, etc. On the other hand it must be the 'simplest' such grammar. To justify a particular grammar, therefore, it is necessary to justify the theory of language and the simplicity measure, which takes us to the second level of justification, that of the theory itself.

Since the general theory and the simplicity measure are the criteria by which particular grammars are established, they cannot derive from the study of particular languages. Thus we are back with the problem of justifying the *a priori* starting point. Here again Chomsky argues that his theory of language is appropriate because it is in some sense the simplest. Thus the evaluation of theories of language, as much as the evaluation of particular grammars, hangs entirely on the criterion of simplicity.

This criterion of simplicity is neither purely formal nor unambiguous. On the one hand, in purely formal terms, it is rarely the case that one theory is unambiguously simpler than another. For example, one theory may provide a simpler description of the corpus than another, while implying a much more complex mechanism for the production and understanding of sentences. One may have a large number of simple rules, another a few complex rules. Thus it is not possible to use a purely formal criterion to evaluate theories.

Simplicity is not something inherent in the theory, it depends on the purposes the theory is designed to serve. In other words one cannot establish the adequacy of a theory without asking what the theory is supposed to be adequate to. A theory which is supposed to provide an economical way of presenting the grammar of a language in a book will be subjected to different criteria from those applied to a theory which is supposed to enable a particular type of computer to reproduce the grammatical sentences of a language, and these will be different in turn from the criteria to be applied to a theory that is supposed to provide an account of the use of language by native speakers or one that is supposed to account for the learning of a language by a child.

This problem of the absence of any non-arbitrary and unambiguous criteria of evaluation of alternative grammars or of alternative theories of language arises because of the purely formal conception of a theory that is associated with the positivist dissociation of language from its context. The problem is that Chomsky, no less than the Bloomfieldians, reduces language to a set of grammatical sentences. However, a set of grammatical sentences, divorced from the context in which they serve a linguistic function, do not constitute a language. If we abstract from the meaning of these sentences and if we abstract from their function within human interaction of communicating meaning then we also are unable to make any significant distinctions between meaningless strings of symbols and the meaningful use of language by human individuals.

Chomsky recognizes that the criterion of simplicity is not unambiguous for his evaluation rule is not purely formal, but refers again to the native speaker's intuition in its reference to 'linguistically significant' generalization. Thus for Chomsky the best theory of language, and the best grammar, is that which accords most closely with the native speaker's intuition of grammaticality. However there is not any absolute and objective way of deciding what is a linguistically significant generalization, for this will depend on the native speaker's, or the linguist's conception of what a language is. Thus what Chomsky's theory of language does is to formalize what Chomsky thinks a language is about.

When it comes down to it Chomsky's conception of language is a very idiosyncratic one. Chomsky regards language as a mechanical model that derives sentences by the automatic application of rules. The form of language, the rules of language, and the generation of sentences are all defined without any reference to the context in which language is learned and used, and so without any reference to the intention to communicate which, for most people, is what gives language its significance.

The way in which Chomsky proposes the problem of linguistics is in terms of the computational problems involved in language learning when faced with a degenerate input of symbols whose meaning is unknown. He argues that the kind of inductive logic proposed by the Bloomfieldians would not allow the computer to learn the language because it would lead to clear errors, matched by the blunders of early translating machines. Thus the computer would have to be programmed with a theory of language which it could then use to establish the grammar of the particular language being presented to it.

In order to establish what kind of programme ('theory of language') would enable the computer to do this satisfactorily Chomsky drew on the most recent advances in mathematical logic that had, until the advent of the computer, been the esoteric concern of philosophical logicians.

The advances in mathematical logic in question had come about because of the positivist concern to develop a purely formal and unified language in which the natural sciences could express their results without being subject to the distortions, ambiguities and misunderstandings that arise from the use of natural languages. This project was at the heart of the neo-positivist enterprise of purifying the language of science and of expunging all traces of metaphysics that had come to be identified with the misuse of language. This project faced two different sets of problems, one the problem of the construction of formal languages, the other the problem of translating natural languages into formal languages without loss of meaning.

In adopting mathematical logic as the means to understand natural languages Chomsky was essentially carrying out the neo-positivist project in reverse. The problem he set himself was that of generating logically the grammatical sentences of a natural language, while neo-positivism had set itself the problem of translating natural languages into the formal system of an artificial logic. The mathematical logic developed by the latter provided a means of achieving this translation. Thus Chomsky used the same logic to achieve the reverse result, to produce a logical device (a grammar and a theory of language) to generate the grammatical sentences of natural language.

Chomsky's theory of language does not, therefore, derive from a consideration of the question how do we understand how people in the course of their social interaction learn and use their language? It derives from the problem of formalization of the rules governing the generation of strings of linguistic symbols, a problem that arises largely because of the impoverished positivist conception of language that serves as the starting point both for Chomsky's linguistics and for the mathematical logic he applies to the solution of his problem. Chomsky's linguistics is as misconceived as was the philosophical project on which it is based.

Chomsky's linguistics has had an impact far beyond the narrow circle of theorists of language. Although few structuralists outside linguistics have taken direct inspiration from Chomsky, his work appears to offer a dramatic confirmation of the power of the structural method and of the possibilities it opens up for acquiring knowledge of the mental foundations of our linguistic capacity and so of our humanity. It is therefore very important to bring out clearly the basis on which Chomsky arrives at his theoretical results.

Chomsky's work has great importance within linguistics both in clearing away the previous naive Bloomfieldian positivism, and in bringing to the attention of linguists many striking, and previously unnoticed, formal properties of natural languages. Whatever the fate of Chomsky's theory these contributions will remain. Beyond linguistics, however, it is the theory that is important and thus, for us, the problem of the arbitrary character of both the theory of language and the grammars derived from it is fundamental to a consideration of the lessons of Chomsky's linguistics.

The weaknesses of Chomsky's linguistics are precisely those aspects that are taken by structuralists to be the key contribution of Chomsky. It seems that Chomsky offers a purely objective and scientific approach to language, the supreme embodiment of human culture, in which language can be treated as an inert object within which objective structures can be uncovered, behind which can be found unconscious mental capacities.

However this model of language is not derived from a consideration of language at all. It derives from a methodological procedure that dissociates the sentences that are the raw material of language from any linguistically relevant context in order to establish an unquestionably 'objective' corpus. This procedure, dictated by the neo-positivist philosophy underlying Chomsky's linguistics and not by any consideration of language, dissociates consideration of the formal properties of the sound sequences that make up the sentences of a language from any consideration of the conditions under which such sound sequences are produced or interpreted, and so of the conditions under which they function as a part of a language. In other words the methodological decision that was taken apparently in the interests of the development of a scientific linguistics in fact achieves a complete dissociation of the form of language from its content and so the results achieved are in turn purely formal, deprived of any linguistic significance. The result is 'scientific' according to the positivist caricature of science, but it is not linguistics, if the aim of linguistics is to achieve knowledge of language.

Chomsky is able to treat language as an inert object, and so to reduce language to a formal structure, because of a methodological decision the price of which is a neglect of everything that makes noises into a language. Linguistically the grammars selected and the theory of language proposed must be arbitrary.

The arbitrary character of Chomsky's theory of language has become increasingly apparent within linguistics in the past decade. It soon became clear, and often to Chomsky before anybody else, that the model Chomsky had developed could not handle natural languages as simply as had been hoped. Once the model began to be modified and made more complex in order to deal with anomalies, in other words as the model came to be confronted more closely with existing natural languages, the fact that the criteria by which alternative theories might be evaluated were linguistically arbitrary became progressively more apparent. Not only was Chomsky's transformational grammar made increasingly complex, but non-transformational grammars were also being developed that were of sufficient power to handle natural languages.

The result has been a proliferation of theories of language in the wake of Chomsky: case grammar, relational grammar, generative semantics. Montague grammar, applicational grammar, systemic grammar, stratificational grammar, etc.: between none of which it is possible to judge on linguistic grounds and all of which are logically equivalent in the sense that each tries to produce a mechanism that can reproduce the grammatical sentences of the language and the proponents of each claim that their model is simpler, more intuitive or more 'natural'.

This proliferation of neo-positivist theories of language over the last decade has led more and more people to question not this or that form of the theory but the positivist approach to language altogether. If positivism leads to theories of language that are purely formal and entirely arbitrary then we are led back to the question of the nature and functions of language and to a rejection of the positivist isolation of language from its context.

If theories are to be judged by their 'naturalness' this can only be in relation to a particular conception of the nature of language. Consideration of this question cannot be divorced from consideration of the intentions of those for whom noises function as a language. This has led to an increasing concern with the phenomenological approach to linguistics, and particularly with the work of the Prague Circle and of Roman Jakobson which combined elements of both the phenomenological and the positivist approaches, using phenomenology for its theoretical inspiration, but rejecting the phenomenological method. Consideration of Prague linguistics is especially important for our purposes because it was from Roman Jakobson that Lévi-Strauss first learnt about structuralism.

# 4 FORM AND FUNCTION: THE PRAGUE LINGUISTIC CIRCLE

Chomsky's linguistics relates strongly to the positivist side of Saussure's approach to language according to which the properties of language derive from unconscious mental structures that are imposed on sound and thought substance. I have argued in the previous sections that this approach to language is unacceptable because the structures uncovered are arbitrary: there is no way in which linguistically significant structural relations can be distinguished from contingent relations that are imposed by the analyst.

Any linguistic theory, even one propounded by a positivist, expresses certain ideas about the nature of language, and so rests on an intuitive understanding of what is involved in speaking and understanding a language. In other words it is not in fact the case that a linguist can treat the language as an inert object, as a set of sentences divorced from the context of use, because the linguist can only formulate a theory of language in accordance with certain ideas about the nature of language.

Once the issue is brought into the open the artificial, and counter-intuitive, character of Chomsky's notion of language becomes apparent. When we consider the nature of language we cannot avoid considering it as a means of communication, and this leads to a quite different approach to language which tries to discover the system of language by relating it to the functions of language as a means of communication. It is this approach that was developed by the Prague Linguistic Circle.

The Prague Circle derived inspiration from a number of sources and emerged, in part, from the concern with language of the Russian Formalists, of whom Jakobson had been a leading theorist. From Saussure they derived a concern with the systematic character of language and with the mechanisms by which language achieved its expressive and communicative ends, but they rejected Saussure's residual psychologism for which introspection could reveal these mechanisms. From neo-positivism they derived a commitment to the 'scientific' analysis of these mechanisms, in sharp reaction to all forms of romanticism, and this informed their concern with structure as the source of meaning immanent in the object, so that they considered not the relation between the meaning-creating subject and language as a pure object, but rather the relations within language that made it possible for language to give meaning an intersubjective existence. However the most important source for the Prague School was probably that of the phenomenology of Edmund Husserl.

From Husserl the Russian Formalists, and the Prague Circle after them, took their opposition to psychologism and to naturalism and this coloured their reaction to Saussure.

For the Prague Circle language has to be treated as an autonomous reality, and not as a psychological phenomenon, so the properties of language cannot be explained simply as the imposition of a psychological form on an acoustic or conceptual substance. Language is an intentional object whose structure is an expression of its function as an instrument of human communication. Linguistics therefore has to be a teleological discipline that seeks the structure of language not through an introspective psychology, as Saussure continued to believe, nor through a search for purely formal connections, as Chomsky later thought, but by relating linguistic form to linguistic function.

The Prague Circle did not take this phenomenological approach to language to its limits. In particular they did not believe that phenomenological methods alone could provide a sound basis for linguistics. Thus refence to the intentionality of language users would provide the means for discovering the structural relations of language and for revealing the linguistic significance of these relations, but the methods of positivism could still be used to verify (or falsify) the resulting hypotheses. Thus the Prague Circle combined a teleological theoretical approach with a rigorously 'scientific' methodology.

It should be noted that observation and experiment has only a restricted role in the Prague canon. Observation can tell us whether or not postulated relationships exist, but it cannot tell us whether or not observed relationships have linguistic significance unless we refer to the linguistic function of the relationship and so to the intention it serves to articulate.

The insistence on the teleological character of linguistics is of fundamental importance to Prague linguistics and it is this that marks it off from the positivism that has dominated other schools of linguistics in this century. For the Prague Circle language is treated as an instrument, and not as an object, so the objective approach to language characteristic of the moment of observation and experiment is only provisional, product of a methodological and not an ontological decision. The teleology of Prague linguistics means that language cannot be understood without reference to the human subjects who communicate by means of language and so the systematic qualities of language cannot be analyzed without reference to meaning.

Moreover it implies that the autonomy of linguistics is also only a provisional autonomy, for language is but one aspect of human social and cultural existence and cannot be analyzed in isolation from that existence. The result is that language is seen as only one system within a 'system of systems' which look at the same reality from different points of view. It is therefore impossible to derive psychological conclusions directly from linguistic facts, since linguistics and psychology look at language from different points of view. Finally it implies that language is an extremely complex reality that can be studied from many different linguistic points of view corresponding to the different functions that language can serve, so the monolithic and static Saussurean model of linguistic structure is undermined. Jakobson has recently insisted that the diversity of language is

'the chief target of international linguistic thought in its endeavours to overcome the Saussurean model of language as a static uniform system of mandatory rules and to supplant this oversimplified and artificial construct by the dynamic view of a diversified, convertible code with regard to the different functions of language. As long as this conception finds its adepts again and again, we must repeat that any experimental reduction of linguistic reality can lead to valuable scientific conclusions so long as we do not take the deliberately narrowed frame of the experiment for the unrestricted linguistic reality'.[11]

For Prague linguistics the aspects of language that concern the linguist are those aspects that are relevant to language's functions. Language is therefore a socially elaborated set of rules adapted to a set of functions. It is these functions that provide linguistics with the *a priori* on the basis of which its systems can be constructed. The functions do not derive from properties of the mind, but from the needs of communication which themselves depend on the social context.

Language is explained theoretically by showing how it is a means of communication adapted to its functions, subject to constraints of physiology (for example the discriminatory powers of hearing), of psychology (for example the capacity of the memory), and sociology (for example the channels of communication, the extent of shared information, the orientation of the communication). Language is, therefore, not an inert object, but a teleological system, that teleology being a social teleology.

The functional approach to language, pioneered in the Prague analysis of the distinctive function of sound, breaks with Saussure's positivism in seeing language as an instrument and not as an object. The concept of function both founds the autonomy of the system and links it to the environment in which it functions. The concept of function makes it possible to identify the system by providing the principle according to which the system is constructed. In this way it makes it possible to identify simultaneously the elements of the system, elements which are defined in relation to their functional role in the system, and to identify the systematic relations between those elements.

It is only the concept of function which makes it possible to distinguish between linguistically pertinent and linguistically non-pertinent relations, and so between linguistically pertinent and linguistically non-pertinent features of the elements of the system. Mounin is characteristically blunt in his insistence on the centrality of the concept of function in structural linguistics:

'There is a structure because there is a choice in the arrangement of the units. What is the criterion of this choice? It is the *function*, a notion fundamental to structural linguistics. Every time anyone refers to structuralism in the human sciences without referring at the same time to functionalism, while claiming to use models provided by structural linguistics, there is reason to believe that one is dealing with pure babbling, or even a completely empty psittacism'.[12]

The intervention of the concept of function implies a decisive break with the psychologism which was still characteristic of Saussure's work. Trubetzkoj, despite early hints of psychologism, was emphatic:

'Recourse to psychology must be avoided in defining the phoneme since the latter is a linguistic and not a psychological concept. Any reference to "linguistic consciousness" must be ignored in defining the phoneme'.[13]

In making explicit the functional basis of language the Prague linguists purged linguistics of any interpretation of language in terms of a psychological reality, whether individual or collective, conscious or unconscious. The relations which constitute the system in question are unambiguously functional and not psychological relations. Investigation of the psychological implications of the findings of linguistics has to be left to psychology, but there is no necessary implication that the system defined by the function has any psychological reality.

In breaking with Saussurean positivism, the Prague linguists also broke with the rigid Saussurean oppositions between *langue* and *parole*, on the one hand, and between synchrony and diachrony, on the other. The former distinction, while of methodological value, constitutes a barrier if elevated to an ontological level.

The opposition to the rigidity of the *langue/parole* division was developed even before the rise of the Prague Linguistic Circle in the work of the Russian Formalists. The Formalists saw speech not simply as a realization of *langue*, but rather as the creative act which brought language to life, in which meaning could be created by breaking rules as well as by merely applying them, and in poetic forms of discourse such means of fully exploiting the resources of language are common.

This leads naturally to the idea of *parole* as permanently innovative, to a dialectic in which every speech act tends to stretch the resources of *langue* and in stretching them to change them. *Langue* is therefore seen as a set of linguistic conventions (or social norms) which are exploited rather than applied, their exploitation underlying the permanence not of linguistic categories and forms but rather of linguistic change. Thus the revised conception of the relation between *langue* and *parole* or the 'code' and the 'message', led naturally to a change in the conception of the relation between synchrony and diachrony.

Jakobson has been very concerned in many of his studies with the relations between the code and message, not only in poetics but also in, for example, his analysis of 'shifters' which integrate code and message. More recently he has referred to the 'indissoluble dialectic unity *langue/parole*' in denouncing the separation of the two, concluding that 'without a confrontation of the code with the messages, no insight into the creative power of language can be achieved'.[14]

Jakobson has been even more emphatic about the need to reconcile synchrony and diachrony. His 1928 theses were unambiguous:

'The opposition between synchronic and diachronic analysis counterposed the notion of system to the notion of an evolution. It has lost its basic importance now that we recognise that every system is necessarily present to us as an evolution, and that every evolution inevitably has a systematic character'.[15]

The abandonment of the positivist view of language for a more dialectical conception which sees objectivism as a methodologically constituted moment of a scientific process which accommodates both subjective and objective elements makes possible the development of a view of language which can get beyond the one-sidedness of the positivist perspective.

Language is no longer seen as a static mental framework but as a socially defined code available to the members of society. This code constitutes a system, but a system which is constantly evolving. Hence there is no opposition between systematic and historical explanation, for both treat of the same thing. Systematic explanation seeks to understand a system *which is evolving*, while historical explanation seeks to understand an evolving *system*. The two are reconciled as soon as it is recognized that the only reality of language is in its use as an instrument by human subjects.

The Russian Formalists first developed the structural approach to language in the analysis of the poetic function, which is defined by a focus on the message for its own sake.

The theoretical reason for this emphasis on the poetic function is very important, because it is only the orientation to the message characteristic of the poetic function that makes it possible to analyze poetic language without reference to any extrinsic meaning: meaning is created by the formation of relationships within language and so the analysis of the poetic function shows how the creation of structural relations within the message produces the poetic meaning of a work.

Jakobson stresses that poetry cannot be reduced to the poetic function or vice versa. In any discourse we are dealing with a hierarchy of functions. In poetry the poetic function is dominant, but different poetic genres imply a different ranking of the various functions, so that, for example, in epic poetry the referential function is strongly implicated, in lyric poetry the emotive function, and so on.

Extreme formalism made the mistake of identifying poetry with the poetic function and so of believing that poetry could be reduced to the structural relations established within a poem, without any reference being made beyond to the other elements of the system of communication. This ignores both the fact that the poetic is only one of several functions and it ignores the fact that the poetic function is only defined within the framework of communication, hence the meaning of the structural relations established within the poem cannot be defined independently of the poet who produces the poem or the hearer for whom it has meaning. The structural relations within the poem are the means by which a poetic meaning is communicated from poet to the hearer of the poem and have no existence outside that functional context.

Within linguistics the Prague Circle concentrated on the sound system of language because, as in the study of the poetic function of language, it was possible here to study an aspect of the structural properties of language without making reference to extrinsic meaning. This is because language is what Martinet has called a 'doubly articulated system', being constituted on the expression plane by the combination of elements (phonemes) which are themselves without meaning. The application of the functional principles of Prague linguistics to phonology was pioneered by Trubetzkoj. Trubetzkoj confines phonology to the study of sound in its referential function, leaving the study of its other functions to phonostylistics. At this level sound features have three functions: culminative, delimitive and distinctive. The distinctive feature is based on the *opposition* between sounds that makes it possible to distinguish linguistic units from one another.

If we concentrate our attention on the distinctive function of the sound system it is clear that the intrinsic characteristics of the sounds of language are irrelevant. All that is important is that the different significant sounds should be distinguished from one another. Thus the sound system of language can be analyzed, from the point of view of the distinctive function, solely in terms of the relations between sounds: the sound system of a given language can be reduced to a series of functional distinctions, a structure of distinctive relations. Correspondingly to learn to speak and to understand a language involves learning to recognize and reproduce these significant distinctions.

This is the importance of Prague phonology for Lévi-Strauss, for it provides a reduction of the sound system to a purely formal structure in which the significance of different sounds is reduced to their relations with other sounds within the system. The system can therefore be reduced to its formal structure.

However this structure is not something inherent in the sound system as an inert object, let alone is it something imposed by the mind, although it must be assimilated by the mind if a language is to be learned and understood. The structure is the product of abstraction, an abstraction that ignores all but the distinctive function of the sound system, so that the structure is isolated on the basis of a functional argument, and cannot be understood in isolation from that function. This is best brought out by observing that not all oppositions between sounds are linguistically significant. In other words not all oppositions are distinctive, and it is only reference to the linguistic function of differentiating meanings, and to the linguistic context within which sounds appear, that can determine which oppositions define *distinctive features* of the sound system.

In any particular context one phoneme will be opposed to others not as a whole, but only by those phonetic features that define its functional distinctiveness. The idea that the distinctive function of sound was served not by the phoneme but by the distinctive opposition between certain features of the phoneme led Jakobson to the conclusion that the phoneme should be analytically dissolved into its constituent features, those features being identifiable only as part of the system of distinctive features. If this could be done the system of phonemes could be reduced to a simpler and more fundamental system of distinctive features, each phoneme then being characterized as a bundle of distinctive features.

If the distinctive features that were isolated could be claimed to be universal a single set of distinctive features could be used to characterize, and to generate, the sound system of every natural language. When Lévi-Strauss met Jakobson in New York in the early 1940s Jakobson was working on the problem of isolating such distinctive features and expressing them in a binary form. It is this structural analysis that Lévi-Strauss felt to be convergent with his work.

It might be thought paradoxical that the Prague School, which insisted on the teleological character of language as a dynamic and dialectical system related to the communication needs of the speech community, should have pioneered an immanent, structural, analysis of sound as a synchronic system. The paradox is resolved when we appreciate that this synchronic structure represents an abstraction from the dynamic system of language, an abstraction legitimated on methodological and not on ontological or epistemological grounds.

This abstraction is legitimate because the double articulation of language, and the correspondingly arbitrary character of the linguistic sign, makes it possible to analyze the distinctive function of the sound system of language without any reference to extrinsic meaning, and so to focus attention, for the limited purpose of investigating that function, on relations internal to the linguistic code. To the extent that the linguistic sign is arbitrary, inherent qualities of the signifier do not play any part in its linguistic function and so the sign can be analyzed in abstraction from consideration of meaning.

It is only reference to the concept of linguistic function that enables us to legitimate the structural method of analysis that is appropriate to the study of the distinctive features of the sound system of language. The concept of function reveals to us that language is a means of communication: there is nothing in the existence of language as an object that tells us this fact, it can only be revealed by reference to an intention to communicate that lies behind linguistic utterances.

It is only the concept of function that reveals to us that positive qualities of sound do not perform an essential linguistic function, but that the primary function of the elementary sounds of language is a distinctive one. At the same time it is only reference to the concept of linguistic function that enables us to set limits to the application of the structural method, in particular revealing that it is only where it is legitimate to abstract from consideration of extrinsic meaning that it is legitimate to confine our attention to internal structural connections.

It is the concept of function, and the integration of form and function in the analysis of language, that underlies all that is productive in Russian Formalism and in Prague linguistics. Russian Formalism isolated the poetic function of language in the analysis of which all reference to extra-linguistic reality could be excluded since the poetic function is served by language taking itself as its signified: it represents the metalinguistic use of language in which new meanings are created by the manipulation of established linguistic meanings which can, for the purposes of analysis, be taken for granted.

Prague Linguistics isolated for special study the distinctive function of sound in language in the study of which, again, extra-linguistic considerations could legitimately be excluded (although the analysis of the sound system cannot in fact be carried out in complete abstraction from meaning: since the phoneme is a functional concept and not a substantive acoustic reality the identity of one phoneme and its difference from others can only be defined functionally, by reference to identity and difference of meaning).

In each case the 'structural' method of immanent analysis, in which the properties of language under review are considered to consist in relations internal to the language (or, in the case of poetry, the metalanguage), is legitimated solely by reference to the concept of function. It is, therefore, not language as such, nor the mind of the language user, that is structural. Rather certain properties of language can be explained in immanent terms.

When we move beyond consideration of the distinctive function of the sound system of language such an immanent structural analysis is no longer legitimate, since it is no longer legitimate to isolate the language from its context, and in particular from considerations of meaning. Within the sound system, for example, the study of prosodic features cannot exclude reference to meaning and cannot confine itself to structural analysis, not least because some such features (intonation, for example) are not discrete and so cannot be defined contrastively. The exclusion of consideration of meaning becomes even less legitimate when we move from the study of the sound system to the study of the syntax of language.

For example, central to Chomsky's enterprise is the belief that it is possible to distinguish between grammaticality and meaningfulness as criteria by which to evaluate the acceptability of sentences. If 'grammatical' is the same thing as 'logical' then there is no problem in distinguishing the criteria: a statement can be logically acceptable but meaningless or wrong. However the grammatical structure of natural languages does not correspond to their logical structure, thus grammaticality can only refer to adherence to the rules of the grammar that govern the language, which leads Chomsky straight into the circularity that I discussed in the last section.

In fact Chomsky has repeatedly changed his mind about the nature of the dividing line between the criteria of grammatical and semantic acceptability, bringing out clearly the arbitrary character of the division in his linguistics. The conclusion seems clear. If we want to understand why the syntactical structure of language does not correspond to its logical structure we have to refer to the function of language.

The function of an artificial scientific metalanguage is to provide an unambiguous form in which to express and to investigate the consistency of a series of statements, and so its syntax is logical. A natural language has a much more varied range of demands placed upon it as means of expression and communication.

Its syntax is subject to a much greater range of pressures, so we would not expect that syntax to correspond to the logical syntax of an artificial language. It is only by investigating the functions of language, and so the constraints to which it is subject in its everyday use, that linguistics can establish the pertinent syntactical relationships within the language. Thus the syntax of a natural language cannot be explored in abstraction from the context within which that language functions as a natural language. It is only because positivism divorces language from this context, and considers it in isolation from the pressures that mould it as a language, that it is then able to reduce language to a formal structure which is, in the last analysis, linguistically arbitrary.

## NOTES

1 F. de Saussure, *Course of General Linguistics*, Fontana, London, 1974, pp. 15, 66.
2 *Ibid.*, p. 122.
3 *Ibid.*, pp. 112–3.
4 *TT*, p. 55.
5 Saussure, *op. cit.*, pp. 81, 90, 99–100.
6 *Ibid.*, pp. 74, 79.
7 R. Jakobson, *Word and Language*, Mouton, The Hague, 1971, p. 711.
8 N. Chomsky, 'Review of B. F. Skinner, *Verbal Behaviour,*' *Language*, 35, 1, 1959, pp. 26–58.
9 N. Chomsky and M. Halle, *The Sound Pattern of English*, Harper & Row, New York, 1968, p. 4.
10 P. Peters and R. Ritchie, 'A Note on the Universal Base Hypothesis', *Journal of Linguistics*, 5, 1969, p. 150.
11 R. Jakobson, 'Linguistics' in *International Study on the Main Trends of Research in the Social and Human Sciences*, Mouton, The Hague, 1970, p. 430.
12 G. Mounin, *Clefs pour la Linguistique*, Seghers, Paris, 1968, p. 96.
13 N. Trubetzkoj, *Principles of Phonology*, University of California Press, Berkeley, 1969, p. 38.
14 Jakobson, 1970, *op. cit.*, p. 458.
15 R. Jakobson and J. Tyanyanov, 'Problems of Literary and Linguistic Studies', *New Left Review*, 37, 1966, p. 60.

# VII. *Lévi-Strauss and the Linguistic Analogy*

## 1 THE ENCOUNTER WITH LINGUISTICS

LÉVI-STRAUSS encountered structural linguistics when he met Roman Jakobson in New York in 1942, where both were attached to the Ecole Libre des Hautes Etudes. Lévi-Strauss attended Jakobson's lecture course 'On Sound and Meaning'[1] and was astonished to find what he regarded as a remarkable convergence between the methods developed by Prague phonology for reducing the diversity of phonological facts to a rational order and the method that he was himself developing in the analysis of kinship phenomena.

For Lévi-Strauss the advance that Jakobson had made on traditional phonology by means of the concept of structure strictly paralleled the advance that he believed himself to be making on the analysis of Granet. Granet had reduced kinship phenomena to a systematic form, but he had not managed to reduce the various systems to modalities of a single order.

I argued earlier that there are few signs of the linguistic inspiration in the body of *The Elementary Structures*. Thus in confronting linguistics Lévi-Strauss was discovering not a new method, but a convergence between tendencies in two different disciplines. However the discovery of this convergence had a major impact on the direction of Lévi-Strauss' work, for it seemed to Lévi-Strauss that the lesson of this convergence was that the structural method could be applied elsewhere within the human sciences. In view of the discussion of the last chapter it is important to uncover precisely what are the grounds on which Lévi-Strauss seeks to legitimate this methodological extension.

There are in fact two different kinds of argument that Lévi-Strauss offers at different times. Firstly, the borrowing can be legitimated on methodological grounds. The functional basis of the structural method can be recognized and the method extended to any system whose function is essentially distinctive. This is the form of argument Lévi-Strauss offers in his earliest borrowings.

However this would give the structural method a very restricted application, as Lévi-Strauss recognizes in his early works. Thus the second argument, based on a supposed identity of object, is much more powerful, if without foundation. This is the argument that linguistics has discovered the basis on which human beings are able to create systems of meaning, this basis being the capacity to introduce structural differentiations into a natural homogeneity.

Linguistics has shown us, on the one hand, the nature of the human mind that makes it possible for us to learn and to apprehend such artificial distinctions, and, on the other hand, the way in which the introduction of such discontinuities make it possible to create systems of meaning. Thus the structural method of linguistics is applicable throughout the human sciences as the method that makes it possible to locate the objective, and for Lévi-Strauss the unconscious, foundations of meaning. The method pioneered in phonology, and discovered independently by Lévi-Strauss in his study of kinship, is the method that makes the scientific study of meaning possible by reducing meanings to relations immanent in the object.

In view of the discussion in the last chapter it is very important to identify which of the two conceptions of linguistics there discussed Lévi-Strauss adheres to. In this section I want to look at Lévi-Strauss' comments on linguistics, where we shall find that despite an early appreciation of the functionalist perspective, Lévi-Strauss soon lapsed into positivist mentalism. In the following sections I shall assess the legitimacy of Lévi-Strauss' borrowings by looking at the contributions of linguistics and the relevance of the structural method to an understanding of mind and of meaning.

Before embarking, however, it is important to note that the methodological convergence that so struck Lévi-Strauss is no indication of the productiveness of the structural method. The enthusiasm for the methods of systematic analysis that swept Europe was recognized by the Prague Circle as a part of a broad intellectual and ideological movement whose achievements, if any, lay in the future. Thus even within phonology Jakobson had not managed to establish that the sound system could be given a structural representation at the time Lévi-Strauss met him, and it would be a long time before Chomsky opened the way to a structural syntax. *Gestalt* psychology was in disarray, phenomonology had collapsed into mysticism, neo-positivism was in a state of permanent revision. As I have argued in earlier chapters in the case both of linguistics and of Lévi-Strauss' analysis of kinship the positive achievements of structuralism in countering the excessive enthusiasm for psychologism and historicism had to be measured against the dangers of formalism and hypostatization that arose if the structure was fetishized and the object under review was isolated from the context within which it functioned. Thus it is important to be aware of the serious limitations of the structural method even in its chosen fields, and not to be carried away by Lévi-Strauss' enthusiasm.

Lévi-Strauss' first self-conscious application of the structural method of phonology was in an article published in 1945. The understanding of linguistics in this article is very limited, as Mounin has shown in an extended critique.[2] In particular Lévi-Strauss wavers between a mentalist and a functionalist conception of linguistics. On the one hand, Lévi-Strauss argues that the study of kinship systems can be assimilated to that of language because both are systems of meaning constituted by the unconscious. On the other hand Lévi-Strauss does introduce the concept of function later in the argument, with interesting results.

Lévi-Strauss argues that, despite first appearances, the method of phonology cannot be applied to the study of the terminology, breaking terms down into smaller units of meaning, and criticized the attempt to do this by Davis and Warner because the method leads only to an abstract system whose elements have no objective reality, which is more complex than the original data, and which has no explanatory power. The reason for this failure is that we do not know the function of the system. At this point, therefore, Lévi-Strauss seems to recognize the importance of the concept of function and the consequences of ignoring it. In particular, and most significantly, when he does so he argues that the structural method is inappropriate to the study of the kinship systems to which *The Elementary Structures* is devoted.

In fact in the 1945 article Lévi-Strauss applies the method to the study of the system of attitudes because there we know the function which is, supposedly, 'to insure group cohesion and equilibrium'. Although Lévi-Strauss does not specify the function more clearly, nor discuss its relation to the structural analysis, the implication is that the function of the prescribed attitudes to kin is purely demarcative. Thus, by a 'formal transposition of method' Lévi-Strauss analyzes this system by means of a series of binary oppositions.

If the function of these attitudes were indeed demarcative, then the transposition of method would be quite legitimate. However there is not much reason to believe that this is the case. The attitudes are in fact prescribed in a positive, and often very detailed, way by the societies in question, and Lévi-Strauss recognizes that to concentrate on the structural relations between the attitudes is to 'oversimplify' them. In fact there is reported to be a preponderance of systems which do fit Lévi-Strauss' scheme so it might be surmised that the attitudes do have a systematic significance, although it is not clear whether this systematic quality is original or derivative and Lévi-Strauss' hypothesis is not really very illuminating.

In the concluding chapter of *The Elementary Structures* Lévi-Strauss also makes some reference to the functional basis of the structural method. Within *The Elementary Structures* the use of the structural method develops spontaneously from the attempt to generalize and formalize Mauss' theory of reciprocity, and does not depend on any analogy with language. It is because Lévi-Strauss sees systems of kinship exclusively as systems designed to establish certain patterns of social relationships that for him the only relevant properties of these systems are the relationships that they establish, and these define the structure to which the system is reduced. Whether or not the theory is adequate to reality, the method is clearly adequate to the theory. The structural analysis is therefore legitimated by the supposed function of the systems.

At the end of *The Elementary Structures* Lévi-Strauss argues that 'the progress of our analysis is . . . close to that of the phonological linguist' in reducing a large number of rules to a small number. The method is analogous because all possibilities are exhaustively established by combining a limited number of elements in a number of different ways. The schema itself has a binary foundation, being engendered by successive dichotomization.

Lévi-Strauss refers to the fact that the structural method is applicable to kinship systems because kinship systems and language share the common function, that he believed unknown in 1945 but which he has now discovered to be the function of communication. However he goes further than this and argues that linguists and ethnologists 'do not merely apply the same methods, but are studying the same thing'.[3] What this thing is varies at different stages of Lévi-Strauss' work, but here it is a system of communication. Thus, according to Lévi-Strauss, we can interpret

'society as a whole in terms of a theory of communication . . . . since the rules of kinship and marriage serve to insure the circulation of women between groups, just as economic rules serve to insure the circulation of goods and services, and linguistic rules the circulation of messages'.[4]

The supposed analogy is in fact extremely misleading, for linguistic rules have nothing whatever to do with the circulation of messages, they are concerned with the *constitution* of messages.

This emphasis on communication gives way in Lévi-Strauss' later work to an emphasis on meaning, and consideration of the functional basis of the structural method disappears almost completely. Even in the earlier works it seems clear that Lévi-Strauss attaches most importance not to these functional arguments but to the argument that linguistics has achieved the breakthrough to a purely formal, and so rational, unconscious, and this is seen as the ultimate foundation of the structural method. Even in the article of 1945 this is what Lévi-Strauss quite erroneously regards as the most important achievement of Trubetzkoj.

In later works Lévi-Strauss places increasing emphasis on the linguistic discovery of the unconscious foundations of the symbolic capacity and so of meaning. In an article of 1946 the contribution of 'psychology and linguistics' was related to the need to set up symbolism 'as an *a priori* requirement of sociological thought'.[5]

By 1949 Lévi-Strauss was arguing that

'the unconscious . . . is reducible to . . . the symbolic function . . . which is carried out according to the same laws among all men, and actually corresponds to the aggregate of these laws. . . . As the organ of a specific function, the unconscious merely imposes structural laws upon inarticulated elements which originate elsewhere . . . these laws are the same for all individuals and in all instances where the unconscious pursues its activities'.[6]

The term 'function' here has a quite different meaning from that found in linguistics, for it has no teleological connotations, referring rather to a particular *capacity* of the organism, as the use of the organic analogy makes clear.

In another article of 1949 the discovery of the unconscious foundation of language is attributed to Boas. In the same article the dissociation of the structural method from its functional foundation is clear. The structures are not to be constructed deductively, on the basis of their function, as they were in *The Elementary Structures*, but rather we 'abstract the structure which underlies the many manifestations and remains permanent throughout a succession of events'.[7]

In the 1950 Introduction to Mauss' *Sociologie et Anthropologie* the lesson of linguistics is again not methodological, but substantive, in showing the unconscious character of the 'fundamental phenomena of the mental life', opening the way to 'a vast science of communication' and making possible an intellectualist psychology, the 'generalized expression of the laws of human thought'.[8]

Linguistics has, Lévi-Strauss writes in a 1951 article inspired by Sapir, 'reached beyond the superficial conscious and historical expression of linguistic phenomena to attain fundamental and objective realities consisting of systems of relations which are the products of unconscious thought processes'. If we could accomplish the same in relation to social phenomena we may be able to 'conclude that all forms of social life are substantially of the same nature . . . (they may S.C.) . . . consist of systems of behaviour that represent the projection, on the level of conscious and socialized thought, of universal laws which regulate the unconscious activities of the mind'. The symbolic capacity is related to 'split representation', and this is the source of exchange. 'Since certain terms are simultaneously perceived as having value both for the speaker and the listener, the only way to resolve this contradiction is in the exchange of complementary values, to which all social existence is reduced'.[9] It seems that now the unconscious has been reduced from the three 'structures' of *The Elementary Structures* to the purely formal principle of opposition.

As Lévi-Strauss assimilated what were, for him, the lessons of structural linguistics, he lost what tenuous grip he had had on the properly functional foundation of the structural method, and instead came to argue that the structural method is universally applicable in the human sciences because it is appropriate to the objective study of systems of meaning that are the product of the formal structuring capacity of the unconscious, condition of possibility of language, thought and culture. Thus Lévi-Strauss espouses a thoroughly positivist, and so formalist, conception of the structural method that parallels that of Bloomfield and Chomsky that I discussed in the last chapter.

Lévi-Strauss' comments on methodology are not to be taken too seriously, but his one significant methodological discussion, of the concept of the 'model' brings out well his positivist conception of the structural method.

For Lévi-Strauss a structure is a particular kind of model which 'exhibits the characteristics of a system'; which offers 'a possibility of ordering a series of transformations resulting in a group of models of the same type'; which properties 'make it possible to predict how the model will react if one or more of its elements are submitted to certain modifications'; and 'finally, the model should be so constituted as to make immediately intelligible all the observed facts'. The model is established by observing facts and elaborating 'methodological devices which permit the construction of models out of these facts'. 'On the observational level, the main . . . rule is that all the facts should be carefully observed and described, without allowing any theoretical preconception to decide whether some are more important than others'. Having established the facts by observation, the model is developed, that model representing the law of construction of the facts.[10]

I have already criticized this crude positivist conception of the model in the last chapter. No model can possibly explain 'all of the facts', and so a theory has to define in advance to which facts the model will be held to apply. In the case of a structural model the facts selected for consideration are a particularly restricted sub-set of 'all of the facts', for the structural model leaves out of account all non-systematic properties and all extrinsic relationships. Thus the application of the structural model presupposes that it is legitimate to exclude all these facts from consideration, and so presumes that the whole under consideration is intelligible in isolation from other wholes and purely in terms of its internal relations. This kind of abstraction has to be legitimated theoretically.

Moreover, even when the facts to be considered have been isolated the problem remains of deciding which structural model to select from the infinite number that could be applied to the data. For Lévi-Strauss 'the best model will always be that which is *true*, that is the simplest possible model which, while being derived exclusively from the facts under consideration also makes it possible to account for all of them'.[11]

Thus the structural model is not something that leaps at us out of the 'facts', it is something that we create in a double analytical movement. Firstly, by isolating certain facts to be explained which constitute an enclosed and self-sufficient system, thus excluding consideration of any extrinsic relationships. Secondly, by selecting one among a series of models according to purely arbitrary criteria of simplicity. There is no doubt that this process of reduction and selection can produce formal models, and that the same formal model can be isolated in the most disparate fields, but we must endorse the conclusion reached by Maybury-Lewis in his evaluation of Lévi-Strauss' application of the device of the model to his study of dualism, which was also the conclusion of the discussion of Chomsky's linguistics above:

'it would seem that the only inference that may be drawn from the comparison of models is that disparate elements drawn from these societies can be represented in identical patterns. But this formal identity of the models has no sociological implications'.[12]

For Lévi-Strauss the structural models are far from being arbitrary. For him the structural model is the mediating link between mind and meaning, for it specifies the structural differentiations and structural connections established by the unconscious mind that in turn provide the objective foundation of the meaning of cultural and linguistic systems. I have argued methodologically that these models are necessarily arbitrary. I now want to look theoretically at the connection between these structural models and the mind, on the one hand, and meaning, on the other. In this chapter I shall look at the question in relation to linguistics. In the following chapters I shall look at the way in which Lévi-Strauss has developed his (mis)understanding of linguistics into a human philosophy and a theory of cultural meaning.

## 2 LANGUAGE AND MIND: THE 'STRUCTURAL UNCONSCIOUS'

For Lévi-Strauss the models isolated by the structural method do not represent empirical reality, and so are not to be confused with the 'structures' studied by Radcliffe-Brown or Murdock. Nevertheless the structures, and the connections they express, are real, even if they correspond to a reality that is not directly observable:

'In my mind models are real, and I would even say they are the only reality. They are certainly not abstractions, . . . but they do not correspond to the concrete reality of empirical observation. It is necessary, in order to reach the model which is the true reality, to transcend this concrete-appearing reality'.[13]

Although we do find conscious models, these are 'by definition poor ones, since they are not intended to explain the phenomena but to perpetuate them'. The true model, therefore, takes us back once again to the unconscious:

'We are led to conceive of social structures as entities independent of men's consciousness of them (although they in fact govern men's existence), and thus as different from the image which men form of them as physical reality is different from our sensory perceptions of it and our hypotheses about it'.[14]

The idea that the structural models developed by linguistics, and by extension by anthropology, refer us back to the unconscious, or the structure of the human mind, is an idea that Lévi-Strauss derived from Jakobson. For Lévi-Strauss Jakobson established that the psychological *a priori* that made possible language, and so meaning, is the formal binary structuring capacity of the mind that is expressed in the binary discrimination of distinctive features in Jakobson's phonology.

It is paradoxical that Lévi-Strauss should draw such conclusions from Jakobson's work, since I have argued that Prague Linguistics was concerned with the autonomy of linguistics and with the establishment of functional and not of psychological connections. However the emphasis on function is not incompatible with the attempt to derive psychological conclusions from the study of language. Indeed it is only the concept of function that can differentiate between the linguistic and the psychological aspects of language and so make it possible to develop a valid psycholiguistics that does not confuse the two.

Jakobson in particular insisted that linguistics should explore language from every point of view, the properly linguistic but also the psychological, sociological, historical, physiological points of view. At the same time he insisted that each of these points of view is distinct and, moreover, that the relationship between them is not a reductionist relation. He insisted that language as an object exists at the intersection of a series of systems, so that language is a 'system of systems', but these systems are not arranged in a reductionist hierarchy for which language expresses thought, which expresses neurological connections, which express organic connections (which is the way in which Lévi-Strauss reformulates Jakobson's conception as the 'order of orders'). The connections between the different points of view are complex and remain to be explored.

Much of Jakobson's work has been concerned with the search for linguistic universals, and part of the motivation for this search is psychological. He has sought linguistic universals at two different levels. On the one hand he has sought laws of implication underlying the structure of all phonological systems which take the form: the presence of A implies that of B (or its absence), leading to the development of an hierarchical structure in the system of distinctive features which can be discovered through studies of language acquisition in children, of linguistic change, and of aphasia.

However the search for such *implicational universals* faces certain problems because their discovery depends on establishing the *objective* character of the phonological description adopted. The search for implicational universals depends on the search for *substantive universals* in the phonological system, and this is where we find the famous binarism.

Implicational universals can only be discovered if the distinctions made by different languages can be reduced to a common 'alphabet' of features. Jakobson has long sought to uncover such an alphabet, but it must be stressed that this search is motivated by a methodological, not a psychological, concern to provide a foundation on which to develop a study of implicational universals. The attempt has not been without some success, but it has proved impossible to give a realistic interpretation of the features, in either acoustic or articulatory terms. To the extent that features are universal this is not likely to be a 'mental' phenomenon, but is 'probably . . . a consequence of the anatomical structure of the human articulatory apparatus and the associated brain formations.'[15]

In trying to develop a universal phonological 'alphabet'

Jakobson sought to express the distinctions between features in binary form. It was, nevertheless, some time before Jakobson managed to express his distinctive features in this form. In 1952 Jakobson, Fant and Halle used ternary oppositions. By 1957 Jakobson and Halle, however, had removed the ternary oppositions by the introduction of additional features, and all oppositions were reduced to a binary form. The important question we have to ask is whether this binarism is an imposition of the analyst, or whether it might not be a characteristic of language, and even ultimately the mind. Certainly in 1957 Jakobson and Halle believed that binarism was characteristic of the language and not the linguist.

The question is not an empirical one, for any opposition can be reformulated in binary form. Hence the justification for the adoption of the binary form must refer to its analytical convenience. It might be thought to be characteristic of language if it also offers the simplest possible description. In fact such a claim is difficult to substantiate in this case since there is no clear gain in simplicity by the adoption of the binary convention. Thus Jakobson and Halle had to increase the number of features in order to achieve the binary form, despite the fact that they claim to be seeking maximum elimination of redundancy by seeking the minimum number of distinctive features needed to distinguish all phonemes.

Halle responded to criticism by clarifying the basis of the binary convention. It transpires that binarism is not in fact adopted on grounds of simplicity at all, but rather in order to establish a straightforward evaluation procedure for alternative linguistic descriptions. It is not therefore dictated by a need to simplify descriptions, but by a need to simplify the evaluation of descriptions. Halle shows that binarism is not a convention which actually constitutes an impediment to the collection of data, and therefore is acceptable as a convenient methodological assumption for the organization of features, but Halle recognizes that this binary solution is not a unique solution to the problem of classifying features.[16] Thus the binary basis of phonological classifications, that is for Lévi-Strauss the supreme psychological discovery of linguistics, is simply a methodological device which is adopted purely and simply in order to provide some, ultimately arbitrary, basis for standardizing phonological descriptions.

It seems clear that Lévi-Strauss can find little support for his claims about the unconscious in the work of Roman Jakobson. On the one hand Jakobson's implicational universals are language specific, asserting, for example, that children when learning a language first make the distinction between vowels and consonants, and then acquire progressively more distinctions in a hierarchical order. On the other hand the much-acclaimed binarism is a methodological device which has no clear implications for psychology. However, the linguist who has claimed to derive knowledge of the mind from the study of language is not Jakobson, but Chomsky. It is therefore as well to look at Chomsky's claims for linguistics. For Chomsky linguistics is essentially a branch of psychology, as it was for Saussure, and the study of language is intended to teach us about the nature of the mind.

Chomsky's theory of language can be related to psychological considerations in two different ways. Firstly, by providing a model of linguistic performance and, secondly, by providing a model of language learning. Chomsky's linguistics is based on the distinction between competence and performance. His structural models provide a formalization of what it is that the native speaker knows, and not an account of how people learn languages or of what they do when they use language. Thus Chomsky's model is a purely formal model constructed on the basis of purely formal criteria, and without consideration either of the nature of language or of the nature of the language speaker.

It is possible to derive a performance model from Chomsky's competence model. However, psycholinguistic research tends to disqualify the transformational model as a model of performance.

Chomsky has often insisted that his theory does not purport to be a performance model, although at times he seems to believe that such a model could be derived from it. Chomsky's attempts to draw conclusions about the nature of the mind from his linguistic theories are not based on consideration of linguistic performance, which is a psychological and not a linguistic concern, but on consideration of what is involved in learning a language, and the argument is a psychological version of his epistemological objection to behaviourism.

Chomsky argues that the inductivist logic of behaviourism can never provide a discovery procedure for the grammars of natural languages. Thus a grammar can only be discovered if the linguist is guided by a theory of language that embodies substantive, formal and organizational universals. The linguist can then formulate hypotheses about the grammatical rules of a particular language, and test these on the linguistic data.

The child, Chomsky believes, is in exactly the same position as the linguist, being presented with a degenerate input made up of grammatical and ungrammatical sentences from which it has to discover the grammar of the language so that it can speak the language correctly. If the child proceeded inductively it would make the same kind of mistakes that the behaviourist would make. Thus if the child is to be able to learn a language it must already have available some knowledge of the nature of language, a theory of language to be precise, on the basis of which it can formulate hypotheses about the grammar of the particular language it is to learn. Thus the theory of language is not simply a construct of the linguist, it must also be innate in the mind of the child: Chomsky believes that his theory of language is also a theory of the innate structure of the mind.

It is essential that we distinguish between two different arguments here. One is the argument that a child must have certain capacities if it is to be able to learn: that learning is an active process which involves the child in going beyond the data immediately presented to it. This is obviously a valid argument and it is one that few would deny. The other argument is that the capacities must be those described by Chomsky's theory of language. This argument is quite without foundation, for two essential reasons.

Firstly, Chomsky's view of the learning process is almost as impoverished as is that of the crudest of behaviourists. Chomsky, like behaviourism, regards language learning as a discovery procedure by which the mind analyzes the formal properties of a linguistic input without any reference to meaning or to context. Because he separates language from its function and its context he deprives the language learner of a large proportion of the information on the basis of which the language is learned. Thus Chomsky deprives the child of all the information required to learn a language, on the one hand, and then argues that this information must be innate, on the other.

The second reason for the inadequacy of Chomsky's theory of

innate universals is that he has no means of discovering what these universals are because in evaluating theories of language he excludes consideration of either functional (linguistic) or psychological criteria. As we have seen, his theory of language is an arbitrary formalism, so there is no justification for the claim that this, rather than some other, formalism is innate in the mind. Thus Chomsky's positivism, that excludes consideration of meaning and intention, and the consequent formalism, that deprives his descriptions of language of linguistic or psychological significance, prevents him from being able to formulate any acceptable hypothesis about the nature of the mind.

Chomsky's approach to linguistics and psychology is very like Piaget's approach to cognition and psychology, and Lévi-Strauss regards Piaget as well as Chomsky as a pioneer of the nativism to which he too subscribes. All three ultimately subscribe to the rationalist view of thought and language that was dominant in the seventeenth and eighteenth centuries, for which language was an expression of thought and thought an expression of innate mental structures.

For the classical rationalists God inscribed a structure on the mind that ensured that human thought and language would be adequate to the world that He had created. For Lévi-Strauss, Piaget and Chomsky it is nature that has so conveniently arranged things. The problem is always the same: we acquire knowledge of God, or of the structure of the mind, by acquiring knowledge of the structure of His products; language and the thought expressed through language. However we have no direct access either to God or to the innate structure of the mind, so we have no way of knowing which of a number of alternative formalizations of the structure of thought or of language corresponds to the innate structure. Thus, even if it is accepted that language and thought express the structure of the mind, this approach to logic and grammar is plagued by indeterminacy and its theories of the mind are necessarily arbitrary.

This classical conception of thought and of language is unacceptable because it isolates thought and language from the subjective and the social context in which they exist, develop and are learned. Thus while Chomsky, Piaget and Lévi-Strauss all recognize the creative power of the subject, they all refuse to entrust this creative power to an empirical, conscious, subject who thinks about the natural and social world around him or her, and who communicates with others about their environment. Instead the creative power of the subject has to be taken away as soon as it is acknowledged and given to a mechanism inscribed in the biological constitution of the mind.

This isolation of thought and language from their mundane context means that all the social and cultural properties of thought and language are attributed uniformly to the innate structure of the mind they supposedly express. Thus Chomsky observes, against behaviourism, that the use of language is necessarily creative, but then looks to innate mental structures to provide the creative mechanism. Piaget observes, against associationism, that the subject must play an active role in the development of conceptual and mathematical knowledge, but then looks to innate mental structures to provide the mechanical foundation for the self-regulation of the mind as a biological system. Lévi-Strauss observes the creative power of culture with regard to its natural foundation, in opposition to naturalism, but then reduces this creative power to a biological mechanism.

In each case the creative power of the empirical human subjects who are doing the talking, thinking and meaning is negated in favour of a simple formal mechanism rooted in the brain, and so the necessarily teleological character of the human sciences is no sooner admitted than it is immediately denied as mechanism replaces teleology.

Once language is seen as a social product and as one aspect of the relationships between social individuals it ceases to be necessary to postulate the existence of complex innate mental structures as the means of access to language. Instead the means of access to language becomes an appreciation of the function of language as the means of communication of meanings. The moment at which a child starts to learn a language is not the moment at which its mental capacities mature, it is the moment at which it comes to grasp the social function of language and to internalize this knowledge in the form of an intention to communicate meanings. The child can then make use of a whole range of non-linguistic information to guide it in learning the language. In exactly the same way the child could learn the structural implications of systems of exchange not by imposing an innate grid on the culture presented to it, but by appreciating the function of the systems as systems of exchange, and so seeing them as social systems, and not as purely formal structures.

Looking at the acquisition of cultural capacities in this way does not abolish the psychological question of the mental capacities that make this possible, but it does transform it. Only when we understand language as a means of human interaction can we ask meaningful questions about the psychological capacities that make it possible.

The conclusion seems clear that Lévi-Strauss can find no support from linguistics for his claim that linguistics has made fundamental discoveries about the nature of the mind. Such discoveries as purport to have been made are in fact the product of an extremely impoverished conception of language that puts into the mind what it has taken out of the context within which language is used. We therefore have to evaluate Lévi-Strauss' psychological hypothesis entirely on its own terms. While his fundamental hypothesis, that the operations of the mind are based on the principle of binary discrimination, is not altogether improbable, the significance of his hypothesis is grossly inflated.

For Lévi-Strauss the principle of (binary) discrimination is the specific defining feature of human culture, and the principle of opposition provides the key to an objective understanding of cultural meanings. It is no doubt the case that the ability to learn or to speak a language, or to participate in cultural activities, does involve the capacity to introduce discriminations or to think relationally. However this capacity is a necessary property of any system for coding, storing or transmitting information. Thus the most elementary forms of aural and visual perception, the transmission of genetic information, the most elementary mechanical, let alone electronic, computers and control systems, and an enormously wide range of human, animal and plant natural (physiological, neurological and genetic) processes necessarily imply a physiological, psychological, neurological, chemical or physical ability to recognize or to impose discriminations. For Lévi-Strauss such evidence from the natural sciences is conclusive proof of his own hypothesis, revealing the natural foundation of culture and the unity of the social and natural sciences.

However, what we are concerned to assess is not the claim that a capacity to discriminate exists, nor that it is necessary for the creation of meaning, but that it is the defining characteristic and the key to the understanding of human symbolic activity. This claim is the claim that meaning can be reduced to a purely formal structure.

# 3 THE STRUCTURAL ANALYSIS OF MEANING

The most fundamental claim of structuralism is that it can provide an objective, scientific, account of meaning. This, for Lévi-Strauss, is the fundamental lesson of linguistics for the human sciences. In fact, however, contemporary linguistics has been based, very largely, on the exclusion of all questions of meaning from its domain. It is only recently that linguists have begun to take up the issues of linguistic semantics. The problems a positivist semantics faces are ones that should by now be familiar.

In looking at Chomsky's linguistics I have noted that his theory of language is based on the neo-positivist separation of syntax from semantics and pragmatics. This separation makes it possible to isolate language as a scientific object from its social context and so to consider it without reference to the communicative intentions of speakers, and so without any reference to any extrinsic meaning. This separation isolates a set of sentence-forms on which the grammar and theory of language can operate so that a syntax can be constructed without introducing any semantic considerations. I have noted that this leads to an arbitrary, and so formalistic, syntax, and I have noted that the separation of syntax from semantics is also arbitrary, as indicated by the impossibility of distinguishing non-arbitrarily between sentences that are syntactically and those that are semantically unacceptable. However this division also makes it possible for Chomsky to leave semantics to one side, so his linguistics has nothing to tell us about meaning.

Prague Linguistics, and Russian Formalism before it, did not accept this separation of semantics from the other dimensions of language, and the integration is expressed in the functionalism to which Prague linguists adhered. However the productive researches of both schools confined themselves to areas within which language could be legitimately considered without regard to extrinsic meaning by isolating functional wholes either below (phonology) or above (poetics and folklore) the level of linguistic meaning.

For both phonology and formalism the meaning of the elements of the system is given unproblematically and the analysis considers what is done with these elements. Thus in phonology only reference to the intentions and understanding of native speakers can establish which phonological distinctions are meaningful, but once the units have been identified in this way the system can be analyzed without reference to meaning. For formalism the 'structural' method of analysis is adapted to the study of the poetic function of language, and this is a metalinguistic function in the sense that the poetic use of language takes linguistic units whose everyday linguistic meaning is given and then combines these units in strange or unconventional ways in order to creat new meanings, or to draw attention to specific nuances of old meanings.

Exactly the same is true of the extension of the method of formalism to other dimensions of folklore and literature: these studies always start from the given meanings of natural language, and then consider the ways in which the formation of new connections can create new meanings. Thus, even though the structural analysis might be said to reveal the objective mechanism by which the poem or folklore creates a meaning, and this mechanism might be shown to be reducible to the formation of particular structural relations, the analysis presupposes as established the primary linguistic meanings which the structure manipulates.

Although formalism does not engage with linguistic meaning, it does provide an analysis of the poetic or folkloric meaning of a text, and as such formalism has been acclaimed as a forbear of structuralism in identifying an objective cultural meaning and in providing the means to a scientific analysis of that meaning in terms of structural relations internal to the text or corpus of texts that make up the culture. This, however, is a misreading of the significance of the achievements of formalism.

Formalism has proved a productive approach to certain genres which are themselves particularly formalistic, notably some forms of poetry and folklore. The formalist analyses show how certain formal relations internal to the texts are the means by which particular poetic or folkloric meanings are constituted, and for a positivist interpretation the analyses have therefore discovered an objective meaning that can be isolated without reference beyond the text to a subject who intends that meaning or to an object that is meant.

Although some formalists were themselves prey to such positivist interpretations of their work it is important to stress that such interpretations are false. A formalist analysis examines the ways in which certain stylistic and rhetorical devices, especially metaphor and metonymy, are used to create new meanings or to accentuate established ones. However these analyses cannot claim to uncover a meaning that has an especially privileged objectivity.

The meaning that is discovered is a product of the analysis, and does not necessarily exist independently of the analysis. It is not a meaning that is inherent in the object, for the analysis represents an interpretation of the text in which the meaning of the elements in natural language is taken as given and certain metalinguistic relationships are then imposed.

It can only legitimately be claimed that this meaning has an existence independent of the analysis if that meaning can be independently identified: either if it is the meaning that the author can be shown to have intended, or if it is the meaning that the readers or hearers can be shown to have perceived. In this case the formalist analysis does not discover the meaning of the text, what it does do is to show the stylistic devices by which the text conveys a previously identified meaning.

In the absence of independent identification of the meaning of the text, the formalist analysis is creating a new meaning, offering a new interpretation to add to those meanings that the text already has in the culture in question. Thus, in either case, there are no grounds for arguing that simply because the meaning is constituted metalinguistically, by relations internal to the text, that this meaning is more objective than any other meaning the text may have. The reason being quite simply that there is no such thing as an objective meaning.

This brings us to the crucial point, which is that meaning cannot be intrinsic to an objective system, even though it might be the effect of relationships that are internal to that system. Meaning can only be a relationship between a subject and something external to that subject: cultural and linguistic meanings can only be meanings for someone, recoverable only through the conscious apprehension of those meanings. This is even the case with so-called unconscious meanings: a meaning can only be claimed to be unconscious if it can be subsequently recovered consciously, and this is the central feature of Freudian analysis (although of course the conscious apprehension of a meaning as one which was previously unconscious is no guarantee that the meaning did in fact exist unconsciously).

Language and culture as objective systems of symbols cannot be said to have any meaning in themselves. They are not meaningful objects, they are the objective *instruments* by means of which meanings are expressed and communicated. To isolate them from the social context in which they function as such instruments is to isolate them from the only context within which they have meaning.

It is this instrumental aspect of language that phenomenological views of language have always counterposed to positivist formalism. For phenomenology language is not an object but a 'gesture' by which the subject signifies the world. Language cannot therefore be dissociated from its ideal aim (to say something) and its real reference (to say it about something). Language cannot be reduced either to the subject (thought, consciousness, the mind, or whatever) or to the object (the natural world) because it is language that mediates the relationship between the two, not only relating subject to the world, but also keeping a distance between them.

It is important to stress that the phenomenological critique of positivism is not simply a metaphysical debating point, expression of some romantic 'humanistic', 'subjectivist', 'irrationalist' rejection of 'science'. Although phenomenology has often degenerated into a subjectivist irrationalism, the core of the phenomenological critique of positivism is a rationalist critique of the irrationalism of so-called 'science' that would seek to understand cultural products without reference to the intentionality that gives those products cultural significance.

Thus the claim is not that the positivist approach to meaning is morally objectionable because it violates human dignity, the claim is that the positivist analysis of meaning is unattainable and its supposed objective findings are spurious. In order to give substance to this claim it is necessary to spell out precisely why such a positivist account of meaning must fail. It must be shown that the supposedly objective account of meaning offered by positivism is in fact arbitrary, at best the systematization of particular subjective interpretations of the system of linguistic meaning.

The fundamental error of the positivist analysis of meaning is the belief that because a certain meaning can be specified without making any reference to an intending subject then that must be the truest, the most objective, or the most real meaning of the text in question. The critique of positivism notes that whatever description of meaning a positivist analysis offers, that description can only be validated beyond the confines of the analysis by reference to the intention of a speaking or hearing subject. Otherwise the meaning exists only in relation to the intention of the analyst, and has no significance beyond the analysis. To see this in more detail it is necessary to consider what is involved in a positivist analysis of meaning.

The analysis of meaning essentially involves the reformulation of the text in such a way as to represent its meaning. The meaning of the text cannot be isolated and presented in its purity, but must be embodied in a new text. Thus any attempt to characterize the meaning system of language will involve the construction of a 'metalanguage', that is to say a language within which to talk about the object language and so within which to describe the meanings of the natural language.

In looking at Russian Formalism I argued that formalism looks at poetry and folklore as metalanguages and that it elucidates the metalinguistic meanings by taking for granted the linguistic meanings of the components of the text. Linguistic semantics has to do the reverse: in order to describe and to analyze the meanings embodied in the object language it is necessary to take the meanings of the metalanguage for granted. Hence the problem of linguistic semantics is the problem of constructing an unambiguous and non-arbitrary metalanguage within which to express the semantic relationships of the object language.

This is the old, and insoluble, problem of neo-positivism of constructing a language of science within which to express our indubitable knowledge of the world. No such language can be constructed for the very simple reason that we need another meta-metalanguage within which to formulate its rules of construction, and so on *ad infinitum*.

The illusion of objectivity is given only by taking for granted the absolute character of the metalanguage. Thus, if the metalanguage is natural language, the effect is to present the presuppositions of our everyday understanding of the world that are embodied in natural language as indubitable objective truths. For example, to say that the objective meaning of 'boy' is 'male child' is not to give an objective account of the meaning of 'boy' unless we presuppose the meanings of 'male' and 'child' to be given objectively, yet the meanings of these terms differ from one individual to another and from one culture to another and so have no privileged objectivity.

We can clarify and exemplify the problems involved in the construction of a metalanguage for linguistic semantics by distinguishing between the syntax and the semantics of the metalanguage. The syntax of the metalanguage will describe the semantic relationships that exist within the natural (object) language, for example it will define semantic contrasts between various terms. For a pure structuralist the metalanguage will have only a syntax, for the meanings of language would be exhausted by these meaning relations. However such a radical structuralism is inconceivable, for meaning is a relationship with something beyond language so the metalanguage must also have a semantics that establishes this relationship in one way or another so as to give the system of linguistic meaning some content as well as form.

The problems raised by the attempt to formulate such a metalanguage are twofold, concerning both the syntax and the semantics of this metalanguage. Firstly, concerning its syntax, the problem is what sort of relationships are to be described by the metalanguage. Here there are basically two alternatives.

The metalanguage may make use of the syntax of analytical logic and describes meaning relations in terms of the logical categories of synonymy, antonymy, inclusion, etc. This is the approach most in favour within linguistics at the moment as the complement to Chomsky's linguistics. It attempts to reduce linguistic meanings through logical analysis to a limited number of meaning elements, variously called 'semantic markers', 'semes' or 'sememes' by analogy with the phonemes as the basic units of sound. Thus if we contrast 'man' with 'woman' we can extract the contrasted semes male/female. Thus the application of analytical logic in this way can reduce every sign in the language to a bundle of ultimate meaning components.

This approach, known as componential analysis, has been pioneered in the analysis of kinship terminologies, which are clearly well-structured systems of signs, and of taxonomies of various kinds. Lévi-Strauss' own analysis of kinship systems is a primitive version of this approach, the fundamental semantic distinction for him being that between the marriageable and the unmarriageable. The method is undoubtedly a convenient approach to the formal description of languages, making the handling of selection restrictions in transformational grammar a relatively simple task.

The alternative approach is to describe the meaning relations of the language not in terms of analytical logic, but in terms of the categories of the language itself. This means that there will not be a universal metalanguage to describe meaning relations in different natural languages, since each natural language will also have its own metalanguage. Moreover the meaning descriptions that emerge will not be 'objective', because they will presuppose a knowledge of the natural language and will be relative to that understanding.

This relativistic approach to natural languages is clearly of much less 'scientific' usefulness. However the pragmatic usefulness of the formalistic approach does not necessarily mean that it gives a more adequate account of the meaning of natural languages. There is no reason to believe that for language users the relationships between different meanings can be expressed in analytical form, so that the semantic structure of natural languages can be reduced to the structure of analytical logic.

Nor, however, is there reason to believe that these relationships are adequately expressed in the categories of natural language, unless thought and language are identified with one another. Thus the problem of devising a metalanguage to describe the meaning system of natural languages is an acute one, and not one that is amenable to a positivistic solution.

Even more problematic than the syntax of this metalanguage is that of its semantics. The metalanguage can describe meaning relations within the language, whether of synonymy or of similarity, but if it is to describe the meanings of the terms of the language it must refer beyond the language. There are many ways in which this might be done. For example Bloomfieldian behaviourism analyzes meaning behaviouristically. Thus the metalanguage relates linguistic terms to their behavioural context. Componential analysis relates its primitive meaning elements to a wider 'culture', which begs the question, or postulates them as universal reflections of the external (or internal) world. Saussure relates the sign system as a whole to the universal continuum of thought on which it is imposed, a conception very like that of Trier's 'semantic field'.

The range of solutions offered should be sufficient to indicate the impossibility of deciding between them on purely formal grounds. But it is not only the form of the solution that is arbitrary in this sense, the content of any one formulation cannot be said to have any inherent objectivity either.

For example, on what basis does componential analysis decide that the terms 'man' and 'woman' should be differentiated as male/female, when these terms have such powerful, complex and changing connotations? To reduce the terms to the gender distinction between their most common referents is to deprive the terms of most of their linguistic and cultural power. Thus the basic semantic units do not emerge objectively, they are abstracted arbitrarily from the infinite set of possible units. Thus even a sympathetic commentator can conclude: 'One cannot avoid the suspicion that the semantic components are interpreted on the basis of the linguist's intuitive understanding of the lexical items which he uses to label them'.[17] Componential analysis tells us more about the impoverished intuition of linguists than it tells us about meaning.

The fundamental problem is that an objective description of the semantics of natural language has to relate elements of language to some extra-linguistic reality, whether it be 'thought' or 'the world'. However the description has itself to make use of linguistic terms to refer to this extra-linguistic reality. Thus, however far a positivist semantics takes its reductionism, even if it goes to the lengths of Bloomfieldian behaviourism in eliminating all reference to meaning, it still has to make use of the meaning system of natural language in its descriptions, and so to presuppose that meaning system. Thus any positivist analysis of the meaning of language has to presuppose its own conclusions, for it must have already established the objectivity of the meaning of natural language in order to have a metalanguage within which to describe that meaning.

It is for this reason that linguistic relativists simply refuse to refer beyond language, revolving within an endless circle from which they cannot escape, and equally unable to explain how anybody could enter the circle by learning a language, and so unable to explain how language could serve as a means of communication.

The dilemma arises because the problem that produces it is a spurious one. The choice, between positivism and relativism, is therefore a false one. The dilemma arises out of the attempt to divorce meaning from the intentionality of people who mean and to give it an existence in an object independent of all human intervention. Positivism seeks, ultimately, to refer meaning back to an objective, pre-linguistic, world. Such an ambition is unrealizable because the relation between meaning and the world can never be formulated unambiguously. If it is formulated within language, it presupposes what it seeks to establish. If it seeks to get beyond (or beneath) language, as in the attempt to base linguistic meaning on 'ostensive' definition, then it ceases to be unambiguous and the attempt to establish a privileged objective meaning founders. Relativism recognizes the impossibility of establishing an unambiguous relationship between language and an external objective world, and so makes language into its privileged object.

As soon as this attempt to exclude intentionality from considerations of meaning is abandoned, the dilemma disappears, and the problem becomes a much more pragmatic one. The linguistic sign only exists as a *linguistic* entity for a speaker or hearer in the context of specific utterances in a particular situation. Hence words are always filled with content, they are never stable, but always changeable and adaptable, their meaning is different for different people, and even for the same person at different points in time. Every word, every phrase, has a history for the individual speaker/hearer, a history that is constantly unfolding. Outside this individual history the elements of language have no linguistic reality, they become only sequences of sounds. Thus the elements of language have no stable, or permanent, or objective meanings to be discovered: such meanings literally and quite simply do not exist.

This does not mean that language can only be related to individual subjects and to individual experience, for language is above all a means of communication of meaning from one subject to another. Thus the subject externalizes an intention in the form of a linguistic utterance in the hope and anticipation that another subject will thereby be able to recover that intention. Thus the meaning of the elements of language has an intersubjective reality:

182 *The Foundations of Structuralism*

some aspects of that meaning are common to more than one language user and have a certain stability. Thus the 'cardinal problem of semantics' is that of how 'the fundamental polysemanticity of the word can be reconciled with its unity'.[18] Positivism seeks to eliminate the polysemanticity, seeing in it only the subjective overtones imposed on some fundamental and static meaning. However it is not sufficient to refer the word back to the individual psyche to recover the polysemanticity of the word because one is then in danger of losing sight of its unity.

The meaning of a linguistic unit for an individual, which is the only meaning that can be said to exist, is the expression of a history, and so the summation of the individual experience of a series of contexts within which the unit has had meaning for that individual. The unity of that meaning can only be a social and historical unity, a shared experience and a shared history in which several individuals have participated and which they have signified by means of their language. The unity of the meaning of the unit is therefore the unity of a speech community. Thus the study of linguistic semantics can never be a formal discipline, it can only be a social and historical one, studying the social and historical conditions within which the world is experienced and signified by social subjects.

## NOTES

1　R. Jakobson, *Six Lectures on Sound and Meaning*, Harvester, Hassocks, 1978.
2　G. Mounin, *Introduction à la sémiologie*, Minuit, Paris, 1970, pp. 202–3. Lévi-Strauss' article is reprinted in *Structural Anthropology*.
3　*ESK*, p. 493.
4　*SA*, p. 83.
5　*FS*, pp. 518, 520.
6　*SA*, pp. 202–3.
7　*SA*, pp. 19, 21.
8　*IM*, pp. xxxi, xxxvi, li.
9　*SA*, pp. 58–9, 62.
10　*SA*, pp. 279–80.
11　*SA*, p. 281.
12　D. Maybury-Lewis, 'Dual Organisation', *Bijdragen tot de Taal-Land-en Volkenkunde*, 116, 1, 1960, p. 35.
13　1953b, p. 115.
14　*SA*, pp. 281, 121.

15  D. Slobin, *Psycholinguistics*, Scott, Foreman, Illinois, 1971, pp. 62–3.
16  R. Jakobson, G. Fant and M. Halle, *Preliminaries to Speech Analysis*, Harvard University Press, Cambridge, Mass., 1952; R. Jakobson and M. Halle, *Fundamentals of Language*, Mouton, The Hague, 1957; M. Halle, 'In Defence of the Number 2', in *Studies Presented to Joshua Whatmough*, Mouton, The Hague, 1957; M. Halle, 'Simplicity in Linguistic Description', in R. Jakobson (ed.), *The Structure of Language and its Mathematical Aspects*, Proceedings of the 12th Symposium in Applied Mathematics, American Mathematical Society, Providence, 1961.
17  J. Lyons, *Introduction to Theoretical Linguistics*, CUP, 1968, p. 480.
18  V. N. Volosinov (M. Bachtin), *Marxism and the Philosophy of Language*, Seminar Press, New York, 1973, p. 80.

# VIII. *The Structural Analysis of Myth*

FROM linguistics Lévi-Strauss learned two lessons. Firstly, that the structural method of analysis that he had developed in his study of kinship could be extended to the study of all cultural phenomena as the method appropriate to the objective study of meaning. Secondly, that behind meaning and culture lay the structuring capacity of the human unconscious. I have examined the validity of these lessons at some length in the last chapter. The first lesson led Lévi-Strauss to develop his structural analysis of myth. The second led him to develop his distinctive human philosophy. I shall look at the former in this chapter and the latter in the next.

Lévi-Strauss' turn to the study of myth followed his discovery of linguistics and coincided with his appointment to the *Ecole Pratique*. It was dictated partly by a desire to apply the new method to non-linguistic cultural phenomena, but more fundamentally by the belief that through the study of symbolic systems Lévi-Strauss would be able to gain access to the human mind.

Although Lévi-Strauss makes use of many terms borrowed from linguistics and makes frequent allusions to linguistics, specific borrowings are rare. Thus many commentators have noted that Lévi-Strauss' allusions to linguistics are largely metaphorical. We have, therefore, to assess his studies on their own terms. As such I shall argue in this chapter that Lévi-Strauss' approach to the objective analysis of mythical meaning runs into exactly the problems that I outlined in the last section of the last chapter.

There is no doubt that Lévi-Strauss can conjure meanings out of the material. However these meanings are, from the analytical point of view, arbitrary. Thus my conclusion will be that the meanings that Lévi-Strauss extracts from the systems of myth under review are no more than a formalization of the very idiosyncratic meanings the material has for Lévi-Strauss.

# 1 EARLY APPROACHES TO MYTH

Although, in the light of his encounter with linguistics, Lévi-Strauss came to interpret *The Elementary Structures* as a work which sought the mark of the unconscious on the social structures which it generated, he was not absolutely confident that these structures were products of the mind alone, for the constraints in question could be 'merely the reflection in men's minds of certain social demands that had been objectified in institutions'. Hence Lévi-Strauss turned his attention to the study of symbolic thought in order to discover the constraints of the unconscious impressed on systems with no apparent 'practical function'.[1]

In studying symbolic thought Lévi-Strauss is seeking to uncover the unconscious through an analysis of the structures displayed in that thought. Symbolic thought offers a 'metalanguage', whose elements have no meaning in themselves, their meaning deriving exclusively from the relations between the elements.

Symbolic thought simply arranges and rearranges a fixed repertory of elements. It is a combinatory thought, which responds to an unconscious 'demand for order'. Since the meaning of symbolic thought is exhausted by its immanent structure it is amenable to an immanent analysis which confines itself to the structural relations between its parts.

The ultimate meaning of symbolic thought does not derive from any reference it makes beyond itself, but from the homologous relation it bears to the mind which produces it:

'Authentic structuralism seeks . . . above all to grasp the intrinsic properties of certain kinds of order. These properties express nothing which would be external to them. Or, if one is determined that they should refer to something external, one should turn to the cerebral organization conceived as a network of which these or those properties are translated by the most diverse ideological systems into the terms of a particular structure, each of which systems in its own way reveals the network's modes of interconnection.
. . . One can thus see how the effacement of the subject represents a necessity of, if one can say it, a methodological order: it scrupulously avoids explaining anything of the myth except in terms of the myth, and consequently excludes the point of view of the judge inspecting the myth from without, inclined for this reason to seek extrinsic causes for it. On the contrary it is necessary to be penetrated by the conviction that behind every mythical system other mythical systems, as predominant determining factors, are profiled: it is they which speak in it and which echo one another'.[2]

This passage brings out very clearly the close connection between the dominant themes of Lévi-Strauss' structuralism: the attempt to discover an objective meaning immanent in the object defined without reference to anything outside the object; the structuralist reduction of that meaning to the formal relations between the parts of the object and so the reduction of content to form; and the theory of the unconscious. The pivot of these themes is the attempt to isolate in practical terms the meaning of the system of mythical thought.

By ruling out any subjective interpretation of the system of mythical thought Lévi-Strauss treats that system as an inert and external object. His aim is to show that the meaning of that object is determined by its structure. To do this he has to isolate, on the one hand, the elements of that object and, on the other, the relations between them. In fact the two tasks cannot be separated from one another since the elements of myth only appear as such within the structure that gives them their mythical meaning, just as distinctive features in phonology exist only in their opposition to other features.

Different versions of the theory of myth are based on different interpretations of the constituent elements of the structure. In the early formulations of the theory this constituent element was defined as a segment of the text of the myth. In 1953 it was called a *theme* or *sequence*, which had no meaning in itself, but which derived its meaning only from its participation in a system. This theme was to be discovered by the application of objective procedures, notably commutation. Later the element was defined as a *mytheme*, which is a segment of the text of subject-predicate form which 'shows that a certain function is at a given time linked to a certain subject'.[3] The mytheme is defined by the relation between subject and function.

In fact we are told that the same mythemes recur throughout a myth, hence the unfolding of the myth is conceived of not as the unfolding of a narrative, but as a repetition. The true mythemes are not, therefore 'isolated relations, but *bundles of such relations*'.

In the later analyses of mythical thought we find that the element changes yet again, being reduced from a proposition to a single sign, as we shall see when we consider *Mythologiques*. This change corresponds to a change in the understanding of the structure of the myth. In the early analyses of myth the structure of the myth is explained by reference to the myth's function which is to develop a logical argument which takes a propositional form. The myth resolves contradictions between conflicting ideological beliefs:

'The purpose of the myth is to provide a logical model capable of overcoming a contradiction (an impossible achievement if, as it happens, the contradiction is real)'.[5]

For Lévi-Strauss the contradiction is concealed by means of an argument by analogy. The initial contradiction will be transformed into another one, which can itself be mediated. The mediation of an analogous contradiction thus 'resolves' the first contradiction. The relation between the two, or more, successive contradictions is a symbolic relation which may be metaphorical or metonymical. Because the initial contradiction is never 'really' resolved it will be mediated time and again, in an incessant attempt to dissolve it by dissipating it. The initial contradiction therefore establishes an interminable series of myths in response to a single ideological problem.

In the Oedipus myth the constitutive contradiction is established outside the myth, deriving from the coexistence of a cosmological belief in the autochthonous origin of man and the empirical observation that man is born of the union of man and woman. The Asdiwal analysis[6] also takes an ideological problem as its starting point. In the latter case the problem is one of legitimating the social order, a legitimation which is achieved by means of two devices. Firstly, the existing order is related to a hypothetical previous order of which it is, in some sense, an inversion. Secondly, the alternative order is shown to be an intolerable one by a *reductio ad absurdum*.

These early analyses open up many interesting lines of inquiry, but they do not establish a purely *immanent* analysis which finds the meaning of myth in its structure. The properties of myth in these cases express something external, for the problems which they take up are problems posed by a cultural need to resolve contradictions between beliefs, or to legitimate the existing order. The structure of the myth develops in response to this cultural problem, hence the structure does not, in the first instance, express the laws of the mind but rather the function of the myth. The meaning of the myth does not derive exclusively from its structure, but derives from its specific content, the contradiction it is called on to resolve.

It is this independence of the contradiction which makes the analysis in principle amenable to empirical control, for we can turn to the cosmology of the society and see if the beliefs attributed to it exist and lead to contradiction. We can then turn to the myth and see if the mythemes have the cultural meaning attributed to them by the analyst. Finally, we can judge whether or not the myth does in fact express, transform and mediate the contradictions in question.

The analysis is not straightforward, especially if we are dealing with a distant culture and lack ethnographic information. It is never a definitive analysis, since it has a large interpretative component. However, it is not arbitrary because means are provided by which we can check the objective existence of the relations posited by the analyst.

It seems that Lévi-Strauss achieves this result despite rather than because of his approach to myth. What happens is that the need to achieve access to the myth as an *intelligible*, cultural, product leads quite spontaneously to an examination of the myth in relation to the culture in which it is found, and so to a view of myth as an instrument of culture rather than a projection of unconscious laws. Although such a development is to be welcomed as a break with the mentalist conception of cultural phenomena, as far as Lévi-Strauss is concerned it must represent a weakness, for it is precisely the latter conception that he is seeking to develop.

If myths are to be subjected to an *immanent* analysis, and the meaning of the elements of myth determined without reference to cultural beliefs or subjective intentions, it is necessary to discover some way of uncovering the meaning of the elements without going beyond the mythical universe. It is necessary to discover the metalinguistic rules of myth which define the mythical meaning of the elements purely in relation to one another. By 'permuting a term in all its contexts . . . one can progressively define a "universe of the tale" analyzable into pairs of oppositions, variously combined within each character, which, far from constituting an entity, is, after the manner of the phoneme, as conceived by Roman Jakobson, a "network of differential elements"'.[7] This investigation of the metalinguistic laws of mythical thought is found in *Totemism* and *The Savage Mind*, works which not only marked a break between the theories of kinship and myth, but also within the study of myth itself.

# 2 THE LOGIC OF UNTAMED THOUGHT

It is in *Totemism* and *The Savage Mind* that structuralist intellectualism definitively replaces sociological functionalism in the analysis of collective representations. It is here that the latter are analyzed as structures which respond to the unconscious 'demand for order'. The problems which dominate mythical thought are no longer ideological problems, but intellectual problems posed by the unconscious, or by myth, to itself.

*Totemism* seeks to demonstrate that 'primitive' thought has its own laws and is as intellectual as is the scientific thought which we value so highly. This is important because totemism has often been explained in irrationalist ways, the adoption of a totem by a clan being explained in terms of some affective or utilitarian relation between clan and totem. Lévi-Strauss wants to provide an intellectualist explanation of the institution of totemism not only so as to uncover the laws of 'primitive' thought, but also to show that these laws are the product of a mind which is capable of thinking analytically.

Lévi-Strauss argues that totemic classifications operate by using a natural series to signify a social series, using a natural model of diversity to conceptualize the diversity of human groups. Totems are not adopted individually by each clan, they are adopted on the basis of an intellectual appreciation of a homology between two series, the natural system of totems and the social system of social groups. The importance of the totem is its power of signifying the clan as a part of a whole, and the affective dimension of the totem, far from being at the origin of totemism, is a response to it.[8]

Social organization and the totemic system are therefore independently products of the mind which are related to one another as transformations. Hence totemism is fundamentally a way of conceptualizing the relation between social groups. This means that the totem is significant only as a part of a system, its positive qualities having no relevance, since it is only significant insofar as it is distinctive: the totem is like the phoneme. Thus content and form are reconciled and the way is open 'to a genuine structural analysis'.

Criticism of this analysis of totemism is twofold. In the first place, Lévi-Strauss is criticized for reductionism, eliminating all content of the institution in order to focus solely on the distinctiveness of the totem and so legitimate a structural analysis. In this vein Leach argues that Lévi-Strauss, in focussing solely on the analytical relation of distinctiveness, eliminates any possibility of explaining the religious dimension of totemism. R. and L. Makarius argue that this reductionism, in 'depriving the ethnography of its factual content' by reducing everything to mere difference, eliminates the possibility of a sociological understanding.[10]

The second criticism doubts the intellectual basis of the totemic classification. The most cogent such critic is Worsley. What is in question is whether the totemic series is constituted by the intellect independently of the social series. Worsley argues, on the basis of his own fieldwork, that the totemic series is not constructed independently, but rather that totems are assigned to groups in an atomistic way, social organization therefore offering the model for a derivative totemic system.

Lévi-Strauss clearly recognizes that the systematic character of the totemic system is by no means obvious. Lévi-Strauss argues that the systems do not appear to be systematic because they tend to get modified over time, particularly in the face of demographic changes. He therefore introduces what he calls the 'theoretical attitude' which reimposes a system in the wake of disruption.[11] The problem of the systematic character of the system is especially acute because, as we shall see, the logic of primitive classification is extremely flexible, so that it is difficult to locate a collection which would not be systematic in Lévi-Strauss' terms. Indeed Lévi-Strauss argued forcefully *against* attributing any systematic significance to totemism on the basis of his own fieldwork.[12]

In *The Savage Mind* Lévi-Strauss broadens his perspective from that of the totemic classification to that of 'primitive' thought in general, and particularly concentrates on identifying the 'logic' of 'primitive' classifications, in order to establish its intellectual credentials.

According to Lévi-Strauss 'primitive' thought makes use of all the resources of symbolism, while scientific thought turns its back on the symbolic. 'Primitive thought' therefore makes extensive use of metaphorical and metonymical relations which would be excluded by science. Objects are assigned to classes not solely on the basis of their possessing the defining attribute of the class, as would be the case with a scientific classification, but also on the basis of symbolic associations with already existing members of the class. Classes are then simply 'heaps' of objects which are not based on the abstraction of one property common to every member of that class. Hence the classifiction can always be exhaustive, although classes will by no means be mutually exclusive. A classification does not have an overall logic, but a series of 'local logics', since items can be associated with one another according to very different criteria. The rules in question are many and varied, and can differ from society to society.

The rules of 'primitive thought' are intellectual, in that they are based on an ability to 'oppose terms' to one another, developing taxonomies on the basis of 'successive dichotomies' which constitute 'binary oppositions'. It seems that it is the oppositional character of these relations, rather than their binary character, which matters most to Lévi-Strauss.

Despite the fact that the enormous variety of the rules makes it difficult, if not impossible, to distinguish thought which would break the rules from thought which did not break them, Lévi-Strauss does show that 'primitive' thought *can* be seen as properly intellectual thought. This does not, however, mean that it actually *is* intellectual. On the one hand, the indeterminacy of the rules makes the claim untestable. On the other hand, the initial exclusion of the affective renders the conclusion tautologous.

It is not clear whether Lévi-Strauss is seeking to establish that the rules underlying these classifications are the same as those underlying scientific classifications, or whether he wants to argue that they are different, without implying any weaker mental capacity on the part of the 'primitive'.[13] Lévi-Strauss probably vacillates because of his identification of laws of thought with laws of the mind. This identification leads easily to the conclusion that, in dealing with two different systems of thought we are dealing with two different mentalities, a 'savage' mentality, in which the mind thinks spontaneously, and a 'civilized' mentality, in which the mind is marked by some kind of training.

The problem arises because of Lévi-Strauss' view of the classification as a product of the mind. Instead of contrasting symbolic thought with scientific thought as two different varieties of 'domesticated' thought, Lévi-Strauss sees the former as a spontaneous product of the mind.[14] In analyzing different 'logics', however, we are not analyzing different mentalities, but different socially elaborated and socially endorsed conventions by which different kinds of thought are ordered. The very differences between different systems of thought should alert us against adopting a mentalist approach and should rather suggest a view of collective representations as cultural products.

For this reason the 'laws' of any particular kind of thought must be related to the end which that thought is designed to achieve, and it is only in relation to those ends that different kinds of thought can be evaluated. Lévi-Strauss finds himself caught between the horns of a dilemma, for in seeking intellectual rather than social foundations for the laws of thought he is led straight to the conclusion which he seeks to avoid, the conclusion that different cultures are characterized by different mentalities. The identification of the 'primitive' with the infantile mentality is difficult to avoid since, as Worsley has noted,[15] the laws of 'primitive' thought according to Lévi-Strauss are remarkably similar to the pre-conceptual thought of the child.

If we compare scientific taxonomies with Lévi-Strauss' characterization of 'primitive' classifications we can easily locate functional differences lying behind the different rules of classification. Scientific taxonomies attempt to classify everything *exhaustively* into *mutually exclusive* classes. Such classifications are extremely difficult to construct on the basis of incomplete knowledge, for there will always be some items which cannot be assigned to a class without ambiguity. When we find some anomalies we know that our classification is inadequate, since the ultimate aim is to use the classification to generate generalizations which will ideally not admit ambiguity or exceptions.

The laws of 'primitive' classification, as described by Lévi-Strauss, sacrifice the condition of mutual exclusiveness of classes to the demand for exhaustiveness. The plurality of rules of assignment of items to classes implies that any item can be assigned to any one of a number of classes. This neglect of the scientific requirement that classes be mutually exclusive is not to be explained by a contrast between an unscientific and a scientific mentality, but rather by a contrast between systems of thought which are elaborated with different ends in view. The 'primitive' classification is not designed to assist in the generation of generalizations, and so the classes need not be mutually exclusive. The requirement imposed on the classification appears to be only that everything should find a place in the ordering of the world, and so mutual exclusiveness is abandoned in order to guarantee exhaustiveness.

Although 'primitive' thought is intellectual, it is not analytical, conceptual thought. It is, in the fullest sense, symbolic thought, making use of concrete images to express abstract conceptions. Lévi-Strauss calls the elements of this thought 'signs', which differ from the concept in being limited in their powers of reference. The meaning of these elements is constituted by the symbolic oppositions into which they enter, and cannot be divorced from those oppositions.

'Primitive' thought has available to it a given stock of symbols, which the thinker can put to use by combining and recombining. However, the concrete basis of the symbol means that new elements cannot be invented to do new things. 'Mythical thought is therefore a kind of intellectual *"bricolage"* '. 'Concepts thus appear like operators *opening up* the set being worked with and signification like the operator of its *reorganization*, which neither extends nor renews it and limits itself to obtaining the group of its transformations'. Meaning is, therefore, reduced to an arrangement, as in the kaleidoscope, which 'can be expressed in terms of strict relations between its parts and . . . these relations have no content apart from the pattern itself'.[16]

The classification represents one exercise of '*bricolage*' by which symbols are related to one another. The meaning of the classification, its 'message', is constituted by the fact that it operates at once a 'totalization' and a 'detotalization', and so can signify both unity and diversity. Hence the totemic classification can express the unity of the society, by the analogy it establishes between the cultural and the natural orders, while at the same time signifying the diversity of social groups by the distinction between species.

This 'message' is at the same time an expression of the relationship between culture and nature, totemism providing 'the means (or hope) of transcending the opposition between them'.[17] Totemism therefore begins by contrasting nature and culture, introducing discontinuity, but then reconciles them with one another by establishing a homological relation between the two.

These classifications are engendered by successive dichotomization. However, the 'concrete classifiers . . . can also, in their sensory form, show that a logical problem has been solved or a contradiction surmounted', and so 'dichotomic linearity becomes the "spiral" of a dialogue of the mind with its own demands which is deepened in a progression which Lévi-Strauss comes to qualify as "dialectical." '[18] The study of classification leads directly into the study of myth.

## 3 *MYTHOLOGIQUES*

The four volumes of *Mythologiques* seek to analyze a body of myths from both North and South America, these myths making up a single universe which is analyzed as a whole. Myths are no longer seen as being generated simply by oppositions, but are seen as transformations of other myths in the same or neighbouring societies. The sequence of opposition, mediation and transformation is not, therefore, found in any one myth, but is dispersed throughout the universe of myths. An opposition may be established in one myth, and mediated or transformed in the myth of a distant society.

Lévi-Strauss argues that this change of perspective is simply a change from a method of 'syntagmatic substitution' to one of 'paradigmatic substitution', a change justified on the grounds that the latter is appropriate only at the beginning of the analysis. The change is, however, more significant than this, for it implies that the oppositions which myths seek to resolve are constituted *within* the universe of myths, which therefore offer a closed universe, although that universe is itself interminable since the possibility of establishing new transformations is always present. The universe of myth therefore represents nothing but a constant rearrangement of terms. Behind the myths we can find a constant structure which generates them. 'Its *growth* is a continuous process, whereas its *structure* remains discontinuous'.[19]

The analysis of *Mythologiques* starts out from a randomly chosen myth and gradually expands to bring in more and more myths from more distant cultures. As each new myth is introduced, and new transformation relations established with the myths already examined, the analysis of the latter is progressively deepened. Although Lévi-Strauss insists that the starting point is not privileged, even if not arbitrary, by the end of *Mythologiques* we find a segment of the reference myth is the objective pivot of the whole system of myths of North and South America. Gradually a picture of the system as a whole is built up in which 'each myth taken separately exists as the limited application of a pattern, which is gradually revealed by the relations of reciprocal intelligibility discerned between several myths'.[20]

Since myths come from societies which have different environments, different societies will use different 'images' to code the same concepts. Each myth will therefore be determined by a double transformation, one which transforms the conceptual content of another myth, and another which takes account of infrastructural differences between the societies which mean that the same concept is expressed by different items:

'Every version of the myth thus betrays the influence of a double determinism: one links it to a succession of earlier versions or to an ensemble of foreign versions, the other acts in a kind of transversal way, through constraints of infrastructural origin which impose a modification of this or that element, from which the result is a reorganization of the system to accommodate these differences to necessities of an external order'.[21]

Hence the myths are now given that immanent analysis which was not achieved in the 1955 analysis. Myths are no longer related to anything outside themselves, other than the objective features of the world which they take up as their means of expression.

'Mythological analysis has not, and cannot have, as its aim to show how men think . . . I . . . claim to show, not how men think in myths, but how myths operate in men's minds without their being aware of the fact (*comment les mythes se pensent dans les hommes, et a leur insu*)'.

'If it is now asked to what final meaning these mutually significative meanings are referring . . . the only reply to emerge from this study is that myths signify the mind which evolves them by making use of the world of which it is itself a part'.[22]

The idea that myths are the products of transformations of other myths leads straight back to those diffusionist hypotheses about the Americas which have concerned Lévi-Strauss throughout his career, and which provided the directly anthropological inspiration for his structuralism. Although these hypotheses only come to the fore in *L'Homme Nu*, they are present from the start of

*Mythologiques*. At first the analysis is confined to the relations between a few Amazonian societies, Bororo mythology being seen as the product of the interaction of Tupi and Gê mythology. As *Mythologiques* develops the net widens to cover the whole continent, and the qualifications and reservations which Lévi-Strauss has in the past attached to his diffusionist speculations are largely dropped.

The idea that we are dealing with a mythical field whose unity is explained by reference to diffusionist hypotheses leads naturally to the search for the archetypal myth, which Lévi-Strauss claims to discover in some myths from Oregon, which may be remnants of the original myth, or which may represent totalizations of the field as a whole, but which provide confirmation of the analysis which would not be available if Lévi-Strauss had to rely solely on a postulated unconscious scheme as genitor of the universe of myths.

In the Oedipus analysis each myth, defined as the sum of its variants, sought to resolve a particular contradiction. Now, however, there is one single problem dominating the mythology of the whole continent:

'Myth is nothing other than the effort to correct or dissimulate its constitutive dissymmetry'.[23]

*Mythologiques* achieves the structuralist programme of subjecting the universe of myth to an immanent analysis in which the properties of myth 'express nothing which would be external to them'.[24] The myth is no longer seen as a culturally elaborated system amenable to explanation in terms of culturally defined ideological functions, but expresses the operation of the precultural unconscious. The myth expresses the laws of the mind. If Lévi-Strauss can establish that the structures produced by his analysis have an objective validity, that they do indeed constitute the objective meaning of the myth, then his claim to have discovered something about the mind will have a certain plausibility. In order to evaluate the theory of myth it is necessary first to spell out more clearly what the theory involves.

The fundamental hypothesis of Lévi-Strauss' developed theory of myth is clear and simple: myths make use of 'signs' to establish, to mediate and to transform oppositions. This power of myth exhausts the meaning of myth, and so the specific content of the myth is a matter of indifference.

The first analytical task is to define the object of the analysis, to specify what is to be explained and what is not to be explained by the analysis. In the first place one has to establish what is and what is not a myth. This is not an empirical but a theoretical question, but one to which Lévi-Strauss fails seriously to address himself. It appears that, with characteristic empiricism, Lévi-Strauss believes that the myth presents itself as such to the analysis, and so reliance is placed on the intuition of the analyst.

However, if we examine his practice it becomes apparent that myth is defined by its structure. This is not surprising, for an immanent analysis requires an immanent definition of the object, and so a definition which does not refer, for example, to the cultural function of myth, nor to indigenous conceptions of myth. Folk-tales are distinguished from myth by their weaker structuring, narrative forms replace structures of opposition by structures of reduplication, so taking a serial form. History is like a myth, but differs in its orientation to time, myths being 'instruments for the suppression of time' and so differ in having a non-reversible structure. Ritual, which the traditional Durkheimian interpretation associates closely with myth, is distinguished sharply from the latter in *Mythologiques*, the verbal glosses on ritual being associated with myth, so that ritual is defined solely as a form of behaviour. Myth and ritual are then contrasted on the basis of their structure.

Hence Lévi-Strauss appears implicitly to define myth as that which is structured like a myth. So long as the object in question can be found to have a structure of reduplicated opposition, mediation and transformation, then it is a myth. This implicit definition leads Lévi-Strauss to introduce a sharp division between the myths which he examines and those which have a historical dimension, the latter demanding a 'refined and transformed structural analysis', if they are in fact amenable to such analysis at all.[25] Hence, far from taking myth as a ready-made object, Lévi-Strauss introduces an original definition which leads him to classify interpretations of myth as part of the corpus, while excluding phenomena which have traditionally been seen as mythical.

The definition of myth does not exhaust the problem of defining the corpus, for the ethnographic reports we have are by no means reliable. Moreover Lévi-Strauss does not take these reports as they stand as his starting point in *Mythologiques*, but has normally summarized these reports even further before including them in his own text. The myth has therefore already been filtered twice before being embodied in the corpus to be analyzed: once by the ethnographer, who will have picked out what he regards as being the essential details, and a second time by Lévi-Strauss. But even this filtered corpus is inadequate to the analysis, and Lévi-Strauss not infrequently has to supplement or correct the text in order to permit the analysis to proceed. This correction and supplementation renders the analysis liable to circularity.

Once the corpus has been defined, the analyst still has to establish what he is to explain. According to Lévi-Strauss the analysis must be exhaustive. The analysis can only be exhaustive in relation to a specification of the features of the object which are to be explained. For example, Lévi-Strauss provides no means of reconstructing the order of sequences in the text, nor the grammatical relations between terms, nor the lexical elements through which concepts will be expressed. These aspects of the myth are regarded as being purely contingent, and so not part of the *explanandum*. All that is to be explained is the structure of the myth, the relations subsisting between the terms. Hence, in response to Ricoeur's criticism that Lévi-Strauss concentrates on the 'syntax' of myth at the expense of its 'semantics' Lévi-Strauss notes that

'as far as I am concerned there is no choice. There is no such choice because the phonological revolution . . . consists of the discovery that meaning is always the result of a combination of elements which are not themselves significant . . . in my perspective meaning is always reducible. In other words, behind all meaning there is a non-meaning, while the reverse is not the case. As far as I am concerned, significance is always phenomenal'.[26]

It is, therefore, the theoretical assertion that the meaning of the myth is exhausted by the formal relations between its parts that underlies the isolation and identification of the object of myth analysis as a body of texts which have a particular kind of structure, and, within those texts, as the formal relations embedded in them. The theoretical assertion itself rests on a specific claim about the nature of the mind and the nature of meaning which itself is not examined, but is the *a priori* starting point of the analysis. The analysis cannot, therefore, result in the *discovery* of the structural character of meaning, since that structural character has already been postulated as the basis on which attention is focussed solely on structural characteristics of the object.

Having defined the object of analysis as the formal relations embedded in the myth, we still require some theoretical principles which will enable us to identify those relations. In the first place we have to discover what it is that the relations relate. In the Oedipus analysis, as we have seen, the element of the myth is the mytheme which relates a subject to a function in a sentence of the text. These mythemes are then related oppositionally. In *Mythologiques* the *subject* has ceased to be a part of the mythemes, and the latter is reduced to a predicate. The element is therefore the 'sign' defined in *The Savage Mind* as union of a concept and an image, the image being the means of expression of the concept which enters into the oppositions and transformations of the myth.

This predicate, moreover, is not itself a part of the text, as it was in the Oedipus analysis, but is discovered underlying the image. Once again Lévi-Strauss' empiricism leads him simply to *assert* that this is the element of mythical thought, and there is no clear explanation of the grounds for this assertion.

The element of the myth exists only in the context of the oppositions into which it enters. Hence the question of the identification of the mythical value of specific elements is that of the identification of the constitutive oppositions of the myth.

Before we can identify oppositions we have to define what is to count as an opposition. It is at this stage that the arbitrary, and so formal, character of the analysis becomes apparent. In the Oedipus analysis myth developed on the basis of a contradiction. In *Mythologiques* the element of the myth is a concept and not a belief, and so the oppositions cannot take the form of *contradictions*. Nor do the oppositions take the form of logical contraries, which could give rise to contradictions if items were discovered which had contradictory attributes. In other words the oppositions do not take the form x/not-x, but rather take the form x/y. Unfortunately Lévi-Strauss does not make the fundamental distinctions between the concepts of binary relation, binary opposition, and binary contradiction. As Makarius notes:

'The binary oppositions . . . revealed by the structuralists cover the whole field from a contradictory opposition to the most fragile and arbitrary opposition that could be sketched by a capricious fantasy'.[27]

It seems that myth develops as a result of the introduction of discontinuity to a continuous world which was effected by the birth of culture. The birth of culture introduces meaning to the world by establishing a system of signs, but only at the expense of distinguishing parts of the world from one another and so threatening the fundamental unity of the world. Hence, for example, magical thought associates smoke and clouds because it posits intellectually an identity between the two which has been broken by the discontinuity implicit in conceptualization. While scientific thought will seek the identity by reference to more fundamental properties of smoke and clouds, magical thought will seek the identity by postulating a symbolic relation rather than a real relation. It is because of the fact that 'primary' qualities are often correlated with 'secondary' qualities that 'primitive' thought can frequently anticipate the results of science.

Symbolic thought, therefore, seeks to restore unity to a world differentiated by the intellect.

'all magical operations rest on the recovery of a unity which is . . . unconscious, or less completely conscious than the operations themselves'.[28]

This unity is achieved statically in a classification, and dynamically in myth and magic.

A very similar view is clearly expressed in *L'Homme Nu*:

'In the course of this last part we have verified that several hundred stories, apparently very different from one another, and each very complex in itself, proceed from a series of linked statements: there is the sky, and there is the earth; between the two parity is inconceivable; consequently the presence on earth of that celestial thing which is fire constitutes a mystery; finally, from the moment that the celestial fire is now found here below in the form of the domestic hearth, it must have been the case that one had had to go from the earth up to the sky in order to find it'.[29]

Myth, therefore, attempts to reconcile diversity with unity by mediating and transforming 'oppositions' which are established on the basis of differences.

If we accept provisionally that the element of the myth has been defined correctly, we next have to ask how the oppositions in play are actually discovered. Although Lévi-Strauss refers to the devices of commutation, of permutation, and substitution, these devices cannot uncover the symbolic value of the opposed elements.

Permutation and substitution can identify the contexts in which a particular sensible form can occur, and it can establish the particular forms which can occur in a given context. However, it cannot establish the symbolic value of the form, not least because the same form has different meaning in different contexts, depending on the function assigned by the code governing that context. Hence the meaning of an opposition can only be established once we have identified the code which serves to assign a meaning to it.

Hence:

'Their meanings can only be "positional" meanings, and it follows that they cannot be available to us in the myths themselves, but only by reference to the ethnographic context, i.e. to what we know about the way of life, the techniques, the ritual and the social organization of the societies whose myths we wish to analyze'.[30]

In going beyond the myth to discover the oppositions it would appear that the structuralist enterprise is threatened, for we have to look beyond myth to culture for its fundamental principle. This problem is only avoided by discovering the opposition in the unconscious mind. Its meaning cannot be discovered by reference to the consciously articulated beliefs of the mythologizing culture, any more than it can be discovered by reference to our own conscious representations:

'Consciousness is the secret enemy of the sciences of man in two respects, firstly as the spontaneous consciousness immanent in the object of observation, and secondly as the reflective consciousness (consciousness of consciousness) in the scientist'.[31]

Far from examining the cosmology, Lévi-Strauss has increasingly come round to the view that the oppositions are pre-conceptual, deriving either from nature or from the natural mechanisms of perception:

'everything happens as though certain animals were more ready than others to fill this role, whether by virtue of a striking aspect of their behaviour, or whether, by virtue of a propensity which would also be natural, human thought apprehends more quickly and more easily properties of a certain type. Both come to the same thing, moreover, since no characteristic is striking in itself, and it is perceptual analysis . . . which . . . confers a meaning on phenomena and sets them up as themes'.[32]

This development completes the dissolution of culture into nature, for even the conceptual operations of culture are now simply the expression of natural mechanisms. Culture is now a 'synthetic duplication of mechanisms already in existence'.[33]

The meaning of an opposition can only be established by inspection of the content of the terms themselves. Lévi-Strauss devotes enormous attention to the ecological environment of the cultures under examination and rather less attention to social structural characteristics, in order to discover objective associations which could provide the basis for symbolic oppositions. In this way the oppositions are discovered without having to make any reference to the conscious beliefs of the culture in question.

When we remember how loosely the term 'opposition' is defined we come face to face with the problem of arbitrariness. The myth could single out any one of a large number of properties associated with a particular item and oppose that item to any other item in the same, or even in a different, myth. Hence any item appearing in a myth can be related to any other item within the universe of myth within a 'binary opposition', for a single difference is sufficient to establish an 'opposition'. When we also remember that ethnographic information is scanty, so that interpolation is often necessary, when we also remember that the oppositions are expressed at an extremely abstract level our doubts are only increased.

Lévi-Strauss does offer a methodological guarantee which should limit the arbitrariness of the analysis. Ethnographic observation can provide an 'external criticism'[34] since the association of concept with sensible quality is not arbitrary but must be founded in the objective world.

However, this guarantee is subsequently undermined by the introduction of the concept of the 'transcendental deduction' in which properties are attributed to an item on the basis of the 'logical necessity' of ensuring the consistency of the connections established by 'empirical deduction' on the basis of empirical judgements. In this way the myth progressively creates new symbolic values in order to maintain its consistency.[35]

The irreverent critic is inclined to suspect that the 'logical necessity' is that of a faulty analysis rather than that of the myth. Such a suspicion is confirmed when we remember a further methodological canon which is that the appearance of a contradiction does not indicate that the analysis is in error, but rather 'it proves that the analysis has not been taken far enough, and that certain distinctive features must have escaped detection'.[36] The introduction of the 'transcendental deduction' therefore makes it possible to retain an analysis which cannot be supported, or even which is contradicted, by ethnographic observation.

The identification of oppositions is also supposedly protected from arbitrariness because oppositions do not exist in isolation, but are related to one another by transformations. The myth takes up one opposition, and then engenders others by successive transformation:

'In order for a myth to be engendered by thought, and to engender other myths in its turn, it is necessary and sufficient for an initial opposition to be injected into experience, from which it follows that other oppositions will be engendered in turn'.[37]

Richard notes optimistically:

'The application of the "principles which serve as the basis of structural analysis" (1958a, p. 233) do not seem to guarantee absolutely that the myth has not been solicited to respond to the *a priori* ideas of the analyst.
Nevertheless the constitution of paradigmatic ensembles, of limited number but containing several relations, on the basis of a syntagmatic chain reduces the risk'.[38]

The risk will, however, only be reduced if the transformations are not in their turn arbitrary. Unfortunately what is true of oppositions is equally true of transformations, for the latter are found as easily as are the former.

Lévi-Strauss uses the term 'transformation' extremely loosely, referring to a transformation relation whenever myths can be related to one another. The simplest form of the transformation is found when a pair of myths share a common element, and one or two differences are then claimed to be correlative. It would be very surprising if we could not discover such transformation relations.

Moreover the transformation relations are never established until the myth has already been interpreted and impoverished to some extent, and often to a very considerable extent. R. and L. Makarius have analyzed the supposed set of myths M 7–12, M14, M273 discussed in *From Honey to Ashes*. They show that Lévi-Strauss has to distort and elaborate on the myths quite outrageously in order to establish a supposed cycle of transformations. Maybury-Lewis has shown the circularity of another supposed cycle.[39] Although there are some sets which appear to be more plausibly related (for example, M23–4 and M26; M55 and M7–12; M15–16 and M20; M188–9 and M191), in other cases Lévi-Strauss appears to conjure transformations out of thin air in order to complete an analysis (e.g. RC, pp. 64, 118).

Because Lévi-Strauss insists that myth is the product of an unconscious to which the analyst has no means of access other than through the myth, the analyst has no means of discovering what are and what are not elements, oppositions and transformations of the myth. There is therefore no means of discovering whether the analyst's constructs in fact pertain to the myth, or whether they are simply his or her own creation. Moreover the terms opposition and transformation are applied so loosely that the structures uncovered could be uncovered anywhere. Hence there is not any way of discovering whether the corpus in question is or is not generated by structural mechanisms of the kind outlined. It might conceivably be the case that they are so structured, but there is absolutely no way of discovering this. Hence, finally, there is no justification whatever for concluding that the structures uncovered can tell us anything about the mind.

The conclusion must be that the analysis of myth offered by Lévi-Strauss is necessarily arbitrary. This is not to say that the oppositions do not necessarily have some objective existence, but 'the problem is to decide between them and to determine the significance of any of them'.[40] Since there is no way in which Lévi-Strauss can legitimise his analysis, the oppositions he uncovers can only come from his own mind. As Wilden notes, 'all the "material entities" and "material relations" he employs come to the analysis already defined'[41] and it is Lévi-Strauss who has defined them. If meaning is relegated to the unconscious, there is no means of recovering that meaning. Instead the interpretation derives from the 'flair, aesthetic perception, a certain intellectual form of intuition' of the analyst:

'Sometimes a sort of recognizable click is produced in the mind such that we suddenly apprehend from within something until then apprehended from without'.[42]

The argument that the structural analysis of myth, as practised by Lévi-Strauss, offers an arbitrary interpretation, one imposed by the analyst is best illustrated by reference to the opposition which Lévi-Strauss regards as being the constitutive opposition of all 'primitive' thought, that between nature and culture.

Despite the fundamental importance of the opposition between nature and culture, Lévi-Strauss, with his insistence on the unconscious foundation of meaning, is unable to establish that this opposition is in fact important, or even present, in the thought of the people whom he is studying.

Totemism supposedly counterposes a natural series to a social series, and yet the totems are by no means necessarily natural entities. Caste is similarly analyzed as being based on the opposition between nature and culture, although Dumont, in a structural analysis, argues that the conceptual 'opposition' which dominates the caste system is that between the sacred and the profane.[43] Laura Makarius goes so far as to argue that 'the antithesis which separates and opposes *society* and *nature* to one another is radically foreign to primitive thought'.[44] Makarius examines an analysis of Georgian myths by G. Charachidze which is based on the culture/nature opposition. She argues very convincingly that this presentation of the opposition is to distort the indigenous conception. In fact she shows that the fundamental opposition is that between the respect for prohibitions, which is the basis of society, and the violation of those prohibitions.

As Makarius points out, and as we find repeatedly, the supposed opposition between nature and culture dominates the thought of Lévi-Strauss, more than that of the peoples whom he is studying. The tragedy which confronts Lévi-Strauss is that we have lost respect for nature, have cut ourselves off from it, and are not prepared to live under its rule. The result is that we have come to dominate nature and to violate its rules. It is the 'primitive' who continues to live in harmony with nature, establishing systems of reciprocity in accord with the dictates of human nature, weaving myths under the guidance of the natural unconscious. The role of the nature/culture opposition in Lévi-Strauss' analysis reveals as clearly as could anything that the meaning which he imposes on myths is not at all located in the impenetrable unconscious of the 'primitive', but rather derives from the philosophy which Lévi-Strauss has developed for himself.

# 4 POSITIVISM AND FORMALISM

In looking at Lévi-Strauss' structural analysis of myth we have reached the same conclusion that we reached in looking at Chomsky's structural linguistics. In both cases the positivist approach to cultural phenomena that seeks to cut off the cultural object from any subjective appreciation and to treat it exclusively as an external inert object leads to an analysis that is *arbitrary*, in that there is no means of determining whether or not the properties identified as properties of the object are in fact such, and that is *formalist*, in that any consideration of content that refers beyond the formal relations internal to the object is excluded not on any principled theoretical grounds, but on the basis of an arbitrary methodological decision to exclude consideration of extrinsic connections.

The discovery that the object can be reduced to a formal structure is already inherent in the methodological decision to define the object by its structure (for Chomsky a language is anything structured like a language, for Lévi-Strauss a myth is anything structured like a myth), while the isolation of the object from any environment within which it has a meaning deprives the structure uncovered of any significance. While Chomsky's analysis of language has the merit of rigour, and so is of some practical use, Lévi-Strauss' analysis of myth has not even got such a limited pretension.

Lévi-Strauss himself denies the charge of formalism, but he does so only by reducing the content of the myth to its form:

'Reality shifts from content towards form or, more precisely, towards a new way of apprehending content which, without disregarding or impoverishing it, translates it into structural terms'.[45]

This reduction excludes from consideration what to most

people appear to be essential parts of the myth. A very obvious aspect of this reduction is the elimination from consideration of the narrative structure of the myth, and so of its temporal dimension. Hence 'structural analysis cannot but reveal myths as timeless'.[46]

In reducing myths by fiat to their formal structure, Lévi-Strauss is indeed able to reduce 'meaning to non-meaning', but in so doing he is simply excluding from consideration the meaningful aspects of the myth. Thus Lévi-Strauss does not provide an objective analysis of meaning, he simply dissolves all specific meanings by reducing all myths to a formal structure, 'an abstract representation which obliterates all their specific characteristics'.[47] In abstracting from all specific meaning, in retreating into the depths of his formal unconscious, Lévi-Strauss is retreating into a world of silence, a world of non-meaning, a world of non-communication, or non-reciprocity. Thus he comes to dissolve culture back into nature.

We are now back at our starting point, not seeking to understand myth, but through myth to seek an understanding of human nature, not seeking to understand this or that human being, but seeking to understand what I have in common with all human beings. *Mythologiques* represents one more attempt to dissolve all differences, all culture, all history, all experience, into a formal unconscious structure which is supposedly the basis of our humanity. Lévi-Strauss' attempt to reduce the meaning of myth to an objective, pre-cultural, unconscious results in the dissolution of all meaning. But this is the meaning that the myth has for Lévi-Strauss: *Mythologiques* is an attempt to interpret the universe of myth in the light of Lévi-Strauss' distinctive, and idiosyncratic, human philosophy. It is to this philosophy that we must now turn.

# NOTES

1  *RC*, p. 10.
2  *HN*, pp. 561–2.
3  *SA*, pp. 210–1.
4  *SA*, p. 211.
5  *SA*, p. 229.

208     *The Foundations of Structuralism*

6  1958h.
7  1960f, p. 26.
8  *Tot*, p. 71; *SM*, p. 10; *HN*, 597–611.
9  *Tot*, p. 86.
10  R. and L. Makarius, 'Ethnologie et structuralisme', *L'Homme et la Société*, 3, 1967, p. 187; E. Leach, 'Telstar et les aborigènes ou la pensée sauvage'. *Annales*, 19, 1964, p. 1111; E. Leach, *Lévi-Strauss*, Fontana, London, 1970, p. 87.
11  P. Worsley, 'Groote Eyland, Totemism and *Le Totemism Aujourd'hui*', in E. Leach (ed.) *The Structural Study of Myth and Totemism*, Tavistock, London. 1967; *SM*, pp. 67, 151–8.
12  1936a, p. 300.
13  *SM*, pp. 11, 13, 161; *SA*, p. 230.
14  *SM*, pp. 219, 248n.
15  Worsley, *op. cit*, p. 153.
16  *SM*, pp. 18, 20, 36.
17  *Tot*, p. 13; *SM*, p. 91.
18  *SM*, p. 143. A. Glucksmann, 'La Déduction de la Cuisine et les Cuisines de la déduction', *Information sur les Sciences, Sociales*, 4, 1965, pp. 207–8.
19  *RC*, p. 307; *HA*, p. 356; *HN*, pp. 565–6, *SA*, p. 229.
20  *RC*, p. 13.
21  *HN*, p. 562.
22  *RC*, pp. 12, 341.
23  1965h, p. 28.
24  *HN*, p. 561.
25  *RC*, p. 16; 1970b, p. 61.
26  1970b, p. 64.
27  R. Makarius, 'Lévi-Strauss et les structures inconscientes de l'esprit', *L'Homme et la Société*, 18, 1970, p. 249.
28  *IM*, p. xlvii.
29  *HN*, p. 539.
30  1970h, p. 60.
31  1964f, p. 537.
32  *HN*, pp. 500–1.
33  *ESK*, p. xxx.
34  *RC*, p. 334.
35  1971e, pp. 19–20.
36  *RC*, p. 162.
37  *HN*, p. 540; *RC*, pp. 333–4.
38  P. Richard, 'Analyse des *Mythologiques* de Cl. Lévi-Strauss', *L'Homme et la Société*, 4, 1967, p. 122.
39  L. and R. Makarius, Des jaguars et des Hommes', *L'Homme et la Société*, 7, 1968. pp. 215–35; D. Maybury-Lewis, 'Review of *Du Miel aux Cendres*', in E. and T. Hayes (ed) *Claude Lévi-Strauss* MIT Press, Cambridge, Mass. 1970.
40  Maybury-Lewis, *op. cit.* 1970, p. 159.
41  Wilden, *System and Structure*, Tavistock. London, 1972, p. 9.
42  1967d, p. 3.
43  L. Dumont, *Homo Hierarchicus*, Weidenfeld & Nicolson, London, 1970.

44 L. Makarius, 'L'apothèose de Cinna: mythe de naissance de structuralisme', *L'Homme et la Société*, 22, 1971.
45 *HA*, p. 466.
46 M. Douglas, 'The Meaning of Myth', in Leach (ed.), *op. cit.* 1967, p. 67.
47 Makarius, 1970, *op. cit.* p. 246.

# IX. *The Structuralist Human Philosophy*

IN earlier chapters I have argued that Lévi-Strauss entered anthropology in order to develop a new human philosophy, and I have further argued that it is this philosophy that is expressed in his studies of kinship and of mythical thought. In these specific studies Lévi-Strauss tells us nothing about kinship or myth, about non-literate cultures or societies. He tells us about his theory of the mind and offers an interpretation of systems of kinship and myth in the light of that theory.

It is now time to look more closely at the human philosophy that Lévi-Strauss has developed and that provides the rationale for all his work. In doing so I want to pick up a theme that was introduced in the first two chapters, that of the complementarity of structuralism and phenomenology. I shall do this by discussing the debate between Lévi-Strauss and Sartre that followed the publication of Sartre's *Critique de la Raison Dialectique.*

Lévi-Strauss' ambition is to discover the human essence as the common denominator, the universal characteristic, of every society, and it is this that leads him to abstract from all specific cultural content and to concentrate his analysis on social forms. In the theory of kinship the universal is the universality of the social relation, in the theory of myth it is the universality of the principle of opposition. The universal mental capacity that makes culture and society possible is the ability to learn to relate and to think relationally, the ability to make binary discriminations. This ability was revealed, for Lévi-Strauss, by the phonology developed by Roman Jakobson.

For Lévi-Strauss this universal mental capacity has a natural foundation. Its emergence is the emergence of culture, but it emerges on the basis of a natural change. Hence the relation between nature and culture is central to Lévi-Strauss' human philosophy.

In his earlier work Lévi-Strauss regarded culture and nature as quite distinct orders, but such a dualistic view was philosophically untenable. Since he renounces idealism, the only solution is a reduction of culture to nature. Hence, in his subsequent work, Lévi-Strauss has come to argue that the distinction between the two orders is 'of primarily methodological importance' to be seen as 'an artificial creation of culture'.[1]

This materialism is an essential complement to Lévi-Strauss' Kantianism, and he himself recognizes this: 'only if they (mental constraints, s.c.) can be linked, even indirectly, to conditions prevailing in man's anatomy and physiology, will we be able to overcome the threat of falling back toward some kind of philosophical dualism'. Hence Lévi-Strauss is right to insist on maintaining his contradictory combination of philosophies: 'Paul Ricouer counts at least three interwoven philosophies at the base of my work: a critical philosophy without a transcendental subject, a biological materialism, and a materialism of *praxis* as intermediary between infrastructure and superstructure. Well, I assume these contradictions, they don't trouble me'.[2]

*The Elementary Structures* already contains the core of Lévi-Strauss' philosophy in its guiding theme of the transition from Nature to Culture. *The Elementary Structures* revealed 'primitive' societies that had developed extremely complex social structures responding, according to Lévi-Strauss, to a need for reciprocity, which was at one and the same time a natural need and condition of possibility of society. The contrast between the 'primitive' societies and our own already stood out. European society had shown itself unable to live by the rule of the other, had abandoned reciprocity, turned its back on nature, and must surely be doomed to extinction. These are the themes which Lévi-Strauss has developed in his subsequent works, either positively and directly, or negatively by his panegyric to the supposedly harmonious world of the 'primitive'.

The discovery of structural linguistics in the wake of *The Elementary Structures* was the discovery of a more adequate theory of the unconscious which could provide the foundation for a thoroughly intellectualist, and so rationalist, human philosophy. The discovery also displaced the concept of reciprocity from the centre of the stage, reciprocity becoming a consequence of the symbolic character of the social fact. The symbolic is itself underlain by the formal structuring capacity of the unconscious, supposedly revealed by structural linguistics.

This purely formal unconscious is universal and atemporal, prior to subjective experience and to the temporal modality of that experience. The concept of the unconscious provides the foundation both for the analysis of symbolic thought, culminating in *Mythologiques*, and for the human philosophy, largely developed in two works devoted respectively to Mauss (IM, 1950) and to Rousseau (JJR, 1962), and implicit in *Tristes Tropiques* which offers its most persuasive expression.

The universality of the unconscious dictates that it be the starting point, and the proving ground of sociological explanation. As foundation of the symbolic capacity it underpins the symbolic relation between self and other, providing a common ground on which both can meet, and so the possibility of society. Finally, as the universal and natural characteristic which defines our humanity, the formal unconscious provides the ultimate meaning of human existence, and the means to criticize society in the name of our inherent humanity.

# 1 LÉVI-STRAUSS' HUMAN PHILOSOPHY

In his Introduction to Mauss' *Sociologie et Anthropologie*, Lévi-Strauss argues that the unconscious provides the point of contact between the social and the psychic. The argument is the basis of a theory which Lévi-Strauss would insist is *intellectualist* without falling into the errors of *psychologism*.

The social cannot be reduced to a matter of individual psychology. The individual does not exist outside society, for the defining characteristic of humanity is its symbolic capacity, and the symbolic system is always collective. It is only through membership of a society that individual behaviour can be symbolic, and so human. The conclusion can only be that both sociologism and psychologism must be rejected, the social and psychological being inseparable:

'the two orders are not in a relation of cause and effect to one another . . . but the psychological formulation is only a translation, at the level of the individual psyche, of a properly sociological structure'.[3]

It is the unconscious which serves to tie together the individual and the social, for it is the unconscious which has both the objectivity of the social and the subjectivity of the psychological.

The social is thus an *objective psychic*, and so unconscious, phenomenon. The unconscious is the 'mediating term between the self and the other'.[4]

This theory of the relation between the psychic and the social has considerable interest in itself. On the basis of this theory Lévi-Strauss formulates a theory of shamanism and neurosis.[5] Lévi-Strauss' aim is to show that abnormal behaviour is dependent on the symbolism of society, and not on an individual symbolism. Hence even the most apparently idiosyncratic psychological activity has a social origin. This provides a link between the individual myth of the neurotic and the socially produced myth of the shaman.

The analogy between shamanism and neurosis has often been noted. However shamanism is clearly not simply identifiable with neurosis, if only because the shaman is integrated into the social consensus, while the neurotic is excluded from it. Moreover the 'symptoms' of the shaman do not coincide with the classic symptoms of neurosis.

Lévi-Strauss does not want to argue that shamanism represents simply a particular way of integrating the neurotic into society, but rather that shamanism and neurosis are equally amenable to sociological explanation as the products of a disjunction between the symbolic systems thrown up by society. Hence shamanism does not represent the social integration of an individual pathological condition, but rather neurosis represents a denial of the social character of the pathology in question.

The theory of neurosis/shamanism is not clearly spelt out. In the first version it is argued that normal and pathological thought are complementary in that normal thought 'continually seeks the meaning of things which refuse to reveal their significance', while pathological thought 'overflows with emotional interpretations and overtones, in order to supplement an otherwise deficient reality'. Normal thought therefore suffers from a 'deficit of meaning', while pathological thought disposes of a 'plethora of meaning'. In this version, therefore, normal and pathological thought are two contrasted kinds of thought.

When we turn to the *Introduction to Mauss* we find that the theory has changed. The theory of the surplus of meaning has become directly a theory of myth. Shamanism is now rather different, for the theory is now explaining pathological thought, and not the institution of shamanism, sociologically. The argument is, basically, that every society comprises a number of symbolic systems which, because of differential development, are 'incommensurable'. Hence no society can actually integrate these systems satisfactorily.

The normal person participates nevertheless in society, at which level the illusion, at least, of coherence is offered (hence it is the normal person who, by submitting to society, is alienated). Pathology followed from the refusal to submit to society in this respect, the neurotic is therefore acting out the incommensurability of the various symbolic systems on an individual level. Hence even the 'mentally ill' are thoroughly implicated in the collective symbolism. In fact they play an integrating role by acting out the inconsistencies of the system.

The theory of shamanism is linked to the theories of myth and of magic because the role of the shaman is to create systems of meaning which are variously mythical or magical systems. The unknown is then brought into these systems, and so made meaningful, if not better known. Magical thinking provides 'a new system of reference, within which the thus-far contradictory elements can be integrated':

'We must see magical behaviour as the response to a situation which is revealed to the mind through emotional manifestations, but whose essence is intellectual. For only the history of the symbolic function can allow us to understand the intellectual condition of man, in which the universe is never charged with sufficient meaning and in which the mind always has more meanings available than there are objects to which to relate them'.[6]

This theory of the individual psyche, although not developed by Lévi-Strauss, is extremely important in the development of structuralism, for it is this theory that inspired the psychoanalyst Jacques Lacan to develop a structuralist reinterpretation of Freud along precisely the lines indicated by Lévi-Strauss.

I have already noted Lacan's attempt to use Lévi-Strauss' theory of kinship to justify his identification of the Oedipus complex as the point at which the individual is introduced into his culture when I looked at Juliet Mitchell's work. However Lacan's debt to Lévi-Strauss is more fundamental even than this, for the Oedipus complex is not simply the psychological expression of the principle of reciprocity, it is the expression of the binary structuring capacity that underlies the integration of the individual into the symbolic orders that make up society.

For Lacan, following Lévi-Strauss, the individual psyche is created in the process of socialization in which the individual is assimilated into these symbolic orders, while at the same time being individuated within them. The individual psyche is therefore the meeting point of the empty unconscious structuring capacity and the symbolic orders of society. Thus subjectivity is an illusion, although it is a necessary illusion. It is simply a way of living out a particular mode of integration (or malintegration) into the symbolic orders of society.

Lacan's psychoanalytic theory is not simply a development of Lévi-Strauss' theory. Although interpretations of Lacan differ enormously, his fundamental orientation is very different from Lévi-Strauss' rationalistic positivism. Lacan takes up Lévi-Strauss' structuralism and combines it with an idiosyncratic reading of Freud, within the overall framework of a Heideggerian phenomenological philosophy of language.

Lacan's structuralism differs from that of Lévi-Strauss in two important respects. Firstly, whereas Lévi-Strauss has what is ultimately a biological reductionist theory of the psyche for which intellectual structures are homologous expressions of the biological foundations of the unconscious, Lacan has a theory which tends much more towards cultural idealism, and in this sense is closer to Durkheim than to Lévi-Strauss in seeing the psyche as the product of a series of systems of collective representations. This cultural idealism is even more pronounced in the comparable approach of Foucault.

Secondly, whereas Lévi-Strauss insists that the unconscious is purely formal and rejects what he sees as Freudian irrationalism, Lacan retains the classic Freudian conception of the unconscious. For this reason Lévi-Strauss is emphatic in dissociating himself from Lacan's structuralism:

'We don't feel at all indulgent towards that sleight-of-hand which switches the left hand with the right, to give back to the worst philosophy beneath the table what it claims to have taken from it above; which, simply replacing the self by the other and slipping a metaphysic of desire beneath the logic of the concept, pulls the foundation from under the latter. Because, in replacing the self on the one hand with an anonymous other, and on the other with an individualized desire (even if it designates nothing), there is no way in which one can hide the fact that one need only stick them together again and turn the whole thing round to rediscover on the other side that self whose abolition one has proclaimed with such a fuss'.[7]

Lévi-Strauss insists that his human philosophy is true to the classic principles of humanism in seeking the natural and universal foundation of our common humanity beneath the superficial differences that separate us from one another. It is the structural unconscious that is the guardian of our humanity. It is on the basis of the unconscious that the self and the other, the observer and the observed, are integrated with one another.

The meaning of human existence is simply our integration into a system that rests on a common unconscious foundation, the content of this system being purely contingent, superficial and, ultimately, meaningless. The common meaning of all human existence is given by the common character of all symbolic systems, the structure that underlies them. It is our common unconscious that gives us access to the experience of the other, even if that other is in a society remote from our own, and so makes it possible for us to put ourselves in the place of the other, and to understand the other as another self.

At the same time this provides the anthropologist with the means of validating his or her constructions by trying them on him or herself. It is this experience that provides the ultimate proof of my construction by proving that it is genuinely human.[8] Thus if we ask for proof we are in the end referred back to an intuition, to a privileged experience which is 'less a proof, perhaps, than a guarantee':

'All we need—and for this inner understanding suffices—is that the synthesis, however approximate, arises from human experience'.[9]

In the last analysis what counts is that a construction is *human*, and not that it is *true*. Hence *Mythologiques* opens with a disclaimer:

'it is in the last resort immaterial whether in this book the thought processes of the South American Indians take shape through the medium of my thought, or whether mine take place through the medium of theirs'.[10]

Lévi-Strauss develops his theory of the self through an interpretation of Rousseau. Lévi-Strauss' thought is dominated by the anthropological concerns of the Enlightenment, as he seeks to discover human nature beneath the diversity of human cultures, without dissolving that diversity into the evolutionary continuum of progress. He seeks to show, above all, that humanity is one, that recognition of the humanity of the other is the condition for the realization of one's own humanity, that beneath the diversity of races and cultures we share a universal essense on the basis of which we can relate to one another.

This universal basis is rational, it is Reason itself, not to be identified with the conscious representation of reason offered by any one society. It is scarcely surprising that it is to Rousseau that Lévi-Strauss turns, although his interpretation of Rousseau is, to say the least, idiosyncratic.

For both Rousseau and Lévi-Strauss the self is to be understood by the comparative study of human differences. However, to understand the self we must go beyond the self in order to understand the self as different from the other. For Rousseau the faculty which makes this possible is compassion, *pitié*, in which the other is recognized as another self through the acknowledgement of his or her capacity for feeling and suffering. At the same time, argues Lévi-Strauss, compassion provides for the transition from animality to humanity, from nature to culture, for it is

'the only psychic state of which the content is indissociably both affective and intellectual, and which the act of consciousness suffices to transfer from one level to the other'.[11]

For Lévi-Strauss, the passage from nature to culture is marked by the transition from the affective to the intellectual. Affective identification with the other makes possible an intellectual differentiation from the other.

This leads to a conception of the self radically different from that of the Cartesian philosophical tradition in which Lévi-Strauss was brought up. The notion of personal identity is acquired only by inference and is always marked by ambiguity, since my intimate experience only provides an *other*, an *other* which seems to be thought in me and makes me doubt whether it is I who thinks. Hence the self can only be understood in relation to the other, and is no more than the sum of all these relations.[12] The human being is incessantly strung between identification with all humans and its own specificity, but without the discontinuity which a Cogito supposes.

Only a consciousness founded on this primitive identification, maintains Lévi-Strauss, can act and distinguish itself as it distinguishes others without breaking the identification. The foundation of this philosophy

'rests in a conception of man which puts the other before the self, and in a conception of humanity which puts life before men'.[13]

In studying distant or different societies one is not leaving one's own society behind. It is only by understanding the other that one can understand one's own society by distancing oneself from it and seeing it as other. This is the theme of *Tristes Tropiques*. We study differences in order to uncover similarities, to discover the natural basis of society which we must respect if we are to reform our own society without offending against the dictates of our human nature. The artist and the sociologist both contribute to this discovery 'for the major manifestations of social life have something in common with works of art: namely that they come into being on the level of the unconscious—*because* they are collective, and *although* works of art are individual'.[14]

Lévi-Strauss' human philosophy leads him to counterpose a universal humanism to the particularistic humanism characteristic of our society, and so leads him to the critique of our society in terms of the universal values embodied in nature and expressed through the unconscious.

In *Race and History* (1952) Lévi-Strauss first developed the relativistic implications of his philosophy, condemning the 'ethnocentric attitude' which seeks to reduce the diversity of cultures. In particular he appeals for caution in the application of the concept of 'progress' to cultures other than our own. The true value of any culture does not lie in its contribution to an evolutionary progression, rather 'the true contribution of a culture consists . . . in its difference from others', and our obligation is to resist the reduction of this diversity.[15]

In *Race and History* Lévi-Strauss links the relativist plea for tolerance towards other cultures to the self-interest of our own culture. In *Tristes Tropiques* the theme is developed, while being turned into a critical weapon with which Lévi-Strauss attacks his own society. The value of diversity now lies not so much in its contribution to the progressive development of humankind as in the knowledge of humans it makes possible, a knowledge which alone makes it possible for us to measure our own society against the demands imposed by human nature.

*Tristes Tropiques* remains an optimistic work, the knowledge of the natural human being acquired by anthropology being applied to the reform of our own society. At the same time, while Lévi-Strauss retains his relativist stance, it is clear where his sympathies lie. It is not our society which offers the closest approximation to a society which accords with the dictates of human nature, but rather is that of the neolithic age which, as Rousseau put it, is 'halfway between the indolence of primitive man and the feverish activity of our self-esteem'.[16] It is in the 'primitive' societies of Brazil that Lévi-Strauss finds the principle of reciprocity expressed, and it is in the thought of these peoples that the world is harmonious and ordered, culture at one with nature. These victims of progress express, within the confines of their small societies, the secret of humanity which our own society denies.

Since 1960 Lévi-Strauss has pushed his critique of his own society to its limits, developing the contrast between our society and that of the 'primitive' into an antithesis. The fall is identified with the introduction of writing which underpins human exploitation of one another and so, by internalizing inequality, gives rise to a cumulative history. Ultimately it is the expansion of population which, by upsetting the balance between humanity and nature, gives rise to ever-increasing exploitation of humans and of nature. Western humanism is the ideological expression appropriate to this society based on the separation of humanity from nature, and so of humans from one another, and on the exploitation of the one by the other.[17]

Our society is, therefore, the very antithesis of those values which are embodied in the 'primitive' society, those values which are imposed on the latter by the unconscious. Our society denies those values, exploitation replacing reciprocity in social life, with social relations becoming increasingly inauthentic as they become increasingly impersonal. Our society is based on 'the total power of man over nature and . . . the power of certain forms of humanity over others'. Our humanism is the converse of that which myth shows to us, a 'well-ordered humanism' which 'does not begin with itself, but puts things back in their place. It puts the world before life, life before man, and the respect of others before love of self'.[18]

An authentic humanism must be based on a rejection of the validity of individual experience and of the manner in which the individual experiences the temporality of his or her existence, in favour of a search for the ultimate meaning of human existence in a universal, objective, and atemporal unconscious. Only thus will a humanism which only validates the self at the expense of the other be a truly universal humanism, a humanism which

'proclaims that nothing human should be foreign to man and so founds a democratic humanism which is opposed to those which have preceeded it: created for the privileged, on the basis of privileged civilizations'.[19]

The basis of this humanism is a recognition of the natural foundation of humanity. It therefore rests more fundamentally on a respect for nature as the presupposition of a respect for the natural ties among men and women.[20]

In *Race and History* anthropology was assigned a reforming role. In *Tristes Tropiques* there was still a possibility of salvation. More recently, however, Lévi-Strauss has concluded that our society has become so large and complex that it is no longer thinkable. Even if we could understand it, we could still not change it. It is, therefore, too late for humanity to be saved. All that the anthropologist can do is to observe and condemn. The only thing we can do is to study the 'primitive' to uncover those ' "values" which have tended to be neglected and which are probably condemned'.[21]

The philosopher's task is not to eulogize the human, it is to 'dissolve' it, to destroy its pretensions, to restore it to nature as an object among objects:

For, if it is true that nature expelled man, and that society persists in oppressing him, man can at least invert the poles of the dilemma to his advantage, *and seek the society of nature there to meditate on the nature of society*'.[22]

## 2 SARTRE'S INCORPORATION OF STRUCTURES IN THE DIALECTIC

As Lévi-Strauss has developed his human philosophy he has

sharpened his antagonism to that liberal humanism of which existentialism is a prime example. He has therefore reacted very sharply to Sartre's attempt to incorporate the findings of *The Elementary Structures of Kinship* into Sartre's own work. This is the basis of the 'debate' between the two.

Sartre's discussion of *The Elementary Structures* in the *Critique* takes up an argument first developed by Lefort.[23] Lefort rejected Lévi-Strauss' attempt to seek an unconscious foundation for exchange and to reduce exchange to a formal structure on the grounds that such an attempt dissolves and denies the experience of exchange which, for Lefort, is the only possible source of the meaning of exchange. For Lefort exchange is the experience of a totalizing *praxis*. It is not a formal mechanism for the resolution of unconscious oppositions, but rather an expression of the mutual recognition of men.

This critique focusses on Lévi-Strauss' inability to explain, or to account for, experience and history. However, Lefort's account has its own weakness, for in assimilating history to experience, and making history the product of the conscious *praxis* of individuals, Lefort is unable to explain the systematic interrelations of contemporaneous events, the structure.

One of the major aims of Sartre's *Critique of Dialectical Reason* is to overcome this weakness, to provide some means of explaining structure as the product of *praxis*, and it is in relation to Lévi-Strauss' work that Sartre raises the question. Sartre is well aware of the threat posed to his philosophy by Lévi-Strauss' structuralism.

Sartre tries to show, with reference initially to *The Elementary Structures*, that the possibility of such a theory is strictly circumscribed, that structure is necessarily subordinate to *praxis*.

While Lévi-Strauss denies that experience and history have any privilege, for Sartre the meaning of human existence is founded precisely in the historicity of the individual conscious experience. For Sartre the meaning of existence is given by the *project* that gives that existence direction. Human activity has meaning because it plays a part in a teleological historical process of which he or she is the subject.

The action is inserted in a system, but that system is one which unfolds diachronically, not one which exists synchronically. It is a system which is continuous, in which the parts are related dialectically, and not one which is discontinuous and in which the parts are related by analytical relations of opposition. Hence Sartre is preoccupied with the problem of the meaning of history, of the meaning of his or her personal history for the individual, and the meaning of their collective history for individual members of the group. The present for Sartre can only be understood as a moment in a continuous, but dialectical, historical development.

Hence Sartre tries to show, in the *Critique*, that the structure is in fact the product of 'organized *praxis*'. The structure only appears as inert and constraining to the outside observer, the demonstration of the necessity of the structure by this observer is 'no more than a mediation'.

The structure is, in fact, the free creation of the praxis of the individual members of the group, who pledge themselves to the group and so accept the structure as the means by which the group will achieve its collective aims. The relationship of the individual to the group, and to its structure, is therefore a reciprocal relationship in which each individual agrees to play his or her part in a common enterprise, the attempt to combat scarcity. The submission of the individual to the structure is, therefore, a free act, and so is a 'freely accepted condition'.

The structure is perpetuated only insofar as each individual *praxis* continues to seek to preserve the existing relation of the individual to the structure, and changes insofar as individuals seek to change that relation. However, because individuals pledge themselves to the group as a means to an end which they share with their fellow members, they treat the group as a '*quasi-object*', but 'the group as a totality or an objective reality does not exist' as anything other than its treatment as such by the individuals who participate in it. It is in this sense that Sartre calls the structures the 'necessity of freedom'.[24]

For Sartre, then, the structure is 'only imposed on us to the extent that it is made by others. To understand how it is made, it is therefore necessary to reintroduce *praxis*, as the totalizing process. Structural analysis must give way to a dialectical understanding'.

For Sartre structure only comes to have meaning when it is integrated into the totalizing activity of a transcendent subject: 'The essence is not what one makes of man, but what he makes of what one has made of him'. The analytic reason which uncovers the objective structure is a constituted reason which can only be validated ultimately by reference to the constitutive reason of the totalizing subject: 'Dialectical reason is itself the intelligibility of positivist Reason'.[25]

For Sartre the human essence is the power of transcendence, the ability to say no, and so to make oneself out of the materials at one's disposal. This is not simply the truth of the human in one particular society, it is the universal truth of humanity: 'Even the most archaic, the most immobile societies . . . have a history'.[26] The way in which people experience this transcendence differs in time and space. In a stagnant society human *praxis* takes the form of a repetition. The fact that in such a society history takes the form of repetition does not mean that the society is without history.

# 3 LÉVI-STRAUSS' SUBORDINATION OF THE DIALECTIC TO STRUCTURE

Sartre does not contest Lévi-Strauss' analysis of kinship in *The Elementary Structures*, and indeed picks up several themes of the latter work (e.g. scarcity, reciprocity). His concern is only with the significance of the structures which Lévi-Strauss claims to have uncovered.

Where Lévi-Strauss assimilates the structures to the objectivity of an inert unconscious, Sartre seeks to grasp them as the residue of the conscious *praxis* of individuals. It is the meaning of human action, and above all the status of experience, which is in question.

Lévi-Strauss denies that the human is transcendent. If the human is not transcendent, argues Lévi-Strauss, then history cannot be dialectical, in Sartre's sense, for we cannot create, we can only reorganize what is given to us.

The subject of history is not a self-conscious historical subject, but is the atemporal structural unconscious. History itself is simply the unfolding through time of systems imposed by the structure of the unconscious. History is simply a transformation, the result of external and contingent forces. History has no meaning and progress is an illusion.

Historical consciousness is simply a myth like any other by which societies such as ours choose to rationalize their existence. Some societies conceptualize time discontinuously, using events in an ahistorical, timeless way, contrasting them with the present. In this kind of myth we find two juxtaposed series, the original series being some kind of transformation of the contemporaneous series, the relation between the two being explicitly conceptualized as discontinuous, a transformation. The 'primitive', or 'cold', society attempts to annul history, it attempts to preserve the structure in the face of threats posed to that structure by events by admitting the latter 'as a form without a content'. In such societies the past is integrated into the present either as a reflection (which may be an inversion) or as a repetition (in the form of periodicity).[27]

In societies such as ours events are not juxtaposed in this way, but are arranged in a succession, characterized by continuity. The present is rationalized as a development out of the past, rather than as a transformation or repetition of the latter. However, these historical myths are no different in form from the 'primitive' kind, they still make use of a code, still introduce discontinuity into the order of events, still select some events which are endowed with historical (mythical) significance and ignore others. This historical consciousness, which Sartre privileges, is derivative in relation to history itself, which is genuinely continuous and infinite, and hence beyond our understanding. It is, therefore, very important not to confuse the myth of historical consciousness with the reality of historical development in imagining that the former can give access to the latter.

As soon as we stand back from the myth of historical consciousness, argues Lévi-Strauss, its mythical character becomes clear. The code on which it is based is not pre-ordained, natural in some way, it is arbitrary. The criteria by which we select events from the past to endow the present with significance, and to inflate our own importance as agents of the development of past through present to future, are culturally defined and constitute the code of the myth of history. Different social groups may experience 'history' according to different codes. For example, the meaning of the French Revolution is quite different for the Left and for the Right.

For Lévi-Strauss Sartre's philosophy is simply an expression of the particular way in which temporality is experienced in his own society. Hence, for Lévi-Strauss, it is not dialectical reason which accounts for analytic reason, but rather analytic reason which accounts for dialectical. Sartre takes the conscious rationalization of his own culture for the ultimate meaning of humanity. Sartre can teach us about his own culture, whose 'dialectical movement' he grasps 'with incomparable artistry',[28] but by confining himself to the conscious expressions of social life he denies himself access to the universality of the unconscious which underlies it. Sartre is, therefore, an historian and not an anthropologist, for

'History organizes its data in relation to the conscious expressions of social life, while anthropology proceeds by examining its unconscious foundation'.[29]

History is concerned with process, which is the modality under which the unfolding of the structural is experienced:

'Structures only appear to the observer from outside. . . . Inversely the outsider can never grasp the processes, which are not analytic objects, but the particular way in which a temporality is experienced by a subject'.[30]

The process with which we are concerned does not represent the temporal development of a transcendent subject making his or her history. It is something passively experienced. Temporality is therefore not a product but an experience of consciousness. Lévi-Strauss uses the term 'history', among other things, to denote this experience, and the study of this experience, and the products of that study.

'The supposed totalizing continuity of the self . . . seems to me to be an illusion sustained by the demands of social life—and consequently a reflection of the external on the internal—rather than the object of an apodictic experience'.[31]

If we are to go beyond the 'practical' to the 'theoretical', if we are to go beyond the weaving of myths to the development of knowledge about humanity we have to recognize that the meaning of the conscious elaborations of social life is purely relative and subjective. Behind it lies a deeper meaning:

'All meaning is answerable to a lesser meaning, which gives it its highest meaning, and if this regression finally ends in recognizing "a contingent law of which one can only say: *it is thus*, and not otherwise" (Sartre, 1960, p. 128), this prospect is not alarming to those whose thought is not tormented by transcendance even in a latent form'.[32]

The only way around the dilemma posed by the alternatives of ethnocentrism and relativism is to found our anthropology on the unconscious, which is objective while underpinning the subjective. The philosophers of the subject are more concerned with retaining the status of the subject than with rendering humanity intelligible:

'they prefer a subject without rationality to a rationality without a subject'.[33]

Instead we must look beyond the conscious and the affective to find behind it the unconscious and the intellectual. Anthropology must dedicate itself to the study of the unconscious processes which underlie social life by understanding societies as different expressions of these unconscious processes.

# 4 THE COMPLEMENTARITY AND IRRECONCILABILITY OF STRUCTURAL AND DIALECTICAL INTELLIGIBILITY

The opposition between Sartre and Lévi-Strauss appears to be total, each recognizing the validity of the other's account, but reducing it to a subordinate moment of a process whose foundation lies elsewhere. For Lévi-Strauss the constructions of the conscious are rationalizations whose true meaning is only reached through a structural analysis which reduces them to their unconscious, and ultimately to their organic, foundation. For Sartre the structures which are produced by this analysis are abstracted from the living *praxis* which produces them, which alone gives them meaning and to which a true anthropology will restore them. While for Lévi-Strauss human existence only becomes meaningful when it is assimilated to the nature from which it emerges, for Sartre nature only has meaning in relation to the projects of the individuals who transcend it.

The opposition between Sartre and Lévi-Strauss also appears to be insurmountable, for each points to fundamental *lacunae* in the other's account. On the one hand, Sartre presents a particular experience as the indubitable foundation of all human existence. It is simply necessary for Lévi-Strauss to cast doubt on the universality of this experience for Sartre's construction to be revealed as a house of cards:

'What Sartre calls dialectical reason is only a reconstruction, by what he calls analytical reason, of hypothetical moves about which it is impossible to know . . .

whether they bear any relation at all to what he tells us about them and which, if so, would be definable in terms of analytical reason alone'.[34]

On the other hand, Lévi-Strauss' own account is deficient in reducing history to the impact of contingency[35] and in reducing experience, including the experience of freedom which is the basis of Sartre's philosophy, to the status of a myth.

Lévi-Strauss' confidence in the determinant character of the unconscious is as unfounded as is Sartre's confidence in the creative historical consciousness. Each seeks to reduce objective social phenomena to processes which render aspects of the object inexplicable. Sartre cannot explain the objective laws of social phenomena, laws which are neither created by conscious subjects, nor which operate through the consciousness of those subjects. Correspondingly, Lévi-Strauss cannot account for such objective laws insofar as they are not reducible to 'an unconscious teleology . . . which rests on the interplay of biological mechanisms . . . and psychological ones',[36] insofar as they are *social* and not simply *natural* laws.

It turns out that both Sartre and Lévi-Strauss offer us anthropological theories based on contrasted philosophies each of which is fundamentally incomplete. For Sartre the objectivity of the social world is dissolved into the subjectivity of lived *praxis*. Lévi-Strauss, in trying to avoid the metaphysical implications of Durkheim's sociology, simply transfers the metaphysical principle from a collective reality beyond to a biological reality beneath the individual. In each case the principle which supposedly regulates social life turns out on inspection to be a moral principle which tells us not what social life is, but what it ought to be, not how society operates, but how the individual should live in society. In each case a moral theory appears in the guise of a scientific theory, a moral imperative is treated as though it were an objective imperative.

At the beginning of this book I indicated that the philosophies of both Sartre and Lévi-Strauss emerged as complementary responses to a common problem. We are now in a position to identify the expression of that initial ideological problem in their philosophies. Moreover we can see that it is in the way that they both pose this problem that the errors they both make are inscribed. Hence the way to go beyond the dilemma which the contrast between Sartre and Lévi-Strauss presents to us is not to attempt to synthesize the work of both, but rather to reformulate the problem with which they began.

Ideologically the problem which confronted Sartre, Lévi-Strauss and their generation was that of establishing a basis on which an isolated individual could relate to a society which offered no point of insertion. The problem appears in the work of Sartre and Lévi-Strauss as that of developing a moral theory in which moral guidance would come solely from within the individual. Hence each tried to develop a moral theory whose starting point is those abstract and universal features which define the individual as human. Each then constructed a world in which human existence represented simply the realization of these human features in the individual's relationship to the world. Finally each sought to demonstrate that the world we live in is characterized by the violation of the human essence, of the defining features of humanity.

The problems faced by the philosophies of Sartre and Lévi-Strauss when they present themselves as theories of society derive from the selection of the supposedly abstract and universal features of the human essence as the starting point, for this initial abstraction of the individual from society leads to the subsequent confrontation of the individual with a society which is abstracted from the individuals who participate in it.

This 'society' is immediately seen to be a metaphysical entity which the philosopher must dissolve at once. For Sartre, 'the group does not possess the metaphysical existence of a form or a *Gestalt*, of a collective consciousness or a created totality', while for Lévi-Strauss the unconscious is introduced precisely to exorcise the Durkheimian collective conscience.[37] Hence society is abolished, formalistically reintegrated into the individual as an abstract category which is either the subjective product of a consciousness or the objective product of an unconscious.

For both Sartre and Lévi-Strauss society is in no sense a *sui generis* reality, for both it is simply an expression of a dialectic inscribed in the individual, conscious or unconscious, psyche. It is, therefore, scarcely surprising that neither is able to provide the basis on which we might begin to explain the laws which govern society, laws which are both objective and meaningful, both things and representations.

In both cases the problems arise because the individual is not defined from the start as a social being, inserted in concrete social relations, but rather as an abstract, asocial and ahistorical individual from whom society must be derived. In each case the idealistic consequences of such arguments are dissipated by metaphysical devices (in the case of Sartre with a metaphysic of scarcity, in the case of Lévi-Strauss with a biological materialism) which present society as the product of the direct relationship of the individual to nature.

For a social science, by contrast, the starting point can only be a social being, the recognition that what sets humans apart from nature is precisely their social character, which is in turn inseparable from their engagement in society. Such a recognition implies immediately that society cannot be derived from the human essance, nor can it be derived from the unmediated relation of humanity to nature, for both the distinction of humanity from nature, and its relation to nature, presuppose the society in which people are engaged, and through which alone they relate to nature.

Sartre and Lévi-Strauss, therefore, offer us complementary philosophics which seek to renounce the social and to rediscover our humanity within the individual. Lévi-Strauss is concerned to uncover a universal and objective meaning, while Sartre seeks a totalizing and subjective meaning. For Sartre there is only a universal meaning if there is a universal totalization, for Lévi-Strauss the subjective meaning is only true if the subject abandons him or herself to the rule of the objective universal. In each case the meaning of human existence is sought in a confrontation of the asocial individual with an inert nature.

While such philosophies are themselves meaningful as responses to a society in which our humanity appears systematically deformed, we must ask whether philosophies which recover this humanity only at the expense of rendering incomprehensible the society in which that humanity has been taken from us are really satisfactory. A satisfactory philosophy must find a meaning for human existence at the point at which the individual engages with the world, the point at which we have meaning for the world of which we are a part, at the same time as the world has meaning for us. It is precisely this point which is abolished by both Sartre and Lévi-Strauss, for it is only in society, in the collective realm of social relations, of language and of culture, that we are integrated into the objective world.

It is only by means of these institutions that as subjectivities we are able to engage with the world, and it is only through these institutions that the objective constraints which the facticity of the world imposes are mediated. If this is the case, then the meaning of human existence must be located in relation to the collective institutions of society through which alone we acquire our humanity. Both Sartre and Lévi-Strauss offer an abstract, contemplative morality which is unable to provide any guidance for those who cannot afford not to live in society precisely because their morality has no point of engagement with society. It is unable either to offer a diagnosis of the evils of the existing society, or to indicate any means of changing it.

Hence an adequate philosophy, no less than an adequate sociology, depends on a renunciation of the dichotomization of the individual and society. It depends on a recognition that the subject is constituted as such in the context of a society which alone articulates the relation between the subject and other subjects and between the subject and nature:

'Both the material of labour and man as the subject, are the point of departure as well as the result of the movement. . . . Thus the *social* character is the general character of the whole movement: *just as* society itself produces *man as man*, so is society *produced* by him. . . . The *human* aspect of nature exists only for *social* man; for only then does nature exist for him as a *bond* with *man*—as his existence for the other and the other's existence for him—and as the life-element of human reality. Only then does nature exist as the *foundation* of his own *human* existence. Only here has what is to him his *natural* existence become his *human* existence, and nature become man for him. Thus *society* is the complete unity of man with nature—the true resurrection of nature—the accomplished naturalism of man and the accomplished humanism of nature'.[38]

# 5 CONCLUSION

The classical philosophical opposition between subject and object offers an unsound basis on which to construct a theory of society. Theories based on either pole of this opposition find themselves unable to grasp the social, which insists on falling between the two terms, not reducible to either. The one-sidedness of theories which base themselves on one pole finds its complement in the one-sidedness of theories which base themselves on the other. The stage is set for an interminable and irresoluble debate, from which society itself is firmly excluded.

In order to come to terms with society it is necessary to overcome this opposition. The opposition cannot, however, be abolished by fiat, for the external and objective character of the typical social relations of our society is something with which sociology must come to terms. It is necessary to uncover the historical relativity of the opposition, to uncover the historic conditions under which social relations assume this objective power, a power which cannot be reduced to the individual will, but which cannot be divorced from it either.

Hegel tried to overcome this opposition between subject and object, but he did so only formalistically, in a speculative way. Instead of offering an account which could establish the 'subjective' and 'objective' as moments of a historical process in which they become dissociated, Hegel identified the two immediately, seeing the latter as the 'immanentization' of the former:

'Thus empirical reality is admitted just as it is and is also said to be the rational; but not rational because of its own reason, but because the empirical fact in its empirical existence has a significance which is other than itself. The fact, which is the starting point, is not conceived to be such but rather to be the mystical result.'[39]

Hegel simply identified the real and the rational, locating the inhuman rationality of the real in the suprahuman Idea. This speculative identification of real and rational was so unsatisfactory that it hardly outlasted Hegel, leaving a rather tired Hegelian dialectic in a 'wholly abstract, "speculative", form', to contest the old metaphysical materialism, which 'held the field by its superiority in positive knowledge', even though it 'had been so annihilated theoretically by Kant and particularly by Hegel'.[40]

Marx realized in the works of his youth that society was the point at which real and rational, subject and object, met one another, and, correspondingly, that it is on the basis of society that we have to understand the opposition between the two, and not *vice versa*.

Marx realized that the opposition between subject and object, rational and real, is not a universal opposition between eternal categories, but is a specific historical product, expressed in classical European philosophy, emerging on the basis of the development of commodity relations. The opposition between subject and object is itself a product of the process of exchange, expressing the contrast between moments of exchange which is established by exchange itself:

'Circulation is the movement in which the general alienation appears as general appropriation and general appropriation as general alienation. As much, then, as the whole of this movement appears as a social process, and as much as the individual moments of this movement arise from the conscious will and particular purposes of individuals, so much does the totality of the process appear as an objective interrelation, which arises spontaneously from nature; . . . Circulation, because a totality of the social process, is also the first form in which the social relation appears as something independent of the individuals, but not only as, say, in a coin or in exchange value, but extending to the whole of the social movement itself. The social relation of individuals to one another as a power over the individuals which has become autonomous . . . is a necessary result of the fact that the point of departure is not the free social individual.'[41]

The concept of the subject developed by classical European philosophy is itself a product of the development of commodity relations:

'Man as a moral subject, that is as a personality of equal worth, is indeed no more than a necessary condition for exchange according to the law of value. Man as a legal subject, or as a property-owner, is a further necessary condition. Finally, these two stipulations are extremely closely connected with a third, in which man figures as a subject operating egoistically.

All three of these seemingly imcompatible stipulations which are not reducible to one and the same thing, express the totality of conditions necessary for the realization of the value relation. . . .

The net result of abstracting these definitions from the actual social relation they express, and attempting to develop them as categories in their own right (by purely speculative means), is a confused jumble of contradictions and mutually exclusive propositions'.[42]

'Because M. Proudhon places eternal ideas, the categories of pure reason, on the one side and human beings and their practical life, which according to him is the application of these categories, on the other, one finds with him from the beginning a *dualism* between life and ideas, between soul and body, a dualism which recurs in many forms. You can see now that this antagonism is nothing but the incapacity of M. Proudhon to understand the profane origin and the profane history of the categories which he defies.'[43]

It is the theory of commodity fetishism, which is the basis of *Capital*, that enables Marx to get beyond the classical opposition by revealing the foundation of that opposition in society. The

supposedly eternal and irreconcilable categories are themselves
but an aspect of commodity fetishism, eternizing an opposition
which is a specific historical result of commodity production. It is
correspondingly the theory of commodity fetishism that is the
foundation of Marx's attempt to understand the external, objective and constraining character of social relations which are
themselves human products. The theory of fetishism not only
showed 'that human relations were veiled relations between
things, but rather that, in the commodity economy, social
production relations inevitably took the form of things and could
not be expressed except through things'.[44] With the theory of
commodity fetishism it became possible to understand society as
an *objective field* of *human activity*.

To argue that the classical philosophical opposition between the
subject and the object is an expression of the development of
commodity relations is not to offer a reductionist argument:

'The economics of value relations provides the key to an understanding of the
juridical and ethical structure, not in the sense of the concrete content of legal or
moral norms, but in the sense of the form itself.'[45]

The content which is expressed through this form can vary, and
has varied, enormously. The same form can mobilize the bourgeois
critique of feudal or socialist social relations in the name of the
freedom and equality of commodity relations. It can mobilize the
petit-bourgeois critique of the socializing tendencies inherent in
capitalist development. It can even mobilize the Utopian socialist
critique of the exploitation characteristic of capitalist production.

The work of Sartre and Lévi-Strauss represents a twentieth-
century version of the Utopian critique. Their critique of
contemporary society is made *from the standpoint of the asocial
individual, in the name of a universal principle of reciprocity between subjects*.
But the apparently universal critic, and the apparently universal
principle are both products of the society to which they are
applied.

The apparently rootless, isolated, asocial individual who experiences society as an alien force is a social product, a specific
'historic result':

'the product on the one side of the dissolution of the feudal forms of society, on
the other side of the new forces of production developed since the sixteenth

century', for whom the 'various forms of connectedness confront the individual as a mere means towards his private purposes, as external necessity. But the epoch which produces this standpoint, that of the isolated individual, is also precisely that of the hitherto most developed (from this standpoint, general) relations'.[46]

The isolated individual, subject of society, is the product of the emergence of commodity exchange which relates these subjects by impersonal, objective bonds.

'But it is an insipid notion to conceive of this merely *objective bond* as a spontaneous, natural attribute inherent in individuals and inseparable from their nature (in antithesis to their conscious knowing and willing). This bond is their product. It belongs to a specific phase of their development. . . . It is the bond natural to individuals within specific and limited relations or production.'[47]

The Utopian socialism of the nineteenth century contrasted the freedom and equality of exchange relations of commodity *circulation* with the exploitation and domination of capitalist relations of production, aspiring to the petit-bourgeois Utopia of a society of independent petty commodity producers. As Marx constantly pointed out, and as the history of Utopian projects revealed, Utopianism took for a *deformation* what is in fact the inevitable *result* of the generalization of commodity relations, and called for the return to a supposed golden age whose historic product was precisely capitalist exploitation.

The philosophies of Sartre and Lévi-Strauss represent, in a sense, a twentieth-century version of this same Utopianism. They criticize their own society from the standpoint of the subject, condemning exploitation and domination, the treatment of the other as an *object*, in the name of the universal human value of reciprocity as the relation between free and equal individual subjects.

However, in the era of monopoly capitalism there is little prospect of a restoration of petty commodity production. Sartre and Lévi-Strauss can only offer, therefore, a contemplative and impotent critique, which bases itself on a truly human exchange, and not on the deformed exchange which is characteristic of a developed capitalist society.

Thus Lévi-Strauss counterposes a ubiquitous exchange (a 'total social fact'), which he finds realized in 'primitive' societies, to the domination which characterizes our own society. Sartre, following

Proudhon in that 'he calls the subjective precisely what is social and he calls society a subjective abstraction'[48] anticipates a contemplative transformation. Contemplation will recapture the essence of social relations as reciprocal relations between free subjects. Even the most downtrodden citizen can recover his or her subjectivity, and so discover his or her own ability to reinstate the rule of reciprocity.

The problems from which Sartre and Lévi-Strauss set off were concrete and specific problems posed to them as isolated intellectuals in a period of social upheaval. In the development of their philosophies too we can trace the impact of concrete events. At the same time the philosophies which are developed in these specific situations claim universal significance. We can now see that this is possible because classical philosophy offers categories which make it possible to translate specific experiences into eternal truths. Problems which represent the specific and very concrete expression of a society based on commodity production find their appropriate intellectual form in the categories of classical philosophy which represent the most abstract expression of the same social relation. In this translation, however, the concrete historical conditions which gave rise to the initial problem are dissolved, and the philosophy developed can do no more than counterpose eternal values to an undifferentiated reality in a contemplative critique.

# NOTES

1 *ESK*, p. xxix.
2 1973c, pp. 19–20; 1967d, p. 16.
3 *IM*, p. xvi.
4 *IM*, pp. xxx–xxxi.
5 1949b; 1949c; *IM*.
6 *SA*, p. 184.
7 *HN*, p. 563.
8 *IM*, p. xxx; 1967e, p. 16; *JJR*, p. 241.
9 1967a, pp. 14, 16.
10 *RC*, p. 13.
11 *Tot*, p. 101
12 *JJR*, p. 242; *HN*, pp. 539–40; 1964a, p. 5.
13 *JJR*, p. 243.
14 *TT*, p. 124.
15 1952a, pp. 21, 42.

236 *The Foundations of Structuralism*

16 Quoted Lévi-Strauss, 1965a, p. 50.
17 1965a, p. 30; 1969a, pp. 30-1; *JJR*, pp. 245-7.
18 *SA*, pp. 366-7; 1958a, p. 30; 1967b, p. 31; 1972a, p. 80, *JJR*, p. 243.
19 1956a.
20 *JJR*, p. 247.
21 1976b, p. 31.
22 *JJR*, p. 245.
23 Cl. Lefort, 'L'échange et la lutte des hommes,' *Temps Modernes*, 6, 64, 1951; Cl. Lefort, 'Sociétés 'sans histoire' et historicité', *Cahiers Internationaux de Sociologie*, 12, 1952.
24 Sartre, 1976, pp. 483-93.
25 J. P. Sartre, *Critique of Dialectical Reason*, NLB, London, 1976, pp. 43, 89, 95.
26 J. P. Sartre, 'J. P. Sartre répond,' *L'Arc*, 30, 1966, p. 90.
27 Lévi-Strauss' reply to Sartre is *SM*, Chapter 8.
28 *SM*, p. 250.
29 *SA*, p. 18.
30 1962a, pp. 44-5.
31 *SM*, p. 256.
32 *SM*, p. 255.
33 *HN*, p. 614.
34 *SM*, p. 254.
35 *SM*, p. 73; *ESK*, p. 268; 1966c, p. 55.
36 *SM*, p. 252.
37 Sartre, 1976, *op. cit.* pp. 496-7; *SA*, p. 65.
38 K. Marx, *Collected Works*, 3, Lawrence & Wishart, London, 1975, p. 298.
39 K. Marx, *Critique of Hegel's Philosophy of Right*, CUP, 1970, p. 9.
40 F. Engels.
41 Marx, 1973, pp. 196-7. K. Marx, *Grundrisse*, Penguin, Harmondsworth, 1973, pp. 196-7.
42 E. Pashukanis, *Law and Marxism*, Ink Links, 1978, pp. 151-2.
43 K. Marx, *The Poverty of Philosophy*, FLPH, Moscow, n.d., p. 183.
44 I. Rubin, *Essays on Marx's Theory of Value* Black and Red, Detroit, 1972, p. 6.
45 Pashukanis, *op. cit.* p. 152.
46 Marx, 1973, *op. cit.* pp. 83-4.
47 *Ibid.*, p. 162.
48 *Ibid*, pp. 164-5.

# Abbreviations used in Bibliography

| | |
|---|---|
| AJS | = American Journal of Sociology |
| Am. Anth. | = American Anthropologist |
| Ann. de l'EPHE | = Annuaire de l'Ecole Pratique des Hautes Etudes, section Sciences Religieuses |
| Arch. Europ. Soc. | = Archives Européennes de Sociologie |
| Bijd. | = Bijdragen tot de Taal-, Land-en Volkenkunde |
| Cah. Int. Soc. | = Cahiers Internationaux de Sociologie |
| H. et S. | = L'Homme et la Société |
| ISSJ | = International Social Science Journal |
| JRAI | = Journal of the Royal Anthropological Institute |
| NNRF | = Nouvelle Nouvelle Revue Française |
| Proc RAI | = Proceedings of the Royal Anthropological Institute |
| TLS | = Times Literary Supplement |
| Soc. Sci. Inf. | = Social Sciences Information |
| TM | = Temps Modernes |
| Trans NY Acad Sci | = Transactions of the New York Academy of Science |

# Abbreviations used for Lévi-Strauss' works

| | |
|---|---|
| ESK | = The Elementary Structures of Kinship. 1969f. |
| FKS | = The Future of Kinship Studies. 1965f. |
| FS | = French Sociology. 1946a. |
| HA | = From Honey to Ashes. 1973b. |
| HN | = L'Homme Nu. 1971a. |
| IL | = The Scope of Anthropology. 1967l. |
| IM | = Introduction to M. Mauss: Sociologie et Anthropologie. 1950a. |
| JJR | = Jean-Jacques Rousseau. 1962a. |
| OMT | = L'Origine des Manières de Table. 1968a. |
| RC | = The Raw and the Cooked. 1969c. |
| SA | = Structural Anthropology. 1968k. |
| SM | = The Savage Mind. 1966h. |
| TT | = Tristes Tropiques. 1961h. |
| Tot | = Totemism. 1964h. |

# The Published Works of Claude Lévi-Strauss

Only major English translations are included

**1936**

a. 'Contribution à l'Etude de l'Organisation Sociale des Indiens Bororo', *Journal de la Société des Américanistes*, XXVIII, 2, pp. 269–304, plates 7–10. (Portuguese version in *Revista do Arquivo Municipal*, III, 27, pp. 5–80, São Paulo).

b. 'Entre os Selvagems Civilizados', *O Estado de São Paulo*, (Coleção do Departimento Municipal de Cultura, 1), São Paulo.

c. 'Os Mais Vastos Horizontes do Mundo', *Filosofia, Ciências e Letras*, 1, São Paulo, pp. 66–9.

**1937**

a. 'A propósito da Civilisação Chaco-Santiaguense', *Revista do Arquivo Municipal*, IV, 42, pp. 5–38, São Paulo.

b. 'La Sociologie Culturelle et son Enseignement', *Filosofia, Ciências e Letras*, 2, São Paulo.

c. 'Poupees Karaja', *Boletim de la Sociedade de Etnografia e de Folklore*, I, São Paulo.

d. 'Indiens du Mato Grosso, Brazil', *Guide-Catalogue de l'Exposition*. etc. (mission Claude et Dina Lévi-Strauss), Paris, Muséum National d'Histoire Naturelle, Musée de l'Homme, pp. 1–14.

**1942**

a. 'Indian Cosmetics', *VVV*, I, I, New York, pp. 33–5.

b. 'Souvenir of Malinovski', *VVV*, I, I, New York, p. 45.

**1943**

a. 'Guerre et Commerce chez les Indiens de l'Amérique du Sud', *Renaissance*, revue trimestielle publiée par l'Ecole Libre des Hautes Etudes, I, 1 and 2, New York, pp. 122–39.

b. 'The Social Use of Kinship Terms among Brazilian Indians', *Am. Anth.*, 45, 3, pp. 398–409.

c. 'The Art of the Northwest Coast at the American Museum of

Natural History', *Gazette des Beaux Arts*, 6th Series, 24, New York pp. 175–82.

d.  'Review of L. W. Simmons (ed.) Sun Chief', *Social Research*, 10, pp. 515–17.

**1944**

a.  'On Dual Organization in South America', *America Indigena*, 4, pp. 37–47.

b.  'The Social and Psychological Aspects of Chieftainship in a Primitive Tribe', *Trans. NY Acad. Sci.*, Series II, 7, 1, pp. 16–32.

c.  'Reciprocity and Hierarchy', *Am. Anth.*, 46, 2, pp. 266–8.

d.  'Review of E. da Cunha: Rebellion in the Backlands', *Am. Anth.*, 46, pp. 394–6.

**1945**

a.  'Le Dédoublement de la Représentation dans les Arts de l'Asie et de l'Amérique', *Renaissance*, II and III, New York, pp. 168–86, 12 plates, [Chapter 13 of *SA*].

b.  'L'Oeuvre d'Edward Westermarck', *Revue de l'Histoire des Religions*, CXXIX, 1 and 2–3, pp. 84–100.

c.  'L'Analyse Structurale en Linguistique et en Anthropologie', *Word*, I, 2, pp. 1–12. [Chapter 2 of *SA*].

**1946**

a.  'French Sociology', in *Twentieth Century Sociology*, G. Gurvitch (ed.), New York, pp. 503–37. [French edition, PUF, Paris, 1947].

b.  'The Name of the Nambikwara', *Am. Anth.*, 48, 1, pp. 139–40.

c.  'La Technique du Bonheur', *Esprit*, 127, pp. 643–52.

**1947**

a.  'La Théorie du Pouvoir dans une Société Primitive', in *Les Doctrines Politiques Modernes*, Brentano, New York, pp. 41–62. [Slightly modified version of 1944b].

b.  'Sur Certaines Similarités Structurales entre les Langues Chibcha et Nambikwara', *Actes du XXVIIIme. Congrès International des Américanistes*, Paris, pp. 185–92.

c.  'Le Serpent au Corps Rempli de Poissons', *id.*, pp. 633–6. [Chapter 14 of *SA*].

**1948**

a.  *La Vie Familiale et Sociale des Indiens Nambikwara*, Société des Américanistes, Paris, 132 pp., 7 plates.

b.  'The Nambicuara', in *Handbook of South American Indians*, J. Steward

(ed.), Bureau of American Ethnology, Smithsonian Institution, Washington, III, pp. 361-9, plates 36-7.
c.   'The Tupi-Kawahíb', *id.*, pp. 299-305, plates 24-6.
d.   'The Tribes of the Upper Zingu River', *id.*, pp. 321-48, plates 27-34.
e.   'The Tribes of the Right Bank of the Guaporé River', *id.*, pp. 371-9, plate 38.
f.   'Review of L. W. Simmons (ed.) Sun Chief', *Année Sociologique*, 3rd Series, 1948-9.

## 1949

a.   *Les Structures Elémentaires de la Parenté*, PUF, Paris, 640 pp., 88 figures. (Prix Paul Pelliot).
b.   'Le Sorcier et sa Magie', *TM*, 41, pp. 3-24. [Chapter 9 of *SA*].
c.   'L'Efficacité Symbolique', *Revue de l'Histoire des Religions*, CXXXV, 1, pp. 5-27. [Chapter 10 of *SA*].
d.   'La Politique Etrangère d'une Société Primitive', *Politique Etrangère*, 2, mai, pp. 139-52.
e.   'Histoire et Ethnologie', *Revue de Metaphysique et de Morale*, 54me année, 3-4, pp. 363-91. [Chapter 1 of *SA*].

## 1950

a.   Introduction, in *Sociologie et Anthropologie*, Marcel Mauss, PUF, Paris, pp. ix-lii. [Also in *Cah. Int. Soc.*, 8, 1950, pp. 72-112.]
b.   'Les Prohibitions Matrimoniales et leur Fondement Psychologique', *Journal de Psychologie Normale et Pathologique*, 43, p. 409.
c.   'The Use of Wild Plants in Tropical South America', *Handbook of South American Indians*, J. Steward (ed.), Bureau of American Ethnology, Smithsonian Institution, Washington, VI, pp. 465-86.
d.   Préface à K. Dunham, *Danses d'Haiti*, Fasquelle, Paris, pp. 7-11.
e.   Préface à C. Berndt, *Women's Changing Ceremonies in Northern Australia, L'Homme*, 1, Hermann, Paris, pp. 3-8.
f.   'Documents Rama-Rama', *Journal de la Société des Américanistes*, XXXIX, pp. 84-100.
g.   'Sur Certains Objets en Poterie d'Usage Douteux Provenant de la Syrie et de l'Inde', *Syria*, XXVII, fasc. 1-2, pp. 1-4.

## 1951

a.   'Language and the Analysis of Social Laws', *Am. Anth.*, 53, 2, pp. 155-63. [Slightly modified version Chapter 3 of *SA*].
b.   'Avant-propos', *Bulletin International des Sciences Sociales*, UNESCO, Paris, 3, 4, pp. 825-9.
c.   'Les Sciences Sociales au Pakistan', *id.*, pp. 885-92.

d.   'La Visite des Ames', *Annuaire de l'Ecole Pratique des Hautes Etudes*, 1951-2, pp. 20-3.

**1952**

a.   *Race et Histoire.* UNESCO, Paris, 52pp. [Also published in English as *Race and History*].

b.   'La Notion d'Archaisme en Ethnologie', *Cah. Int. Soc.*, XII, pp. 3-25. [Chapter 6 of *SA*].

c.   'Les Structures Sociales dans le Brésil Central et Oriental', in *Proceedings of the 29th International Congress of Americanists*, III, University of Chicago Press, pp. 302-10.

d.   'Le Père Noël Supplicié', *TM*, 7me année, 77, pp. 1572-90.

e.   'Kinship Systems of Three Chittagong Hill Tribes', *SWJ Anth.*, 8, 1, pp. 40-51.

f.   'Miscellaneous Notes on the Kuki', *Man*, 5, 284, pp. 167-9.

g.   'Le Syncrétisme Religieux d'un village mɔg du territoire de Chittagong', *Revue de l'Histoire des Religions*, CXLI, 2, pp. 202-37.

h.   'Recherches de Mythologie Américaine', *Ann. de l'EPHE*, 1952-3, pp. 19-21.

**1953**

a.   'Social Structure', in *Anthropology Today*, A. L. Kroeber (ed.), University of Chicago Press, pp. 524-58 [Modified version as Chapter 15 of *SA*].

b.   'Contributions to Discussion', in *An Appraisal of Anthropology Today*, Sol Tax, *et al.* (eds.), University of Chicago Press.

c.   'Panorama de l'Ethnologie', *Diogène*, 2, pp. 96-123. [English edition pp. 69-92].

d.   Chapter 1, in Results of the Conference, etc., *Supplement to International Journal of American Linguistics*, 19, 2, pp. 1-10. [Modified version as Chapter 4 of *SA*].

e.   'Recherches de Mythologie Américaine (Suite)', *Ann. de l'EPHE*, 1953-4, pp. 27-9.

f.   'Structure Sociale', *Bulletin de Psychologie*, VI, 5, 358-90 [French version of 1953a].

**1954**

a.   'Rapports entre la Mythologie et le rituel', *Ann. de l'EPHE*, 1954-5, pp. 25-8.

b.   'L'Art de Déchiffrer les Symboles', *Diogène*, 5, pp. 128-35. [English edition pp. 102-8].

c.   'Place de l'Anthropologie dans les Sciences Sociales et Problèmes Posés par son Enseignement', in *Les Sciences Sociales dans l'Enseignement*

*Supérieure* (rapports préparés par C. W. Guillebaud, *et al.*), UNESCO, Paris, 32 pp. [Chapter 17 of *SA* is a slightly modified version].

d. 'Qu'Est ce qu'un Primitif?', *UNESCO Courier*, 8–9, pp. 5–7.

e. Obituary notice of M. Leenhardt, *Ann. de l'EPHE*, 1954–5, pp. 21–2.

## 1955

a. *Tristes Tropiques*, Plon, Paris, 462 pp., 54 figures, 62 illustrations.

b. 'Les Prohibitions du Marriage', *Ann. de l'EPHE*, 1955–6, pp. 39–40.

c. 'Les Structures Elémentaires de la Parenté', in *La Progenèse, etc.*, Centre International de l'Enfance, Masson, Paris, pp. 105–10. (Travaux et Documents VIII).

d. 'The Structural Study of Myth', *Journal of American Folklore*, 68, 270, pp. 428–44. [Chapter 11 of *SA* is modified version. Also reprinted in T. Seboek, *Myth: A Symposium*. University of Indiana Press, 1965].

e. 'How the Gift Started', *UNESCO Courier*, December 1955, pp. 8–9.

f. 'Diogène Couché', *TM*, 110, pp. 1187–220.

g. 'Des Indiens et leur Ethnographie', *TM*, 116, pp. 1–50. [Part of 1955a].

h. 'Réponse à Roger Caillois', *TM*, 111, pp. 1535–6.

## 1956

a. 'The Family', in *Man, Culture and Society*, H. L. Shapiro (ed.), Oxford University Press, pp. 524–58.

b. 'Les Organisations Dualistes Existent-ils?', *Bijd.*, 112, 2, pp. 99–128. [Chapter 8 of *SA*].

c. 'Review of G. Balandier, Sociologie des Brazzavilles Noires', *Revue Française de Sciences Politiques*, VI, 1, pp. 177–9.

d. 'Sorciers et Psychanalyse', *UNESCO Courier*, July–August, pp. 8–10.

e. 'Structure et Dialectique', in *For Roman Jakobson, Essays on the Occasion of his Sixtieth Birthday*, Mouton, The Hague, pp. 289–94. [Chapter 12 of *SA*].

f. 'Jeux de Société', *United States Lines, Paris Review* (special issues on games).

g. 'La Fin des Voyages', *L'Actualité Littéraire*, 26, pp. 29–32.

h. 'Les Trois Humanismes', *Demain*, 35.

j. 'Le Droit au Voyage', *L'Express*, 21 September, p. 16.

k. 'Recherches Récentes sur la Notion d'Ame', *Ann. de l'EPHE*, 1956–7, pp. 16–18.

l. 'The Mathematics of Man', *ISSJ*, 6, 4, pp. 581–90. [Also in *Esprit*, 24, 10, pp. 525–38].

m. 'Sur les Rapports Entre le Mythe et le Rituel', *Bulletin de la Société Francaise de Philosophie*, 50, 3, pp. 99–125.

## 1957

a. 'Le Symbolisme Cosmique dans la Structure Sociale et l'Organisation Cérémonielle de Plusiers Populations Nord et Sud-Américaines', in *Le Symbolisme Cosmique des Monuments Religieux*, Roma, IsMEO, pp. 47–56. (Série Orientale Roma, Vol. 14) (Istituto Italiano per il Medio ed Estremo Oriente.)

b. 'Review of R. Briffaut – B. Malinovski, Marriage: Past and Present', *Am. Anth.*, 59, 5, pp. 902–3.

c. 'Le Dualisme dans L'Organisation Sociale et les Représentations Réligieuses', *Ann. de l'EPHE*, 1957–8, pp. 32–5.

d. 'These cooks did not spoil the broth', *UNESCO Courier*, 10, pp. 12–3.

e. 'Letter to A. Breton', in *L'Art Magique*, A. Breton and G. Legrand, Paris, p. 56.

## 1958

a. *Anthropologie Structurale*, Plon, Paris, 454 pp., 23 figures, 13 illustrations.

b. Préface to M. Bouteiller, *Sorciers et Jeteurs de Sorts*, Plon, Paris, pp. i-vi.

c. 'Review of R. Firth (ed.): *Man and Culture'*, *Africa*, 28, pp. 370–1.

d. 'Dis-moi quels Champignons', *L'Express*, 10 April, p. 17.

e. 'One World, Many Societies', *Way Forum*, March, pp. 28–30.

f. Le Dualisme dans l'Organisation Sociale et les Représentations Réligieuses', *Ann. de l'EPHE*, 1958–9, pp. 50–3.

g. 'Documents Tupi-Kawahib', in *Miscellanea Paul Rivet*, 2, Mexico, pp. 323–38.

h. 'La Geste d'Asdiwal', *Ann. de l'EPHE*, 1958–9, pp. 3–43. [Also published in *TM*, 179, March 1961].

j. *Titres et Travaux*, Projet d'Enseignement, Centre de Documentation Universitaire, Paris.

## 1959

a. 'Amérique du Nord et Amérique du Sud', in *Le Masque*, Musée Guimet, Paris.

b. 'Le Masque', *L'Express*, 443, 10 Dec., pp. 46–7.

c. 'Mauss, Marcel', *Encyclopaedia Brittanica*.

d. 'Passage Rites', *Encyclopaedia Brittanica*.

e. Préface to D. Talaysesva, *Soleil Hopi*, Plon, Paris, pp. i-x.

## 1960

a. 'Four Winnebago Myths. A Structural Sketch', in *Culture and History*

S. Diamond (ed.) University of Columbia Press, New York, pp. 351–362.

b.  'La Chasse Rituelle aux Aigles', *Ann. de l'EPHE*, 1959–60, pp. 38–42.

c.  'L'Anthropologie Sociale devant l'Histoire', *Annales*, July–August, pp. 625–637. [Part of 1960l].

d.  'Méthodes et Conditions de la Recherche Ethnologique Française en Asie', *Colloque sur les Recherches, etc.*, Fondation Singer-Polignac, Paris, pp. 111–25.

e.  'Les Trois Sources de la Refléxion Ethnologique', *Revue de l'Enseignement Supérieure*, pp, 43–50.

f.  'La Structure et la Forme. Reflexions sur un Ouvrage de Vladimir Propp', *Cahiers de l'Institut de Sciences Economique Appliquées*, (Recherches et Dialogues Philos. et Econ., 7), 9, Paris, pp. 3–36. Also as: 'L'Analyse Morphologique des Contes Russes', *International Journal of Slavic Linguistics and Poetics*, 3, pp. 122–49.

g.  'On Manipulated Sociological Models', *Bijd.*, 116, 1, pp. 45–54.

h.  'Ce que l'Ethnologie Doit à Durkheim', *Annales de l'Université de Paris*, 30 (1), pp. 47–52.

j.  'Résumé des Cours et Travaux (1959–60)', *Annuaire du Collège de France*, pp. 191–207.

k.  'Le Problème de l'Invariance en Anthropologie', *Diogène* 31, pp. 23–33. [English edition pp. 19–28.] (Part of 1960m).

l.  *Lecon Inaugurale Faite le Mardi 5 Janvier 1960*, Collège de France, Paris. 47pp.

m.  Interview with J-P Weber, *Figaro Littéraire*, 14 March.

n.  Interview, *L'Express*, 20 October.

## 1961

a.  'Comment on Goody, Classification of Double Descent Systems', *Current Anthropology*, 2, p. 17.

b.  'Recherches d'Ethnologie Religieuse', *Ann. de l'EPHE*, 1960–61.

c.  'Today's Crisis in Anthropology', *UNESCO Courier*, 14 (11), 12–17.

d.  'Le Métier d'Ethnologue', *Annales*, revue mensuelle de lettres françaises, 129, pp. 5–17.

e.  'Résumé des Cours et Travaux (1960–1)', *Annuaire du Collège de France*, pp. 191–205.

f.  Various reviews in *L'Homme*, 1, 1, pp. 111–4, 127–9, 142–3; 1, 2, pp. 128, 132–5, 137, 138, 142–3; 1, 3, p. 129.

g.  (Charbonnier, G.), *Entretiens avec Claude Lévi-Strauss*, Plon-Julliard, Paris.

h.  *Tristes Tropiques*, translated by J. Russell, Criterion Books, New York. [Omits chapters 14, 15, 16, 39 of original.]

1962

a.  *Le Totémisme Aujourd-hui*, PUF, Paris, 154 pp.
b.  *La Pensée Sauvage*, Plon, Paris, 389 pp., 11 figures, 8 illustrations.
c.  (With R. Jakobson), 'Les Chats de Charles Baudelaire', *L'Homme*, 2, 1, pp. 5–21.
d.  'Jean-Jacques Rousseau, Fondateur des Sciences de l'Homme', in *Jean-Jacques Rousseau*, La Baconnière, Neufchatel, pp. 239–48.
e.  'Les Limites de la Notion de Structure en Ethnologie' in *Sens et Usages du Terme Structure*, R. Bastide (ed.), Januâ Linguarum, Mouton, The Hague, pp. 40–5 and 143–5, 150, 157, 159.
f.  'Résumé des Cours et Travaux (1961–2)', *Annuaire du Collège de France*, pp. 211–17.
g.  'Sur le Caractère Distinctif des Faits Ethnologiques', *Revue des Travaux de l'Académie des Sciences Morales et Politiques*, 115me annee, 4me série, Paris, pp. 211–9.
h.  Various reviews in *L'Homme*, 2, 2, pp. 139–41; 2, 3, pp. 134–47, 141–3.
j.  'La Antropologia, Hoy: Entrevista a Claude Lévi-Strauss, by Eliseo Veron', *Cuestiones de Filosofia*, 1, 2–3, Buenos Aires.
k.  1. 'Les Fondements Philosophiques de l'Anthropologie', 2. 'Recherches Sémiologiques', *Ann. de l'EPHE*, 1961–2, pp. 40–2.
l.  'L'Ethnologue Avant l'Heure', *Les Nouvelles Littéraires*, 29 November.
m.  'Le Temps Retrouvé', *TM*, 191, pp. 1402–31. [Chapter 8 of 1962b.]

1963

a.  (With N. Belmont) 'Marques de Propriété dans Deux Tribus Sud-Américaines', *L'Homme*, 3, pp. 102–8.
b.  'Résumé des Cours et Travaux (1962–3)', *Annuaire du Collège de France*, pp. 223–7.
c.  'Les Discontinuités Culturelles et le Développement Economique et Sociale', *Table Ronde sur les Prémices Sociales de l'Industrialisation* (1961), UNESCO, Paris. [Also in *Social Sciences Information*, 1963, pp. 7–15.]
d.  'Réponses a Quelques Questions', *Esprit*, 322, pp. 628–53.
e.  'The Bear and the Barber, The Henry Myer Memorial Lecture', *Journal of the Royal Anthropological Institute*, 93, Pt.1, pp. 1–11.
f.  'Rousseau, the Father of Anthropology', *UNESCO Courier*, 16, 3, pp. 10–14.
g.  Various reviews, *L'Homme*, 3, 1, p. 140; 3, 2, pp. 136–8; 3, 3, pp. 126–7, 133–4.
h.  'Compte Rendu d'Enseignement', *Ann. de l'EPHE*, 1962–3, pp. 40–3.
j.  'Compte Rendu d'Enseignement', *Ann. de l'EPHE*, 1963–4, pp. 42–5.
k.  (With R. d'Harcourt) 'A. Métraux (1902–63)', *Journal de la Société des Américanistes*, n.s. 52, pp. 301–11.

l. 'Conversazioni con Cl. Lévi-Strauss (a cura di P. Caruso)', *Aut Aut*, 77, Milan.

m. 'Where Does Father Xmas Come From', *New Society*, 64, 19 December, pp. 6–8. [Adaptation of 1952d.]

**1964**

a. *Mythologiques: Le Cru et le Cuit*, Plon, Paris, 402 pp., 20 figures, 4 illustrations.

b. 'Alfred Métraux, 1902–63', *Annales de l'Université de Paris*, 1.

c. 'Lucien Sebag,' *Journal de la Société des Américanistes*, LIII, p. 182.

d. 'Hommage à Alfred Métraux', *L'Homme*, 4, 2, pp. 5–8.

e. 'Résumé des Cours et Travaux (1963–4)', *Annuaire du Collège de France*, pp. 227–31.

f. 'Criteria of Science in the Social and Human Disciplines', *International Social Science Journal*, XVI, 4, pp. 534–52. [French edition pp. 579–97].

g. 'Compte Rendu d'Enseignement', *Ann. de l'EPHE*, 1964–5, pp. 51–6.

h. *Totemism*, translated by R. Needham, Merlin, London.

**1965**

a. 'Présentation d'un Laboratoire Sociale', *Revue de l'Enseignement Superieure*, 3, pp. 87–92.

b. 'Résumé des Cours et Travaux (1964–5)', *Annuaire du Collège de France*, pp. 269–73.

c. 'Les Sources Polluées de l'Art', *Arts-Loisirs*, 7–13, April, p. 4.

d. 'Réponse à un Questionnaire (sur la critique dite "structurale")', *Paragone*, n.s. 2, 182, Milan, pp. 125–9.

e. 'Réponse à un Questionnaire (sur 25 témoins de notre temps)', *Figaro Litéraire*, 1023, p. 9.

f. 'The Future of Kinship Studies', Huxley Memorial Lecture, 1965, *Proceedings of the Royal Anthropological Institute*, London, pp. 13–22.

g. 'Entretien avec Claude Lévi-Strauss' (by M. Delahaye and J. Rivette), *Les Cahiers du Cinéma*, XXVI, 4, pp. 19–29.

h. 'Le Triangle Culinaire', *L'Arc*, 26, Aix-en-Provence, pp. 19–29.

j. 'Compte Rendu d'Enseignement', *Ann. de l'EPHE*, 1965–6), pp. 51–6.

k. 'Man Has Never Been So Strange As He Is Today', *Réalités*, 175, pp. 48–51.

l. Review, *L'Homme*, 15, 2, p. 147.

m. 'Civilisation Urbaine et Santé Mentale', *Cahiers de l'Institut de la Vie*, 4, pp. 31–6.

n. Interview with P. Caruso, *Rinascita*, Supplemento Culturale, 5, 29/3.

**1966**

a. *Mythologiques 2: Du Miel aux Cendres*, Plon, Paris, 450pp.

b. 'Anthropology: Its Achievements and Future', *Nature*, 209, pp. 10–13.

c. 'Resume des Cours et Travaux (1965–6)', *Annuaire du College de France*, pp. 269–73.

d. Interview accorded to *Cahiers de Philosophie* (special issue on anthropology), 1, pp. 47–56.

e. (G. Steiner), 'A Conversation with Claude Lévi-Strauss', *Encounter*, 26, 26 April, pp. 32–8.

f. 'Compte Rendu d'Enseignement', *Ann. de l'EPHE* 1966–7, pp. 61–3.

g. 'The Culinary Triangle', *New Society*, 22 December, pp. 937–40. [Translation of 1965h].

h. *The Savage Mind*, translated by Anon, Weidenfeld & Nicolson, London. [Omits appendix from original].

j. 'The Scope of Anthropology', *Current Anthropology*, 7, 2, pp. 112–23. [Part of 1967l].

k. 'Humanity, what is it?' Interview with Cl. Lévi-Strauss, *Kroeber Anthropological Society Papers*, 35, pp. 41–53. [English translation of 1960n.]

l. Interview with Cl. Lévi-Strauss by P. Caruso, *Atlas*, April, 245–6.

m. 'The Work of the Bureau of American Ethnology and its Lessons' in *Knowledge Among Men*, Smithsonian Institution, Washington.

n. 'A Propos d'une Retrospective', *Arts* 60, 16–22 November.

o. 'The Disappearance of Man', *New York Review of Books*, 28 July.

**1967**

a. *Les Structures Elémentaires de la Parenté*, 2nd revised and corrected edition, Mouton, The Hague.

b. A Contre-Courant, 'Interview with G. Dumur', *Nouvel Observateur*, 25 January, pp. 30–2.

c. 'Résumé des Cours et Travaux (1966–7)', *Annuaire du Collège de France*, pp. 267–74.

d. Interview with Gilles Lapouge, *Figaro Littéraire*, 1085, pp. 3, 16.

e. 'La Sexe des Astres', in *Mélanges Offerts à Roman Jakobson pour sa 70me Année*, Mouton, The Hague.

f. 'Présentation du Laboratoire d'Anthropologie Sociale', *Sciences*, 47, pp. 115–28.

g. 'Vingt Ans Après', *TM*, 256, pp. 385–406. [New preface to 1967a].

h. 'Compte Rendu d'Enseignement', *Ann. de l'EPHE*, 1967–8, pp. 61–3.

j. Interview with R. Bellour, *Les Lettres Francaises*, 1165, pp. 1, 3–5, 7.

k. 'The Story of Asdiwal', translated by N. Mann, in *The Structural Study of Myth and Totemism*, E. Leach (ed.), Tavistock, London.

l.  *The Scope of Anthropology*, translated by S.O. and R.A. Paul, Cape, London. [Translation of 1960m.]
m.  'The Savage Mind', *Man*, 2, 3, p. 464.
n.  'Comments', *Current Anthropology*, 8, 4, pp. 359–61.
o.  'Une lettre de Cl. Lévi-Strauss', *Cahiers pour l'analyse*, 8, October, p. 90.
p.  'Entretien de F. Malet', *Magazine Littéraire*, February, pp. 42–4.
q.  'The Particular Task of Anthropology', in *Culture and Consciousness*, G. B. Levitas (ed.), Braziller, New York.
r.  'Les clefs du mystère humain', *Le Patriote Illustre*, 35.

## 1968

a.  *Mythologiques 3: L'Origine des Manieres de Table*, Plon, Paris.
b.  'Hommage aux Sciences de l'Homme', *Soc. Sci. Inf.*, 7, 2, pp. 7–11.
c.  'Religions Comparées des Peuples sans Ecriture', in *Problèmes et Méthodes d'Histoire des Religions*, PUF, Paris, pp. 1–7.
d.  'La Grande Aventure de l'Ethnologie', *Nouvel Observateur*, 166. [Part of 1970e].
e.  'The Concept of Primitiveness', in *Man the Hunter*, R. Lee and I. DeVore (eds.), Aldine, Chicago, pp. 349–52.
f.  'Contributions to Discussions', in R. Lee and I. DeVore, *id*.
g.  'Résumé des Cours et Travaux (1967–8)', *Annuaire du Collège de France*, pp. 305–17.
h.  'Compte Rendu d'Enseignement', *Ann. de l'EPHE*, 1968–9, pp. 65–6.
j.  (With J. Guiart), 'Evènement et Schéma', *L'Homme*, 8, 1, pp. 80–7.
k.  *Structural Anthropology*, translated by C. Jacobson and B. G. Schoepf, Allen Lane, London.
l.  Speech on receiving the Gold Medal of the CNRS, *Le Monde*, 13 January, p. 9.
m.  'Vivre et Parler. Un Debat entre F. Jacob, R. Jakobson, Cl. Lévi-Strauss et P. l'Heritier', *Les Lettres Francaises* 1221, 14 and 21 February.
n.  'Entretien avec Claude Lévi-Strauss', *Témoignage Chrétien*, 8, 8/4.
o.  'Le structuralisme sainement pratiqué ne prétend pas formuler une nouvelle conception du monde et même de l'homme', *Le Monde*, 12 January.
p.  'Sur les divers usages du structuralism. Réponse à Gadoffre', *Le Monde*, 14 November.

## 1969

a.  'Conversation with P. Caruso', in *Conversazioni con Lévi-Strauss, Faucoult, Lacan*, U. Mursia, Milan, pp. 25–90.
b.  'Reports of Seminars Conducted by Sperber, Sahlins, Monod,

Pouillon, Cresswell, Maranda, Kutuldjian, et al.,' *Ann. de l'EPHE*, 1969–70, pp. 109–28.

c. *The Raw and the Cooked*, translated by J. and D. Weightman, Cape, London.

d. *Conversation with Claude Lévi-Strauss*, by G. Charbonnier, translated by J. and D. Weightman, Cape, London.

e. 'Résumé des Cours et Travaux (1968–9)', *Annuaire du Collège de France*.

f. *The Elementary Structures of Kinship*, translated by J. H. Bell and J. R. V. Sturmer, edited by R. Needham, Eyre & Spottiswood, London.

**1970**

a. 'Les Champignons dans la Culture. A Propos d'un Livre de M.R.G. Wasson', *L'Homme*, 10, 1, pp. 5–17.

b. 'A Confrontation', *New Left Review*, 62, pp. 57–74. [Translation of 1963d].

c. 'Résumé des Cours et Travaux (1969–70)', *Annuaire du Collège de France*, pp. 299–305.

d. 'Compte Rendu d'Enseignement', *Ann. d l'EPHE*, 1970–1, pp. 95–102.

e. 'Texte de l'Emission de Michel Tréguer Consacrée a Lévi-Strauss, dans la Série *Un Certain Regard*' (Winter 1968) in *Claude Lévi-Strauss ou la structure de la malheur*, C. Backès-Clément, Seghers, Paris, pp. 172–88.

f. Letter in C. Backès-Clément, *op. cit.*, p. 170–1.

g. 'La théorie', *VH 101*, 2.

h. Interview, *Mademoiselle*, LXXI, pp. 236–7, 324.

j. Interview, *University Review*, X, p. 21.

k. 'Myth and Meaning', *Sunday Times*, 7694, 15 November, p. 27.

**1971**

a. *Mythologiques 4: L'Homme Nu*, Plon, Paris.

b. 'Der Humanismus Bedroht den Menschen', Interview, *Der Spiegel*, 53, pp. 93–7.

c. 'Comment Meurent les Mythes', in *Science et Conscience de la Société. Melanges en l'honneur de Raymond Aron*, 1, Calmann-Lévy, Paris, pp. 131–43. Also in *Esprit*, 39 (402), 1971, pp. 694–706.

d. 'Le Temps du Mythe', *Annales*, May–August, pp. 533–40.

e. 'The Deduction of the Crane', in *The Structural Analysis of Oral Tradition*, P. and E. K. Maranda (eds), University of Pennsylvania Press.

f. 'Boléro de M. Ravel', *L'Homme*, 11, 2, pp. 5–14.

g. 'Compte Rendu d'Enseignement', *Ann. de l'EPHE*, 1971–2, pp. 65–80.

h. 'Résumé des Cours et Travaux (1970–1)', *Annuaire du Collège de France*, pp. 277–84.

j. 'Rapports de Symétrie entre Rites et Mythes de Peuples Voisins', in T.O. Beidelman (ed.), *The Translation of Culture, Essays in Honour of E. E. Evans-Pritchard*, Tavistock, London, pp. 161–78.

k. 'Race and Culture', *ISSJ*, XXIII, 4, pp. 608–25.

l. 'L'Express Va Plus Loin avec Lévi-Strauss', *L'Express*, 15–21 March, pp. 60–6.

m. 'Interview with Edwin Newman' (WNBC TV), *Speaking Freely*, 12 September, pp. 1–23.

n. 'Le problème ultime des sciences de l'homme', *Magazine Littéraire*, 58, pp. 22–9.

o. Préface to L. Sebag, *L'invention du monde chez les indiens pueblos*, Maspero, Paris.

p. Interview, *Le Monde des Livres*, 8339, pp. 17–20.

q. Interview, *Les Lettres Françaises*, 1406, pp. 3–4, 1407, pp. 6–7.

r. Interview, *Les Nouvelles Littéraires*, 2297, pp. 14–15.

s. 'De quelques rencontres', *L'Arc*, 46, pp. 43–7.

## 1972

a. Various reviews, *L'Homme*, 12, 4, pp. 97–102.

b. 'Interview with Claude Lévi-Strauss', *Psychology Today*, May, pp. 37, 39, 74, 78–80, 82. [English version of interview in *Psychologie*.]

c. 'Compte Rendu d'Enseignement', *Ann. de l'EPHE*, 1972–3.

d. 'Résumé des Cours et Travaux (1971–2)', *Annuaire du Collège de France*, pp. 329–49.

e. 'La Mère des Fougères', in *Langues, Techniques, Nature et Société*, T. Barran *et. al.* (eds), Klincksieck, Paris, pp. 367–9.

f. 'The Tempering of our Pride'. Interview excerpted from *Diacritics* 1, 1 (Cornell University), *New York Times*, 21 January.

g. Interview, *Figario Littéraire*, 1338, pp. 13, 16.

## 1973

a. Interview with *Nouvelle Critique*, n.s. 61, pp. 27–36.

b. *From Honey to Ashes*, translated by J. and D. Weightman, Cape, London.

c. 'Structuralism and Ecology', *Social Sciences Information*, XII–I, pp. 7–23. [Gildersleeve Lecture at Barnard College, New York, 28 March 1972. First published in *Barnard Alunnae*, Spring, 1972.]

d. 'Réflexions sur l'Atom de Parenté, *L'Homme*, XIII, 3, pp. 5–29.

e. *Anthropologie Structurale Deux*, Plon, Paris. [Contains 1952a (corrected version), 1956h, 1958h, 1960a (adaptation), 1960f, 1960g, 1960h,

1960m, 1962d, 1963c, 1964f, 1965c, 1965d, 1965e, 1965m, 1966m, 1966n, 1967e, 1968c, 1970a, 1971c, 1971j, 1973d.]

f.  'Contribution to Musiques en Jeu' (transcription of ORTF broadcast), *Musique en Jeu*, 12, pp. 101–9.

g.  *Tristes Tropiques* translated by J. and D. Weightman, Cape, London.

h.  'Le problème des sciences humaines au collège de France', *Nouvelle Revue des deux Mondes*.

j.  'Dieu existe-t-il?', in *Dieu existe-t-il?* C. Chabonis *et. al.*, Fayard, Paris.

k.  'Comte Rendu d'Enseignement', *Annuaire de l'EPHE*, 1973–4.

l.  Obituary of E. Lot-Falck, *Annuaire de l'EPHE*, 1973–4, pp. 39–41.

m.  'Résumé des Cours et Travaux (1972–3)', *Annuaire du Collège de France*, pp. 269–84.

## 1974

a.  Various Reviews, *L'Homme*, XIV, 3–4, pp. 161–2.

b.  *Discours prononcés* dans la séance publique tenue par l'Académie française pour la reception de M. Claude Lévi-Strauss le 27 Juin 1974. Institut de France, Paris. [English summary *TLS* 12 July].

c.  Interview, *Le Monde*, 2 June.

d.  Interview, *Le Monde*, 15 November.

e.  Interview, *Il Ponte*, XXX, pp. 65–7.

## 1975

a.  'Anthropology', *Diogène*, 90, pp. 1–25 (abridged version of an article prepared for the *Enciclopedia Italiana*.)

b.  *La Voie des masques*, 2 vols, Skira, Genève.

c.  (With M. Augé et M. Godelier), 'Anthropologie, Histoire, Idéologie', *L'Homme*, XV (3–4), pp. 177–89.

d.  'Propos retardataires sur l'enfant créateur', *Nouvelle Revue des Deux Mondes*, January.

e.  'Histoire d'une structure', in *Explorations in the Anthropology of Religion. Essays in Honour of Jan Van Baal*, M. Nijhoff, The Hague.

f.  'Un ethnologue dans la ville', *Le Figaro*, 7 March and 9 May.

g.  'De Chrétien de Troyes à Richard Wagner, Programme *de Parsifal*', Beyreuther Festspiele.

## 1976

a.  'Cosmopolitisme et schizophrénie', in *L'Autre et l'ailleurs. Hommage à R. Bastide*, Berger-Levrault, Paris.

b.  'Une préfiguration anatomique de la gémillité' in *Mélanges offerts à Germaine Dieterlen*, Hermann, Paris.

c.  'Structuralisme et Empirisme', *L'Homme*, XVI, 2.

d. 'Hommage à E. Benveniste', *L'Homme*, XVI, 4, p. 5.
e. Review, *L'Homme*, XVI, 1, p. 166.
f. 'Hommage à Jean Piaget', in *Hommages à Jean Piaget*, Klett Verlag, Stuttgart.
g. Review, *Times Literary Supplement*, 26 November, p. 1457.
h. Préface to R. Jakobson, *Le Son et le sens*, Seuil, Paris.
j. 'Réflexions sur la Liberté', *Nouvelle Revue des deux Mondes*, November.
k. Review, *Times Literary Supplement*, 26 November, p. 1475.
l. 'Résumé des Cours et Travaux (1975–6)' *Annuaire du Collège de France*, pp. 387–98.

**1977**

a. 'Les Dessous d'un masque', *L'Homme*, XVII, 1, pp. 5–29.
b. 'Réponse à E. Leach' *L'Homme*, XVII, 2–3, pp. 131–4.
c. Reviews, *L'Homme*, XVII, 1, pp. 139–41.
d. *Discours de Réception d'Alain Peyrefitte à L'Académie française et Réponse de Claude Lévi-Strauss*, Gallimard, Paris.
e. 'Résumé des Cours et Travaux (1976–7)', *Annuaire du College de France*, pp. 455–63.
f. *L'identité*, Seminaire dirigée par Claude Lévi-Strauss (1974–5), Grasset, Paris.

# Bibliography

THE bibliography that follows is intended to provide a guide to further reading for those who wish to follow up the discussion in the text without immersing themselves in the specialist literature. The bibliography is organized according to chapters in the text, although there is some overlap.

## CHAPTER I.

I have argued in the text that a number of writers can be described as 'structuralists' on the basis of their adherence to the fundamental postulate of structuralism that systems of meaning can be given an objective analysis without reference either to an external reality or to a subject that exist independently of the system of meaning. However different thinkers have developed this fundamental postulate in very different ways. Thus Louis Althusser has used it as the epistemological basis for a reconstruction of Marxist social theory. Nicos Poulantzas has developed this reconstruction in the area of the theory of the state, while in Britain Barry Hindess and Paul Hirst have pushed Althusser's epistemology to its rationalist limits. Jacques Lacan has used the structuralist postulate as the basis for a reconstruction of psychoanalysis and Michel Foucault for the history of ideas. Roland Barthes and the *Tel Quel* group have developed a structuralist approach to literature whose initial inspiration came directly from linguistics rather than from Lévi-Strauss, although the latter has subsequently influenced their work. Jacques Derrida has developed the most esoteric version of the structuralist philosophy as a reintegration of positivism and phenomenology. The phenomenological inspiration of these later versions of structuralism is very important: both Lacan and Derrida were directly inspired by Heidegger, while Poulantzas, Foucault and perhaps Althusser came to structuralism through the work of Sartre. Thus any development of the structuralist theme takes us far afield.

The writers mentioned are best represented by the following works:

L. Althusser: *For Marx*, Allen Lane, 1969.
——: *Reading Capital*, NLB, 1970.

———: *Lenin and Philosophy*, NLB, 1971.

R. Barthes: *Mythologies*, Paladin, 1973.

———: *Elements of Semiology*, Cape, 1967.

———: *S/Z*, Cape, 1974.

J. Derrida: *Of Grammatology*, Johns Hopkins University Press, 1976.

———: *Writing and Difference*, University of Chicago Press, 1978.

———: *Positions*, Minuit, 1972.

M. Foucault: *The Order of Things*, Tavistock, 1970.

———: *The Archaeology of Knowledge*, Tavistock, 1972.

———: *Discipline and Punish*, Allen Lane, 1977.

B. Hindess and P. Hirst: *Pre-Capitalist Modes of Production*, Routledge & Kegan Paul, 1975.

———: *Modes of Production and Social Formations*, Macmillan, 1977.

——— and A. Cutler and A. Hussein: *Marx's Capital and Capitalism Today*, Routledge & Kegan Paul, 1978.

J. Lacan: *Ecrits*, Seuil, 1966 (selections in translation published by Tavistock, 1977).

N. Poulantzas: *Political Power and Social Classes*, NLB/Sheed & Ward, 1973.

The following general surveys of some aspects of later structuralism are thorough:

T. Bennet: *Formalism and Marxism,* Methuen, 1979.

R. Coward and J. Ellis: *Language and Materialism*, Routledge & Kegan Paul, 1977.

C. Sumner: *Reading Ideologies*, Academic Press, 1979.

I have criticized the substantive theories, rather than the specifically structuralist foundations, of the work of Poulantzas and Althusser: S. Clarke: 'Marxism, Sociology and Poulantzas's Theory of the State', *Capital and Class*, 2, 1977.

———: 'Althusserian Marxism', in S. Clarke, T. Lovell. K. McDonnell, K. Robbins and V. Seidler: *One-Dimensional Marxism*, Allison & Busby, 1980.

The latter volume also includes valuable critical discussion of the psychoanalytic versions of structuralism developed in Britain by the writers associated with the journal *Screen*.

General works of more direct relevance to the theme of this book include:

R. Bastide: *Sens et Usages du Terme 'Structure' dans les Sciences Sociales*, Mouton, 1962.

J. Broekman: *Structuralism*, Reidel, 1974.

M. Ducrot, et al.: *Qu'est ce que le Structuralisme?*, Seuil, 1968.

M. Dufrenne: *Pour L'Homme*, Seuil, 1968.

M. de Gandillac, L. Goldmann and J. Piaget: *Entretiens sur les Notions de Genèse et Structure*, Mouton, 1965.

G. Granger: *Pensée Formelle et Sciences de l'Homme*, Aubier-Montaigne, 1960.

F. Jameson: *The Prison House of Language*, Princeton University Press, 1972.

D. Lecourt: *Marxism and Epistemology*, NLB, 1975.

H. Lefebvre: *Position: Contre les Technocrates*, Gonthier, 1967.

——: *Au Dela du Structuralisme*, Anthropos, 1971.

R. Macksey and E. Donato: *The Languages of Criticism and the Sciences of Man*, Johns Hopkins University Press, 1970.

R. Makarius: 'Structuralism: Science or Ideology', *Socialist Register*, 1974.

M. Marc-Lipiansky: *Le Structuralisme de Claude Lévi-Strauss*, Payot, 1973.

J. Parain-Vial: *Analyses Structurales et Idéologies Structuralistes*, Privat, 1969.

J. Piaget: *Structuralism*, Routledge & Kegan Paul, 1971.

D. Robey: *Structuralism: an Introduction*, Clarendon, 1973.

L. Sève: 'Méthode Structurale et Méthode Dialectique', *Pensée*, 1967.

——: 'Marxisme et Sciences de l'Homme', *Nouvelle Critique*, 1967.

Y. Simonis: *Claude Lévi-Strauss ou la Passion de l'Inceste*, Aubier-Montaigne, 1968.

J. Viet: *Les Méthodes Structuralistes dans les Sciences Sociales*, Mouton, 1965.

A. Wilden: *System and Structure*, Tavistock, 1972.

## CHAPTER II

S. de Beauvoir: *Memoirs of a Dutiful Daughter*, Penguin, 1963.

——: *The Prime of Life*, Penguin, 1965.

——: *Force of Circumstance*, Penguin, 1968.

H. Bergson: *Creative Evolution*, Macmillan, 1964.

——: *Matter and Memory*, Allen & Unwin, 1962.

——: *Time and Free Will*, Allen & Unwin, 1959.

L. Brunschvig: *Idéalisme Contemporain*, Alcan, 1905.

T. Clark: *Prophets and Patrons*, Harvard University Press, 1973.

F. Coplestone: *History of Philosophy*, 9, Burns Oates, 1975.

A. Cresson: *Bergson*, PUF, 1964. (Cresson was Lévi-Strauss' philosophy teacher).

H. Hughes: *The Obstructed Path*, Harper & Row, 1968.

H. Lefebvre: *La Somme et le Reste*, La nef de Paris, 1959.

L. Lévy-Bruhl: *Primitive Mentality*, Allen & Unwin, 1923.

M. Merleau-Ponty: *Signs*, Northwestern University Press, 1964.

E. Morot-Sir: *La Pensée Française d'aujourdhui*, PUF, 1971.

P. Nizan: *Aden-Arabie*, Rieder, 1932.

——: *Les Chiens de Garde*, Rieder, 1932.

W. Redfern: *Paul Nizan*, Princeton University Press, 1972.

J-P. Sartre: *Being and Nothingness*, Methuen, 1957.

———: *Situations*, Heinneman, 1965.

———: *Between Existentialism and Marxism*, NLB, 1974.

## CHAPTER III

C. Bougle: *Bilan de la Sociologie Française Contemporaine*, Alcan, 1935.

S. de Beauvoir: 'Les structures élémentaires de la parenté', *Temps Modernes*, 1949.

E. Durkheim: *The Division of Labour in Society*, Free Press, 1964.

———: *The Rules of Sociological Method*, Free Press, 1964.

———: *Elementary Forms of the Religious Life*, Collier, 1961.

———: *Essays on Sociology and Philosophy*, Harper & Row, 1960.

R. Hertz: *Death and the Right Hand*, Cohen & West, 1960.

I. Kant: *The Moral Law*, Hutchinson, 1948.

R. Lowie: *Primitive Society*, Routledge & Kegan Paul, 1953.

S. Lukes: *Emile Durkheim: His Life and Works*, Allen Lane, 1973.

M. Mauss: *The Gift*, Cohen & West, 1966.

———: *Sociology and Psychology*, Routledge & Kegan Paul, 1979.

## CHAPTER IV

J. A. Barnes: *Three Styles in the Study of Kinship*, Tavistock, 1971.

M. Boden: *Piaget*, Fontana/Harvester, 1979.

S. Clarke: 'The Structuralism of Claude Lévi-Strauss' PhD thesis, University of Essex, 1975.

A. Coult: 'The Determinants of Differential Cross-Cousin Marriage', *Man*, 1962.

K. Davis and W. Warner: 'Structural Analysis of Kinship', *American Anthropologist*, 1937.

G. Davy: 'Review of *ESK*', *Année Sociologique*, 3rd Series, 1949.

L. Dumont: *Introduction à Deux Théories d'Anthropologie Sociale*, Mouton, 1971.

R. Fox; *Kinship and Marriage*, Penguin, 1967.

S. Freud: *Totem and Taboo*, Routledge & Kegan Paul, 1950.

M. Granet: 'Catégories Matrimoniales et Relations de Proximité dans la Chine Anciènne', *Année Sociologique*, série B, 1939.

G. Homans and D. Schneider: *Marriage, Authority and Final Causes*, Free Press, 1955.

J. de Josselin de Jong: *Lévi-Strauss' Theory of Kinship and Marriage*, Medenlingen van het Rijksmuseum voor Volkenkunde, 10, 1952.

K. Koffka: 'Gestalt', *Encyclopedia of the Social Sciences*, VI, Macmillan, 1930.

W. Köhler: *Gestalt Psychology*, New American Library, 1966.

F. Korn: *Elementary Structures Reconsidered*, Tavistock, 1973.

E. Leach: *Rethinking Anthropology*, Athlone Press, 1961.

R. Lee and I. DeVore (eds): *Man The Hunter*, Aldine, 1968.

M. Merleau-Ponty: *The Structure of Behaviour*, Methuen, 1965.

R. Needham (ed.): *Rethinking Kinship and Marriage*, Tavistock, 1971.

D. Schneider: 'Some Muddles in the Models', in *The Relevance of Models for Social Anthropology*, Tavistock, 1965.

H. Scheffler: 'The Elementary Structures of Kinship', *American Anthropologist*, 1970.

E. Terray: *Le Marxisme devant les Societés 'Primitives'*, Maspero, 1969.

## CHAPTER V

S. de Beauvoir: *The Second Sex*, Bantam, 1961.

I. Buchler and H. Selby: *Kinship and Social Organization*, Macmillan, 1968.

A. Coult: 'The Determinants of Differential Cross-Cousin Marriage', *Man*, 1962.

L. Dumont: 'The Dravidian Kinship Terminology as an Expression of Marriage', *Man*, 1953.

———: *Hierarchy and Marriage Alliance in South Indian Kinship*, RAI, 1957.

———: 'Descent or Intermarriage?', *Southwestern Journal of Anthropology*, 1966.

———: 'Marriage Alliance', *International Encyclopedia of the Social Sciences*, 10, 1968.

———: *Homo Hierarchicus*, Weidenfeld & Nicolson, 1970.

E. Evans-Pritchard: *The Nuer*, OUP, 1940.

———: *Kinship and Marriage Among the Nuer*, Clarendon, 1951.

———: *Social Anthropology and Other Essays*, Free Press, 1962.

C. Hart: 'Review of *ESK*', *American Anthropologist*, 1950.

A. Kuper: *Anthropologists and Anthropology*, Allen Lane, 1973.

E. Leach: 'The Structural Implications of Matrilateral Cross-Cousin Marriage', *JRAI*, 1951.

———: *Political Systems of Highland Burma*, Bell, 1954.

———: 'Concerning Trobriand Clans and the Kinship Category "Tabu"', in J. Goody (ed.): *The Developmental Cycle in Domestic Groups*, CUP, 1958.

———: *Pul Elija*, CUP, 1962.

———: *Lévi-Strauss*, Fontana, 1970.

R. Makarius: 'Parenté et Infrastructure', *Pensée*, 1970.

———: 'Dialectique de la Parenté', *Pensée*, 1973.

J. Mitchell: *Psychoanalysis and Feminism*, Allen Lane, 1974.

R. Needham: 'A Structural Analysis of Aimol Society', *Bijdragen tot de taal-land- en Volkenkunde*, 1960.

———: 'Descent Systems and Ideal Language', *Philosophy of Science*, 1960.

———: *Structure and Sentiment*, University of Chicago Press, 1962.

———: 'The Future of Social Anthropology: Disintegration or Metamorphosis?' *Anniversary Contributions to Anthropology*, Brill, 1970.

——: 'Introduction' and 'Remarks on the Analysis of Kinship and Marriage', in R. Needham (ed.) *Rethinking Kinship and Marriage*, Tavistock, 1971.

——: *Belief, Language and Experience*, Blackwell, 1972.

——: 'Prescription', *Oceania*, 1973.

——: *Remarks and Inventions*, Tavistock, 1974.

S. Orther: 'Is Female to Male as Nature is to Culture?', in M. Rosaldo and L. Lamphere (eds): *Woman, Culture and Society*, Stanford University Press, 1974.

D. Sperber: 'Edmund Leach et les Anthropologues', *Cahiers Internationaux de la Sociologie*, 1967.

## CHAPTER VI

P. Achinstein and S. Barker (eds): *The Legacy of Logical Positivism*, Johns Hopkins University Press, 1969.

M. Bloomfield: *Language*, Allen & Unwin, 1957.

E. Cassirer: 'Structuralism in Modern Linguistics', *Word*, 1945.

N. Chomsky: *Syntactic Structures*, Mouton, 1957.

——: 'Review of B. F. Skinner: *Verbal Behaviour*', *Language*, 1959.

——: *Aspects of the Theory of Syntax*, MIT Press, 1965.

——: *Topics in the Theory of Generative Grammar*, Mouton, 1966.

——: *Cartesian Linguistics*, Harper & Row, 1966.

——: *Current Issues in Linguistic Theory*, Mouton, 1967.

——: *Studies on Semantics in Generative Grammar*, Mouton, 1972.

—— and M. Halle: *The Sound Pattern of English*, Harper & Row, 1968.

M. Cohen: 'Quelques notations historiques et critiques autour du structuralisme en linguistique', *Pensée*, 1967.

B. Derwing: *Transformational Grammar as a Theory of Language Acquisition*, CUP, 1973.

J. Dubois: 'Structuralisme et linguistique', *Pensée*, 1967.

V. Erlich: *Russian Formalism*, Mouton, 1955.

J. Fodor and J. Katz (eds): *The Structure of Language*, Prentice Hall, 1964.

P. Garvin: *On Linguistic Method*, Mouton, 1964.

G. Harman (ed.): *On Noam Chomsky*, Doubleday, 1974.

Z. Harris: *Methods in Structural Linguistics*, University of Chicago Press, 1951.

L. Hjelmslev: *Prolegomena to a Theory of Language*, Waverly Press, 1953.

C. Hockett: *The State of the Art*, Mouton, 1968.

S. Hook (ed.): *Language and Philosophy*, New York University Press, 1969.

E. Holenstein: *Roman Jakobson's Approach to Language*, Indiana University Press, 1976.

R. Jakobson: 'The Notion of Grammatical Meaning According to Boas', *American Anthropologist*, memoir 89, 1959.

—— (ed.): *The Structure of Language and its Mathematical Aspects*, Proceedings of the 12th Symposium in Applied Mathematics, American Mathematical Society, 1961.

——: 'Linguistics and Poetics', in T. Sebeok (ed.): *Style in Language*, MIT Press, 1966.

——: *Selected Writings*, Mouton, 1966.

——: 'Linguistics', in *International Study on the Main Trends of Research in the Social and Human Sciences*, Mouton, 1970.

——: *Word and Language*, Mouton, 1971.

——: *Six Lectures on Sound and Meaning*, Harvester, 1978.

—— and J. Tynyanov: 'Problems of Literary and Linguistic Studies', *New Left Review*, 37, 1966.

J. Katz: 'Mentalism in Linguistics', *Language*, 1964.

——: *The Philosophy of Language*, Harper & Row, 1966.

L. Kolakowski: *Edmund Husserl and the Search for Certitude*, Yale University Press, 1975.

J. Krige: *Science, Revolution, Discontinuity*, Harvester, 1979.

G. Lepschy: *A Survey of Structural Linguistics*, Faber, 1970.

J. Lyons: *Introduction to Theoretical Linguistics*, CUP, 1968.

——: *Chomsky*, Fontana, 1977.

A. Martinet: *A Functional View of Language*, OUP, 1962.

G. Mounin: *Clefs pour la Linguistique*, Seghers, 1968.

——: *Saussure*, Seghers, 1968.

P. Peters and R. Ritchie: 'A Note on the Universal Base Hypothesis', *Journal of Linguistics*, 1969.

W. Quine: *Word and Object*, MIT Press, 1960.

F. de Saussure: *Course of General Linguistics*, Fontana, 1974.

J. Searle: 'Review of N. Chomsky: *Reflections on Language*', *Times Literary Supplement*, 10 September, 1976.

E. Stegmüller: *Main Currents in Contemporary German, British and American Philosophy*, Reidel, 1969.

N. Trubetskoi: *Principles of Phonology*, University of California Press, 1969.

J. Vachek (ed.): *A Prague School Reader in Linguistics*, Indiana University Press, 1964.

V. Volosinov (M. Baxtin): *Marxism and the Philosophy of Language*, Seminar, 1973.

Y. Wilks: 'Review of N. Chomsky: *Current Issues*', *Linguistics*, 1967.

——: *Grammar, Meaning and the Machine Analysis of Language*, Routledge & Kegan Paul, 1972.

## CHAPTER VII

F. Boas: Introduction to *Handbook of American Indian Languages*, University of Nebraska Press, 1968.

N. Chomsky: *Language and Mind*, Harcourt Brace, 1968.

H. Coubreras: 'Simplicity, Descriptive Adequacy and Binary Features', *Language*, 1969.

W. Goodenough: 'Componential Analysis and the Study of Meaning', *Language*, 1956.

M. Halle: 'In Defence of the Number 2', in *Studies Presented to Joshua Whatmough*, 1957.

——: 'Simplicity in Linguistic Description' in R. Jakobson (ed.): *The Structure of Language and its Mathematical Aspects*, American Mathematical Society, 1961.

D. Hymes (ed.): *Language in Culture and Society*, Harper & Row, 1964.

R. Jakobson: *Six Lectures on Sound and Meaning*, Harvester, 1978.

——: *Child Language, Aphasia and Phonological Universals*, Mouton, 1968.

——, G. Fant and M. Halle: *Preliminaries to Speech Analysis*, MIT Press, 1952.

—— and M. Halle: *Fundamentals of Language*, Mouton, 1957.

J. Katz: *Semantic Theory*, Harper & Row, 1972.

—— and J. Fodor: 'The Structure of a Semantic Theory', *Language*, 1963.

F. Korn and R. Needham: 'Permutation Models and Prescriptive Systems', *Man*, 1970.

H. Lefebvre: *Le Langage et la Société*, Gallimard, 1966.

F. Lounsbury: 'A Semantic Analysis of the Pawnee Kinship Usage', *Language*, 1956.

J. Lyons: *Structural Semantics*, Blackwell, 1964.

——: *Semantics*, 2 vols, CUP, 1977.

D. Maybury-Lewis: 'Dual Organisation', *Bijdragen tot de taat- land- en Volkenkunde*, 1960.

O. Moore and D. Olmsted: 'Language and Professor Lévi-Strauss', *American Anthropologist*, 1952.

G. Mounin: 'Linguistique, structuralisme et marxisme', *Nouvelle Critique*, 1967.

——: *Introduction à la Sémiologie*, Minuit, 1970.

O. Paz: *Claude Lévi-Strauss: an Introduction*, Cape, 1971.

P. Ricoeur: 'New Developments in Phenomenology in France: the Phenomenology of Language', *Social Research*, 1967.

B. Rotman: *Jean Piaget, Psychologist of the Real*, Harvester, 1977.

D. Schneider: 'American Kin Terms and Terms for Kinsmen: a Critique of Goodenough's Componential Analysis', *American Anthropologist*, 1965.

D. Slobin: *Psycholinguistics*, Scott, Foresman, 1971.

B. Whorf: *Language, Thought and Reality*, MIT Press, 1956.

## CHAPTER VIII.

G. Bachelard: *Psychoanalysis of Fire*, Routledge & Kegan Paul, 1964.

I. Buchler and H. Selby: *A Formal Study of Myth*, University of Texas Press, 1968.

E. Durkheim: 'Sur le Totémisme', *Année Sociologique*, 1902.

—— and M. Mauss: *Primitive Classification*, University of Chicago Press, 1963.

A. Glucksmann: 'La déduction de la cuisine et les cuisines de la déduction', *Social Sciences Information*, 1965.

A. Greimas: *Semantique Structurale*, Larousse, 1966.

——: *Du Sens*, Seuil, 1970.

E. Hammel: *The Myth of Structural Analysis*, Addison Wesley Modules, 1972.

R. Jakobson: 'On Russian Fairy Tales', in *Russian Fairy Tales*, Pantheon, 1945.

G. Kirk: *Myth: its Meaning and Functions*, CUP, 1970.

S. Körner: *Categorial Frameworks*, Blackwell, 1970.

E. Leach: 'Telstar et las aborigènes', *Annales*, 1964.

—— (ed.): *The Structural Study of Myth and Totemism*, Tavistock, 1967.

——: *Genesis as Myth and Other Essays*, Cape, 1969.

——: *Lévi-Strauss*, Fontana, 1970.

L. Makarius: 'L'apothéose de Cinna: Mythe de naissance de structuralisme', *L'Homme et la Société*, 1971.

—— and R. Makarius: 'Ethnologie et structuralisme', *L'Homme et la Société*, 1967.

——: 'Des jaguars et des hommes', *L'Homme et la Société*, 1968.

R. Makarius: 'Lévi-Strauss et les structures inconscients de l'esprit', *L'Homme et la Société*, 1970.

P. and E. Maranda: *The Structural Analysis of Oral Tradition*, University of Pennsylvania Press, 1971.

D. Maybury-Lewis: 'Review of *Du Miel aux Cendres*', *American Anthropologist*, 1969.

B. Nathhorst: *Formal or Structural Studies of Traditional Tales*, Bromma, 1969.

R. Needham: 'Introduction to E. Durkheim and M. Mauss', *op. cit.* 1963.

——: 'Review of *The Savage Mind*', *Man*, 1967.

——: *Right and Left*, University of Chicago Press, 1974.

V. Propp: *Morphology of the Folktale*, University of Texas Press, 1968.

A. Regnier: 'De la théorie des groupes à la Pensée Sauvage', *L'Homme et la Société*, 1968.

P. Richard: 'Analyse des *Mythologiques* de Cl. Lévi-Strauss', *L'Homme et la Société*, 1967.

——: 'A propos de *L'Origine des Manières de Table* de Cl. Lévi-Strauss', *L'Homme et la Société*, 1969.

P. Ricoeur: 'Structure et Hermeneutique', *Esprit*, 1963.

——: 'Le symbolisme et l'explication structurale', *Cahiers Internationaux de Symbolisme*, 1964.

L. Sebag: 'Le Mythe: Code et message', *Temps Modernes*, 1965.

V. Turner: *The Forest of Symbols*, Cornell University Press, 1967.

## CHAPTER IX

R. Aronson: 'Sartre's Individualist Social Theory', *Telos*, 1973.

J. Culler: 'Phenomenology and Structuralism', *Human Context,* 1973.

J. Derrida: 'Nature, culture, écriture', *Cahiers pour l'Analyse*, 1966.

F. Engels: 'Karl Marx: *A Contribution to the Critique of Political Economy*', in K. Marx and F. Engels, *Selected Works*, I, FLPH, 1962.

H. Lefebvre: 'La notion de totalité dans les sciences sociales', *Cahiers Internationaux de Sociologie*, 1955.

——: 'Réflections sur le structuralisme et l'histoire', *Cahiers Internationaux de Sociologie*, 1963.

——: 'Claude Lévi-Strauss et le nouvel Eléatisme', *L'Homme et la Société*, 1967.

Cl. Lefort: 'L'échange et la lutte des hommes', *Temps Modernes*, 1951.

——: 'Sociétés sans histoire' et historicité', *Cahiers Internationaux de Sociologie*, 1952.

K. Marx: *Critique of Hegel's Philosophy of Right*, CUP, 1970.

——: *The Poverty of Philosophy*, FLPH, n.d.

——: *Grundrisse*, Penguin, 1973.

——: *Economic and Philosophical Manuscripts* in *Collected Works*, 3, Lawrence & Wishart, 1975.

E, Pashukanis: *Law and Marxism*, Ink Links, 1978.

J. Pouillon: 'L'oeuvre de Cl. Lévi-Strauss', *Temps Modernes*, 1956.

——: 'Sartre et Lévi-Strauss', *L'Arc*, 26, 1967.

N. Poulantzas: 'Vers une théorie marxiste', *Temps Modernes*, 1966.

P. Ricouer: 'La structure, le mot, l'evénement', *Esprit*, 1967.

J. Rousseau: *The Social Contract and the Discourses*, Everyman, 1963.

I. Rubin: *Essays on Marx's Theory of Value*, Black and Red, 1972.

J-P. Sartre: 'J-P Sartre répond', *L'Arc*, 30, 1966 (English version *Telos*, 1971).

——: 'L'Anthropologie', *Cahiers de Philosophie*, 1966.

——: *Between Existentialism and Marxism*, NLB, 1974.

——: *Critique of Dialectical Reason*, NLB, 1976.

L. Sebag: *Marxisme et Structuralisme*, Payot, 1964.